SAP® S/4 HANA Product Cost Planning—Costing with Quantity Structure

Tom King

Thank you for purchasing this book from Espresso Tutorials!

Like a cup of espresso coffee, Espresso Tutorials SAP books are concise and effective. We know that your time is valuable and we deliver information in a succinct and straightforward manner. It only takes our readers a short amount of time to consume SAP concepts. Our books are well recognized in the industry for leveraging tutorial-style instruction and videos to show you step by step how to successfully work with SAP.

Check out our YouTube channel to watch our videos at https://www.youtube.com/user/EspressoTutorials.

If you are interested in SAP Finance and Controlling, join us at http://www.fico-forum.com/forum2/ to get your SAP questions answered and contribute to discussions.

Related titles from Espresso Tutorials:

- Stefan Eifler: **Quick Guide to CO-PA (Profitability Analysis)**
  http://5018.espresso-tutorials.com
- Paul Ovigele: **Reconciling SAP CO-PA to the General Ledger**
  http://5040.espresso-tutorials.com
- Ashish Sampat: **First Steps in SAP Controlling (CO)**
  http://5069.espresso-tutorials.com
- Marjorie Wright: **Practical Guide to SAP Internal Orders (CO-OM)**
  http://5139.espresso-tutorials.com
- Ashish Sampat: **Expert tips to Unleash the Full Potential of SAP Controlling**   http://5140.espresso-tutorials.com
- John Pringle: **Practical Guide to SAP Profit Center Accounting**
  http://5144.espresso-tutorials.com
- John Pringle: **Practical Guide to SAP Cost Center Accounting**
  http://5192.espresso-tutorials.com
- Stefan Eifler, Christoph Theis: **Value Flows into SAP ERP FI, CO, and CO-PA**   http://5199.espresso-tutorials.com
- Tom King: **Practical Guide to SAP CO Templates**
  http://5262.espresso-tutorials.com
- Tom King: **SAP S/4HANA Product Cost Planning—Configuration and Master Data**   http://5376.espresso-tutorials.com

Provide effective SAP training for your team
without travel costs and external trainers

- 150+ eBooks and video tutorials
- Regularly updated with new content
- Access via web browser or app (iOS/Android)
- Pricing based on number of users

Try a free 7-day, no obligation trial:
http://free.espresso-tutorials.com

Get a quote for your team today:
http://company.espresso-tutorials.com

Tom King
SAP® S/4 HANA Product Cost Planning—Costing with Quantity Structure

ISBN:	978-3-96012-535-8
Editor:	Karen Schoch
Cover Design:	Philip Esch
Cover Photo:	iStockphoto.com	sykono No. 171301497
Interior Book Design:	Johann-Christian Hanke

All rights reserved.

1st Edition 2019, Gleichen

© 2019 by Espresso Tutorials GmbH

URL: *www.espresso-tutorials.com*

All rights reserved. Neither this publication nor any part of it may be copied or reproduced in any form or by any means or translated into another language without the prior consent of Espresso Tutorials GmbH, Bahnhofstr. 2, 37130 Gleichen, Germany.

Espresso Tutorials makes no warranties or representations with respect to the content hereof and expressly disclaims any implied warranties of merchantability or fitness for any particular purpose. Espresso Tutorials assumes no responsibility for any errors that may appear in this publication.

Feedback
We greatly appreciate any feedback you may have concerning this book. Please send your feedback via email to: *info@espresso-tutorials.com*.

Table of Contents

Introduction		**9**
1	**BOM and routing advanced features**	**11**
1.1	Fixed and variable activity allocations	11
1.2	Unit of measure conversions	12
1.3	Component allocation to an operation	17
1.4	Specifying a quantity structure for costing	19
1.5	Scrap	22
1.6	Recursion	38
2	**Costing with special procurement**	**41**
2.1	Special procurement keys	41
2.2	Plant to plant transfers	45
2.3	Withdrawal from another plant	47
2.4	Manufactured in another plant	51
2.5	In-house manufacturing	53
2.6	Phantom assemblies	55
3	**Subcontracting and external processing**	**59**
3.1	Subcontracting description	59
3.2	Subcontracting master data	59
3.3	Subcontracting cost estimate	67
3.4	External processing description	70
3.5	External processing master data	71
3.6	External processing cost estimate	74
4	**Costing and variant configuration**	**81**
4.1	Configurable materials	81
4.2	Variants	83
4.3	Super BOMs	86
4.4	Super routes	89
4.5	Variant cost estimate	93

5 Applying overhead to cost estimates — 97
- 5.1 Overhead and cost estimates — 97
- 5.2 Overhead costing sheets — 97
- 5.3 Template allocation — 112

6 Mixed-price costing — 123
- 6.1 Mixed-price cost estimate — 123
- 6.2 Defining procurement alternatives — 126
- 6.3 Mixed-price costing configuration — 131

7 Additive cost estimates — 137
- 7.1 How additive cost estimates work — 137
- 7.2 Maintaining additive cost estimates — 138
- 7.3 Additive cost estimate configuration — 149

8 Co-products — 157
- 8.1 Joint production — 157
- 8.2 Apportionment structures — 162

9 Costing run — 173
- 9.1 Costing run — 173
- 9.2 Creating a costing run — 179
- 9.3 Selection — 180
- 9.4 Costing — 186
- 9.5 Analysis — 189
- 9.6 Marking — 191
- 9.7 Cost updates — 193
- 9.8 Deleting costing runs — 195

10 Alternative costing variants — 197
- 10.1 Reference variants — 197
- 10.2 Inventory costing — 201
- 10.3 What-if costing — 207
- 10.4 Group costing — 211

11	**Cost estimate reorganization**	**217**
	11.1 Deleting cost estimates	217
	11.2 Archiving cost estimates	221
12	**Standard costing reports**	**223**
	12.1 Summary reports	223
	12.2 Object comparison	226
	12.3 Detail reports	227
	12.4 Cost estimate tables for queries	228
A	**The Author**	**234**
B	**Index**	**235**
C	**Disclaimer**	**239**

Introduction

The SAP Product Cost Planning (CO-PC-PCP) module defines a methodology used to help determine the expected costs for manufactured and procured materials. This includes the ability to assign standard costs to a material, to provide a means to simulate costs, and to develop additional cost estimates for special purposes. This is the second book of a two-book set that started with "SAP® S/4HANA Product Cost Planning Configuration and Master Data". The first book introduced costing variants, the cost component split, the primary master data driving the costing process, and the two methodologies used for creating material cost estimates. Unit costing, also known as cost estimates without quantity structure, provides a means of entering product costs without referring to bills of material, manufacturing routings, or purchasing information. This is a very manual method for assigning costs to materials and has only limited application. The real power of the SAP CO-PC-PCP module lies in the topic of product costing with quantity structure. This was introduced in the first book, but only at a fundamental level.

This book continues where the first book left off and delves deeper into important topics associated with costing with quantity structure. Different costing scenarios are investigated, and the additional configuration that enables these scenarios to work is covered in detail. Products from the fictitious company Universal Writing Utensils are again used to demonstrate the effects of configuration choices.

This book is written from the perspective of S/4HANA, which is SAP's latest version of the ERP software, and it contains up-to-date information from release 1809. The majority of the screen shots come from the many Fiori apps available for product costing. However, some functions do not yet have a Fiori equivalent, and SAPGUI screenshots are used for these. Although this book is written primarily with S/4HANA product costing in mind, the topics covered are still applicable to older ERP versions. A few differences exist, and where practical, these are discussed in the text.

Finally, I want to express my gratitude to the staff at Espresso Tutorials for their invaluable aid in making these two books a reality. Martin Munzel and Alice Adams both have been most supportive during the project making sure that I have gotten the help I have needed when I needed it. Johann Hanke provided valuable assistance in setting up the Fiori screen shots used in the book. My special thanks goes to my editor Karen Schoch, who has helped keep my prose clear and hopefully simple enough to follow.

We have added a few icons to highlight important information. These include:

Tips

Tips highlight information that provides more details about the subject being described and/or additional background information.

Examples

Examples help illustrate a topic better by relating it to real world scenarios.

Attention

Attention notices highlight information that you should be aware of when you go through the examples in this book on your own.

Finally, a note concerning the copyright: all screenshots printed in this book are the copyright of SAP SE. All rights are reserved by SAP SE. Copyright pertains to all SAP images in this publication. For the sake of simplicity, we do not mention this specifically underneath every screenshot.

1 BOM and routing advanced features

Bills of materials (BOMs), routings, and recipes provide the means to assign manufacturing costs when creating a cost estimate with quantity structure. The basic structure of how these costs are allocated was covered in the first book of this set. However, there are many additional features available to enhance the accuracy of the calculated costs.

1.1 Fixed and variable activity allocations

Work center formulas are used to calculate the allocation quantity for each activity type associated with an operation. These can be defined to have a **fixed** portion and a **variable** portion. The fixed portion does not refer to any parameter that is associated with the base quantity of the routing operation. The variable portions include at least one parameter that is assigned to that base quantity.

```
Formula key        ZPMIXL  Labor w/ Premixing

Formula
ZPMMIN * ZPMPRS +
SAP_03 * SAP_09 / SAP_08 / SAP_11
```

Figure 1.1: New formula with user-defined fields

The formula in Figure 1.1 has a fixed portion (ZPMMIN * ZPMPRS) and a variable portion (SAP_03 * SAP_09 / SAP_08 / SAP_11). Parameter SAP_08 is associated with the routing master data that is assigned to the base quantity field (BMSCH). The order of operations separates these two portions of the formula because multiplication and division take precedence over addition. When a formula is defined in this manner, the activity allocation is split into two parts on the cost estimate. ZPMMIN is assigned to a user field and has the value 30 MIN. ZPMPRS is also assigned to a user field and is set to 2 PRS. The formula is assigned to the LABRHR activity type in the MIXER work center definition.

ItmNo	I...	Resource		Resource (Text)	Cost Element	Total COCr	Quantity	Un
1	E	200101	MIXER SETUP	Mix Ink	94303000	87.94 USD	1.5	HR
2	E	200101	MIXER MACHHR	Mix Ink	94301000	262.49 USD	5.833	HR
3	E	200101	MIXER LABRHR	Mix Ink	94311000	22.75 USD	1.0	HR
4	E	200101	MIXER LABRHR	Mix Ink	94311000	218.01 USD	9.583	HR

Figure 1.2: Fixed and variable allocations of LABRHR

The result of using formula ZPMIXL is seen in Figure 1.2. Section ❶ shows the calculation of the portion that is not associated with the base quantity. This takes ZPMMIN and multiplies it by ZPMPRS–30 MIN multiplied by 2 PRS equals 60 MIN (1 HR). Because the unit of measure PRS is non-dimensional, it does not affect the conversion of MIN to HR in the result. Section ❷ shows the variable portion of the calculation and uses the labor time (parameter SAP_03) divided by the base quantity (SAP_08) to give the result of 9.583 HR. The quantity calculated at ❶ remains 1 HR regardless of the costing lot size used. This means that the cost per unit of this item becomes greater when the costing lot size is low. The value assigned at ❷ changes with the lot size and its impact on the cost per unit is not affected by the lot size used for the cost estimate.

1.2 Unit of measure conversions

The unit of measure that is used for confirmations in routings and recipes does not have to be the same as the base unit of measure. For example, confirmations can be in gallons or even kilograms for certain operations even though the base unit of measure is in liters. When there is a difference in the unit of measure for the operation compared with the base unit of measure of the material, a conversion factor must be assigned to the operation. Standard unit of measure conversions for units with the same dimension are not automatically used in the same way as in other areas of the system. This is because there can be a conversion factor loaded even if the operation unit of measure is the same as the base unit of measure.

Shrinkage and stretch in the textile industry

Routings for textile finishing operations can be complex. Due to the nature of processing, the length of the fabric entering an operation may be different at the end due to tension placed on the fabric or shrinkage that

> can occur when heat is applied. The finished fabric can have a much different length than the fabric that entered the process. Because operations usually require confirmation using a length unit of measure such as M (meters), there must be a conversion factor loaded at each operation to represent the amount of shrinkage or stretch associated with the process, even though the same unit of measure is used throughout. The quantity counted at the end of each operation can only reflect the current length of the fabric. There must be a relationship defined for the M reported at operation xx versus the finished M of fabric.

The recipe for material H101 at the UWU2 plant (Los Angeles) has standard values that were mistakenly assigned per 1,000 liters (L) instead of 1,000 gallons (GAL). The incorrect cost estimate is shown in Figure 1.3

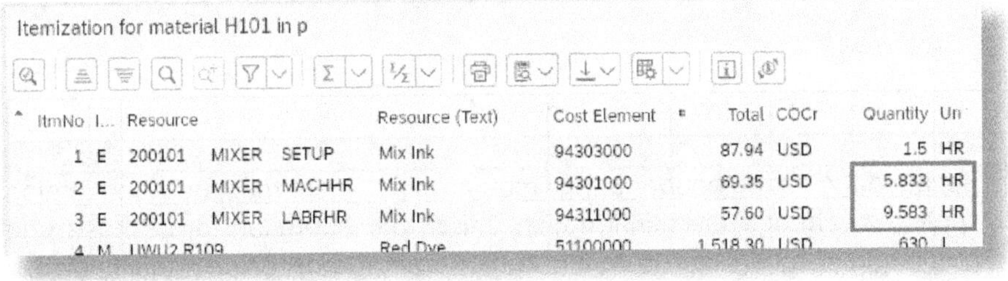

ItmNo	I...	Resource			Resource (Text)	Cost Element	Total COCr		Quantity	Un
1	E	200101	MIXER	SETUP	Mix Ink	94303000	87.94	USD	1.5	HR
2	E	200101	MIXER	MACHHR	Mix Ink	94301000	69.35	USD	5.833	HR
3	E	200101	MIXER	LABRHR	Mix Ink	94311000	57.60	USD	9.583	HR
4	M	UWU2 R109			Red Dye	51100000	1,518.30	USD	630	L

Figure 1.3: Itemization with base quantity set to 1,000 L

The times specified are correct for 1,000 GAL but not for 1,000 L. The base quantity for the operation in the recipe is changed from L to GAL shown in Figure 1.4.

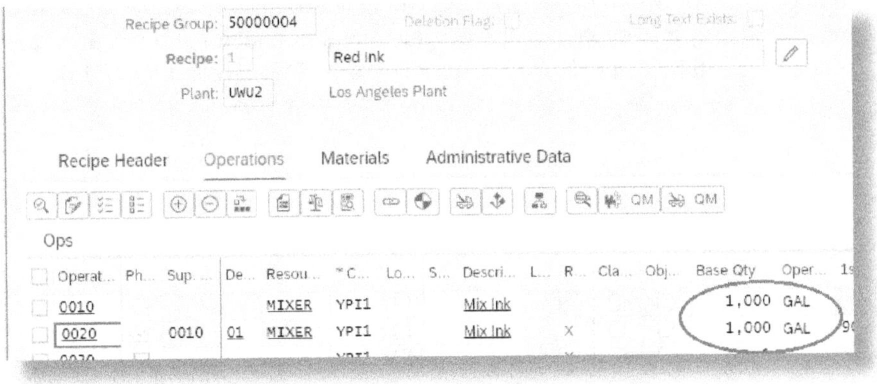

Operat...	Ph...	Sup...	De...	Resou...	~C...	Lo...	S...	Descri...	L...	R...	Cla...	Obj...	Base Qty	Oper...
0010				MIXER	YPI1			Mix Ink					1,000 GAL	
0020		0010	01	MIXER	YPI1			Mix Ink	X				1,000 GAL	90

Figure 1.4: Operation with unit of measure GAL

The recipe header contains the unit of measure that is normally used by the operations of the recipe. Figure 1.5 shows the location of the default task list unit of measure (TskL Unit). The base unit of measure of material H101 is L, and this becomes the default unit of measure for the operations in the recipe.

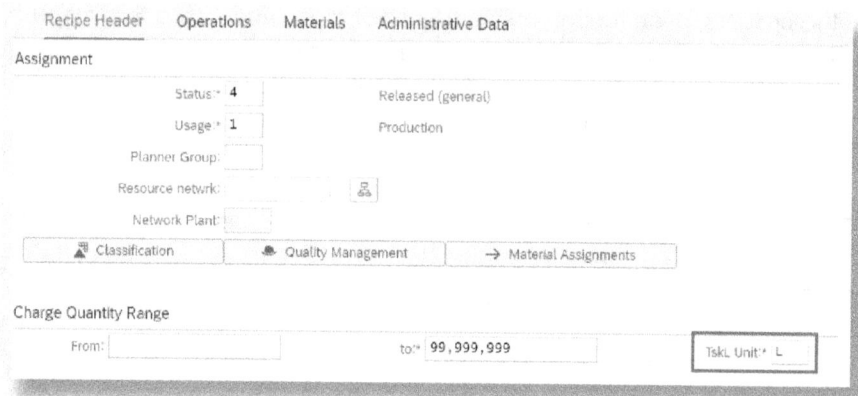

Figure 1.5: Recipe header with task list unit of measure

Because the recipe header unit of measure is L, there must be a conversion applied to change the confirmation unit in the operation to the base unit. This is found by drilling down into the operation. For recipes, this is on the STANDARD VALUES tab, as shown in Figure 1.6. The highlighted area shows a value for CHARGE QUANTITY and one for OPERATION QTY. The standard unit of measure conversion of liters to gallons is 3.785412 L to 1 GAL. Unfortunately, only whole numbers can be used when defining the conversion factors. Rounding up the L portion to 4, to make the conversion 4 L to 1 GAL, would result in large inaccuracies in the result. Another solution is to multiply both by 1,000 to get 3,785 L, which is equal to 1,000 GAL, giving a much better approximation of the actual conversion factor. A more accurate result is found by using 15,206 L, equaling 4,017 GAL (see Figure 1.6).

BOM AND ROUTING ADVANCED FEATURES

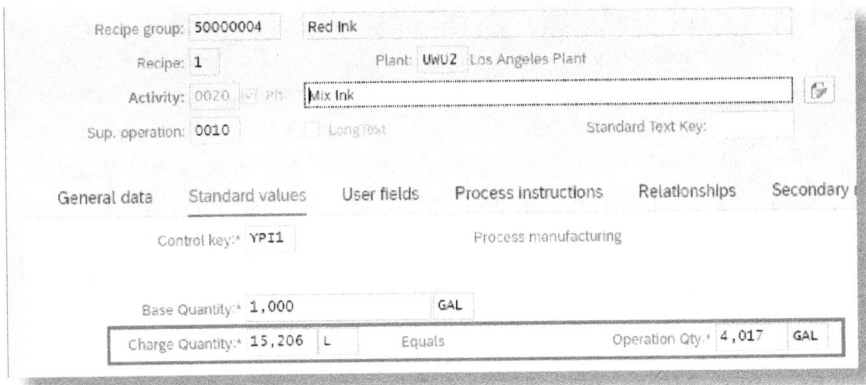

Figure 1.6: Recipe unit of measure conversion

Decide how much accuracy is required when defining the values to use. Other common imperial to metric unit of measure conversions are: 1,250 LB is equal to 567 KG, and 1,250 YD is equal to 1,143 M.

The resulting cost estimate has reduced quantities of the MACHHR and LABRHR activities allocated with the change of the base quantity from 1,000 L to 1,000 GAL. Figure 1.7 shows this. Compare this result with Figure 1.3. The new calculation uses the conversion factor. The quantity calculation for LABHR is 575 MIN (from the standard value) multiplied by 1,000 L (from the costing lot size) divided by 1,000 GAL (from the base quantity) multiplied by 4,017 GAL (from the operation quantity) divided by 15,206 L (from the charge quantity) divided by 1 (number of splits). This results in a value of 151.899 minutes (2.532 hours).

ItmNo	I...	Resource			Resource (Text)	Cost Element	B	Total COCr		Quantity	Un
1	E	200101	MIXER	SETUP	Mix Ink	94303000		87.94	USD	1.5	HR
2	E	200101	MIXER	MACHHR	Mix Ink	94301000		69.35	USD	1.541	HR
3	E	200101	MIXER	LABRHR	Mix Ink	94311000		57.60	USD	2.532	HR
4	M	UWU2 R109			Red Dye	51100000		1,518.30	USD	630	L

Figure 1.7: Itemization with base quantity set to 1,000 GAL

15

> **Rounding in work center calculations**
>
>  Work center formula calculations always round to three decimal places. If a unit of measure is defined to round to fewer than three decimal places, the result is affected. For example, if the unit GAL is defined for rounding to 0 decimal places, then, in this instance, the resulting 2.532 HR for LABRHR calculates to 2.540 HR. If the results don't match a manual calculation, check the definition of the units of measure in transaction CUNI.

The conversion factors for routings work in the same way as for recipes. The lot size unit of measure in Figure 1.8 defaults to the material's base unit of measure, but it can be changed to an alternative unit of measure that is defined in the material master, or that has a predefined conversion factor within the same unit of measure dimension.

Figure 1.8: Route header unit of measure

Drill down into the routing operation to update the conversion factors. This is found in Figure 1.9. Section ❶ shows the unit of measure used for confirmations of the operation. Section ❷ shows the factor for the routing unit of measure. Section ❸ shows the factor for the operation with the operation unit of measure. The task list unit of measure is PC, but the operation unit of measure is DZ (dozens). There are 12 PC to 1 DZ. Note that the conversion factor is always defined as the units expected to be processed at this operation as compared to the base units received into inventory at the end of the routing.

BOM AND ROUTING ADVANCED FEATURES

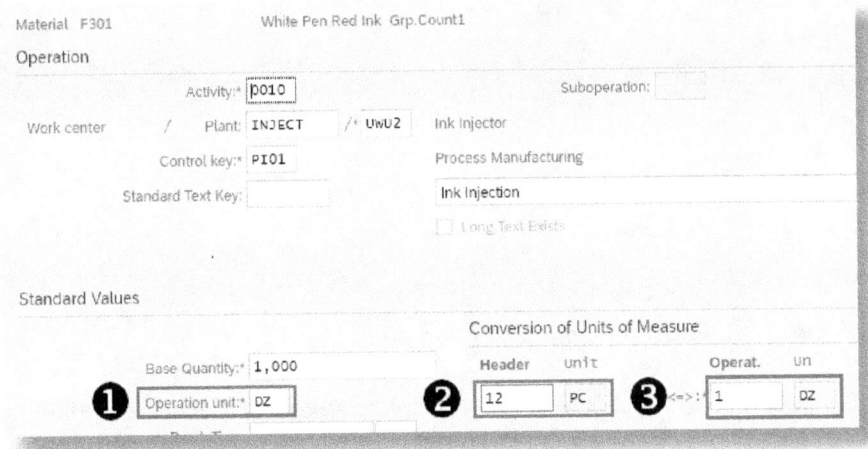

Figure 1.9: Route operation unit of measure conversions

BOM quantities and operation unit of measure conversions

 Unit of measure conversions in operations do not affect the quantities of components that are included in the cost estimate. The component quantity in the BOM should be defined based on the quantity associated with the end of the routing.

1.3 Component allocation to an operation

Component allocation is the assignment of specific components to be issued at a specific operation in the routing or recipe. Not all components have to be issued at the first step in a manufacturing order. In the Universal Writing Utensils scenario, ink is injected into the ink reservoir in the first step of the final pen assembly operation. The ink and the ink reservoir are issued into the first step in the routing. The pen barrel does not become a part of the final product until a later step in the procedure. Figure 1.10 shows the operations for manufacturing material F302 in plant UWU3.

Material	F302			White Pen Blue Ink Grp.Count4								
Sequence:	0											

Operation Overview

	Ope...	Work cen...	Plant	"C...	St...	Description	Lo...	PRT	Cl...	O...	Pe...	Su...	Base...	Un...	Set
☐	0010	INJECT	UWU3	YBP1		Inject Ink							1,000	PC	50
☐	0020	ASSEMBLY	UWU3	YBP1		Assemble pen							1,000	PC	25
☐	0030	PACK	UWU3	YBP3		Packaging							100	DZ	10

Figure 1.10: Routing for manufactured pen

Operation 0010 injects the ink into the ink reservoir, and operation 0020 assembles the barrel and the ink reservoir together to make the pen. Figure 1.11 highlights the component allocation of the routing.

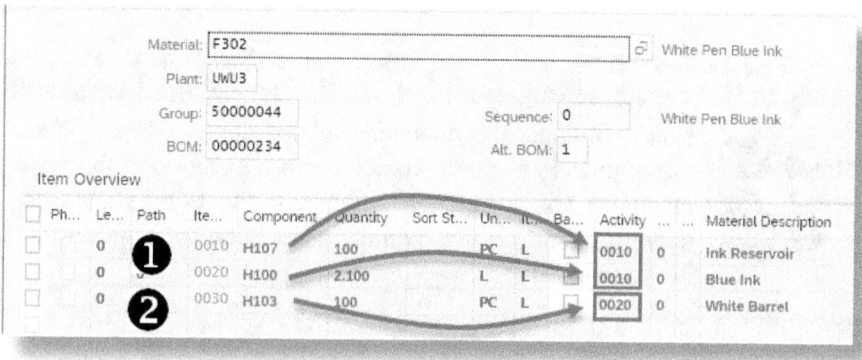

Figure 1.11: Component allocation

Section ❶ shows the first two components (H107 – INK RESERVOIR and H100 – BLUE INK) being allocated to operation 0010 of the routing. This is the ink injection operation. Section ❷ shows component H103 – WHITE BARREL allocated to operation 0020. The resulting cost estimate itemization is shown in Figure 1.12. The operation number has been included in the report layout.

Section ❶ shows the first two components grouped with the activities of operation 0010. Section ❷ shows the white barrel component grouped with the activities of operation 0020. Although the materials are placed in the itemization with the operations to which they are allocated, there is no impact on the cost unless operation scrap is involved. See Section 1.5.4 for a description of how this affects the resulting cost estimate.

ItmNo	...	OpAc	Resource			Resource (Text)	Cost Element	Total Value	COCr	Quantity	Un
1	E	0010	300104	INJECT	SETUP	Inject Ink	94303000	45.76	USD	0.833	HR
2	E	0010	300104	INJECT	MACHHR	Inject Ink	94301000	19.31	USD	0.750	HR
3	E	0010	300104	INJECT	LABRHR	Inject Ink	94311000	18.28	USD	0.750	HR
4	M	0010	UWU3 H107			Ink Reservoir	54300000	668.34	USD	1.000	PC
5	M	0010	UWU3 H100			Blue Ink	54300000	33.76	USD	21	L
6	E	0020	300104	ASSEMBLY	SETUP	Assemble pen	94303000	22.91	USD	0.417	HR
7	E	0020	300104	ASSEMBLY	MACHHR	Assemble pen	94301000	25.75	USD	1.0	HR
8	E	0020	300104	ASSEMBLY	LABRHR	Assemble pen	94311000	24.38	USD	1.0	HR
9	M	0020	UWU3 H103			White Barrel	54300000	189.03	USD	1.000	PC
10	E	0030	300105	PACK	SETUP	Packaging	94303000	9.54	USD	10	MIN
11	E	0030	300105	PACK	MACHHR	Packaging	94301000	8.84	USD	0.486	HR
12	E	0030	300105	PACK	LABRHR	Packaging	94311000	25.03	USD	0.972	HR
								1,090.93	USD		

Figure 1.12: Cost estimate showing component allocation

1.4 Specifying a quantity structure for costing

A specific production version, BOM, or task list can be defined for use in costing regardless of the normal quantity structure selection process. This provides the ability to see the cost impact of using a specific method for manufacturing, compared to the standard method. There are two ways to accomplish this.

The first method is to use the defaults that are found on the COSTING 1 tab of the material master. Material F302 at plant UWU3 has four different routings and two different BOMs. There are currently only two production versions defined: 0001 and 0002. The difference is in which BOM they use. Assuming that the lot sizes and the dates match, the normal selection methodology chooses production version 0001, which comes first alphabetically (production versions are alphanumeric). To force production version 0002, the definition needs to be set in the COSTING 1 tab of the material master. Figure 1.13 shows the QUANTITY STRUCTURE DATA section of the COSTING 1 tab for material F302 at plant UWU3.

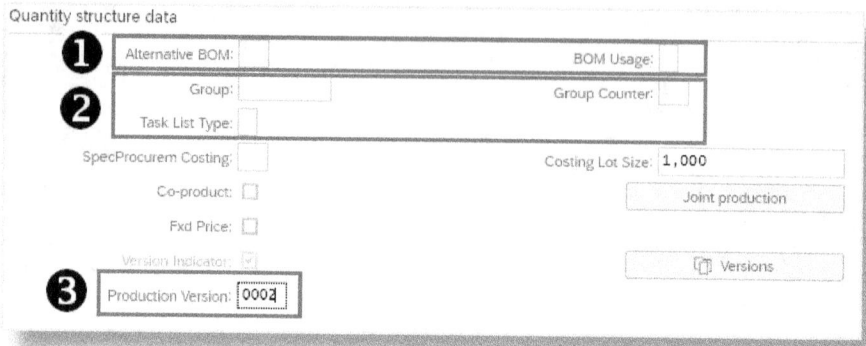

Figure 1.13: Quantity structure data from Costing 1 tab

In section ❶, a specific ALTERNATIVE BOM and a BOM USAGE can be selected for use within the cost estimate. The fields in section ❷ indicate the selection of a specific routing or recipe. Section ❸ defines a specific PRODUCTION VERSION to be used. In this case, production version 0002 is selected. The resulting cost estimate is shown in Figure 1.14 with the PRODUCTION VERSION highlighted.

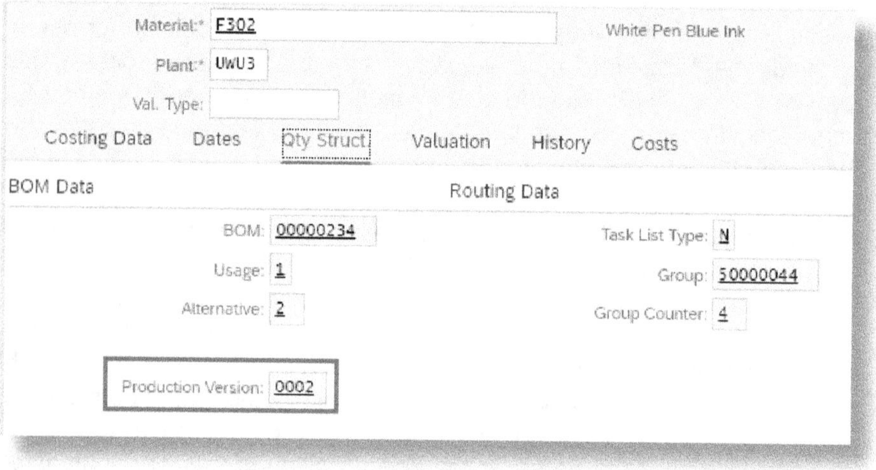

Figure 1.14: Cost estimate showing production version selection

Quantity structure selections

 If both a production version and a BOM/routing combination are defined in the material, the production version takes priority. If a specific BOM or routing is defined with no production version, that BOM or routing is used instead. If it is associated with one or more production versions, then the first valid production version is selected and used for the cost estimate. If it is not assigned to a production version, then no production version is used for the cost estimate.

The second method is to specify the quantity structure when creating a cost estimate using either the Create Material Cost Estimate Fiori tile or transaction CK11N. After entering the main costing information on the COSTING DATA tab, select the QTY STRUCT. tab. A specific BOM, routing task list, or production version can be selected at this time (see Figure 1.15).

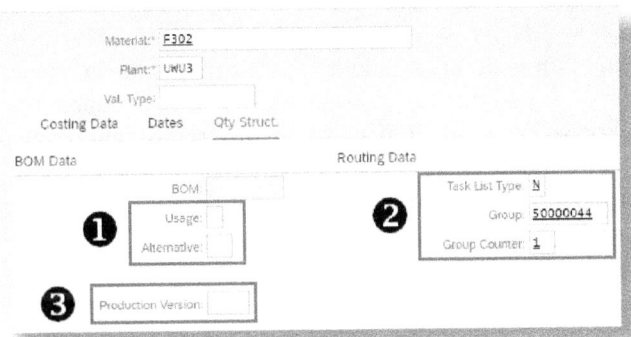

Figure 1.15: Quantity structure selection in cost estimate

Section ❶ shows the BOM information. Only BOM USAGE and ALTERNATIVE can be selected. Section ❷ shows the task list information. Only one of the selections is necessary to define a routing task list. For example, GROUP 50000044 has four task lists assigned to it. If only GROUP COUNTER is entered, then the system uses that group counter, assuming it is assigned to one of the groups used by that material. In section ❸, the production version is chosen. Figure 1.16 shows that the requested task list information was used for the cost estimate. Note that this task list is not yet assigned to a production version, so the production version is blank, and the BOM was selected using the standard selection process.

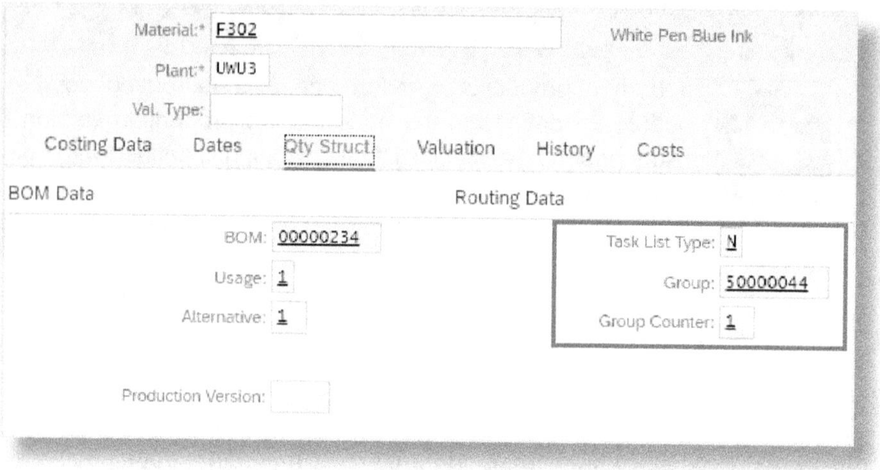

Figure 1.16: Routing task list selection in cost estimate

1.5 Scrap

The processes used in manufacturing are not perfect, and events can occur which cause a portion of the production to be unusable. This unusable portion of production is known as *scrap*. If this is a normal part of manufacturing certain products, then the amount of scrap can be accounted for in cost estimates. Scrap can occur at any operation within a routing and can also be associated with components being issued to the product.

SAP uses three different classifications of scrap:

- *Component scrap* accounts for the quantity of a component that is unable to be used in the product due to either quality issues or manufacturing constraints that prevent using 100% of the component. Component scrap increases the quantity of the component by the percentage assigned.

- *Operation scrap* describes the amount of production that is lost at specific operations in the routing. This reduces the amount that is delivered from an operation, based on the quantity that entered the operation, by the specified percentage. This affects the final costing lot size.

- *Assembly scrap* represents the amount of product that does not meet the required standards for that product. In effect, this increases the quantity of components and manufacturing activities used by the percentage defined. Costing lot size is unaffected.

1.5.1 Component scrap

Master data defining component scrap percentages is found in two places. Figure 1.17 shows that, as defined in the material master, component H100 normally loses 10% of the quantity issued into the order. This means that 10% more of the component must be accounted for in the product cost.

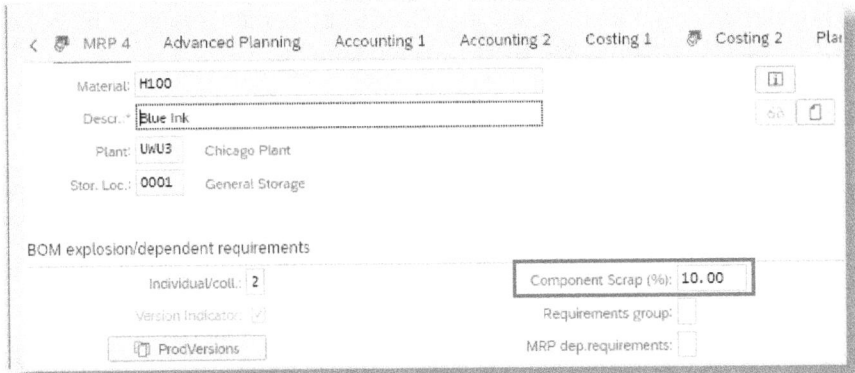

Figure 1.17: Component scrap definition on MRP 4 tab

The impact of scrap in the cost estimate can be seen in the costing structure. Figure 1.18 shows the result of the component scrap calculations in the costing structure of the cost estimate.

Resource			Quantity	Co...	Scrap ...	U...	Scrap...	Total val...	Comp.S...	Scrap	Cur...
UWU3 F302			1,000	0	0	PC	0.000	1,324.30	0.00	0.00	USD
300104	INJECT	SETUP	0.833	0.0	0.0	HR	0.000	45.76	0.00	0.00	USD
300104	INJECT	MACHHR	0.750	0.0	0.0	HR	0.000	19.31	0.00	0.00	USD
300104	INJECT	LABRHR	0.750	0.0	0.0	HR	0.000	18.28	0.00	0.00	USD
UWU3 H107			1,000	0	0	PC	0.000	668.34	0.00	0.00	USD
UWU3 H100			23.100	2.100	0	L	10.000	37.14	3.38	0.00	USD
300104	ASSEMBLY	SETUP	0.417	0.0	0.0	HR	0.000	22.91	0.00	0.00	USD
300104	ASSEMBLY	MACHHR	1.0	0.0	0.0	HR	0.000	25.75	0.00	0.00	USD
300104	ASSEMBLY	LABRHR	1.0	0.0	0.0	HR	0.000	24.38	0.00	0.00	USD
UWU3 H103			1,000	0	0	PC	0.000	189.03	0.00	0.00	USD
300105	PACK	SETUP	10	0	0	MIN	0.000	9.54	0.00	0.00	USD
300105	PACK	MACHHR	0.486	0.0	0.0	HR	0.000	8.84	0.00	0.00	USD
300105	PACK	LABRHR	0.972	0.0	0.0	HR	0.000	25.03	0.00	0.00	USD
UWU3 V500			1,000	0	0	PC	0.000	230.00	0.00	0.00	USD

Figure 1.18: Component scrap quantity and value

Of the 23.1 L of material H100 in the cost estimate, 2.1 L account for the 10% component scrap defined for the material. The value of the scrap is 3.38 USD for lot size 1,000. Only use component scrap defined at the material level, if that is the normal loss, regardless of the product in which it is used.

The second place that component scrap can be defined is in the BOM. Drill down into the component. The component scrap percentage is found in the QUANTITY DATA section of the BASIC DATA tab (see Figure 1.19).

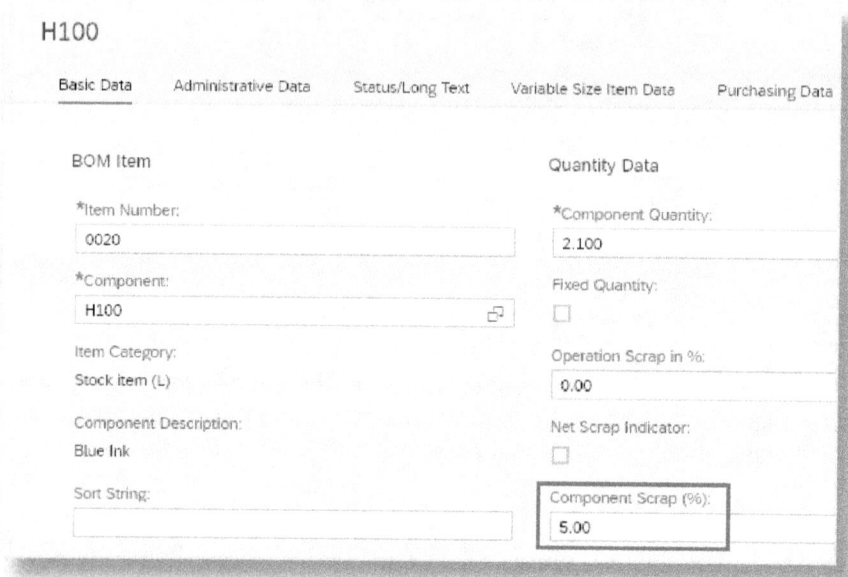

Figure 1.19: Component scrap in the BOM

Component scrap defined in the BOM supersedes the scrap defined in the material master. In this case, BOM component scrap is set to 5%, whereas the value in the material master is set to 10% (see Figure 1.17). Compare Figure 1.20 with the costing structure in Figure 1.18. In this case, the scrap percentage now shows 5% instead of the 10% from the material master.

Resource			Quantity	Co...	Scrap ...	U...	Scrap...	Total val...	Comp.S...	Scrap	Cur...
UWU3 F302			1.000	0	0	PC	0.000	1,322.63	0.00	0.00	USD
300104	INJECT	SETUP	0.833	0.0	0.0	HR	0.000	45.76	0.00	0.00	USD
300104	INJECT	MACHHR	0.750	0.0	0.0	HR	0.000	19.31	0.00	0.00	USD
300104	INJECT	LABRHR	0.750	0.0	0.0	HR	0.000	18.28	0.00	0.00	USD
UWU3 H107			1.000	0	0	PC	0.000	668.34	0.00	0.00	USD
UWU3 H100			22.050	1.050	0	L	5.000	35.45	1.69	0.00	USD
300104	ASSEMBLY	SETUP	0.417	0.0	0.0	HR	0.000	22.91	0.00	0.00	USD
300104	ASSEMBLY	MACHHR	1.0	0.0	0.0	HR	0.000	25.75	0.00	0.00	USD
300104	ASSEMBLY	LABRHR	1.0	0.0	0.0	HR	0.000	24.38	0.00	0.00	USD
UWU3 H103			1.000	0	0	PC	0.000	189.03	0.00	0.00	USD
300105	PACK	SETUP	10	0	0	MIN	0.000	9.54	0.00	0.00	USD
300105	PACK	MACHHR	0.486	0.0	0.0	HR	0.000	8.84	0.00	0.00	USD
300105	PACK	LABRHR	0.972	0.0	0.0	HR	0.000	25.03	0.00	0.00	USD
UWU3 V500			1.000	0	0	PC	0.000	230.00	0.00	0.00	USD

Figure 1.20: Component scrap from BOM

One other BOM item setting that can have an effect on the calculation of the component scrap is the NET SCRAP INDICATOR. If this checkbox is selected, then the scrap assigned for the item is not affected by the assembly scrap. This is covered in Section 1.5.3.

1.5.2 Operation scrap

Operation scrap is applicable to either routing operations or BOM components. The effect of operation scrap depends on where it is assigned. Like component scrap, operation scrap can be defined for a BOM component. In this case, the operation scrap only affects the amount of component, and works similarly to component scrap. When used for a component, it represents the amount that is lost associated with being issued to the operation. BOM operation scrap is defined in the same area as BOM component scrap (see Figure 1.21). If operation scrap is defined for a component, NET SCRAP INDICATOR must be selected.

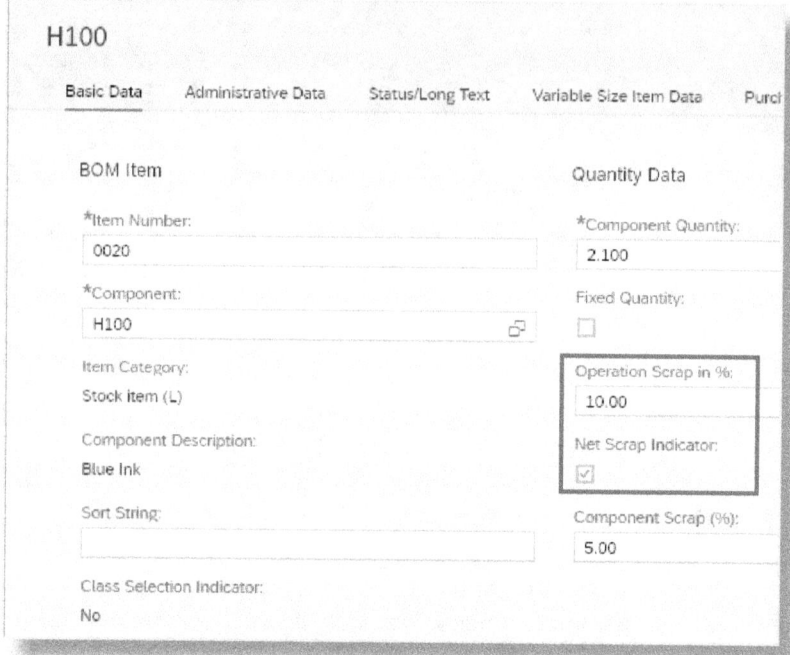

Figure 1.21: Operation scrap for a BOM component

If both operation scrap and component scrap are defined for a component, the operation scrap is processed first. Component scrap is calculated based on the total component quantity after the operation scrap is applied. In this example, the component quantity per 100 is 2.1 L. First, apply the 10% operation scrap: 2.1 L plus 0.21 L becomes 2.31 L. The 5% component scrap is applied to that total: 2.31 L multiplied by 0.05 is 0.1155 L. The cost estimate costing lot size is 1,000, and for that quantity the numbers are multiplied by 10. The results are shown in Figure 1.22. For 1,000 PC, the operation scrap quantity is 2.1 L and the component scrap quantity is 1.155 L.

When operation scrap is assigned to the routing, the effect is different. The quantity produced by that operation is reduced by the scrap percentage. The final quantity after applying all operation scrap percentages becomes the costing lot size. Figure 1.23 shows the position for defining scrap on an operation in the route. 10% is assigned to the last operation. If the costing lot size for the material is 1,000, the effective costing lot size becomes 900 (1,000 minus 1,000 multiplied by 0.10).

BOM AND ROUTING ADVANCED FEATURES

Resource		Quantity	Co...	Scrap...	U...	Scrap...	Total val...	Comp.S...	Scrap	Cur...
UWU3 F302		1,000	0	0	PC	0.000	1,326.15	0.00	0.00	USD
300104	INJECT SETUP	0.833	0.0	0.0	HR	0.000	45.76	0.00	0.00	USD
300104	INJECT MACHHR	0.750	0.0	0.0	HR	0.000	19.31	0.00	0.00	USD
300104	INJECT LABRHR	0.750	0.0	0.0	HR	0.000	18.28	0.00	0.00	USD
UWU3 H107		1,000	0	0	PC	0.000	668.34	0.00	0.00	USD
UWU3 H100		24.255	1.155	2.100	L	5.000	38.99	1.86	3.38	USD
300104	ASSEMBLY SETUP	0.417	0.0	0.0	HR	0.000	22.91	0.00	0.00	USD
300104	ASSEMBLY MACHHR	1.0	0.0	0.0	HR	0.000	25.75	0.00	0.00	USD
300104	ASSEMBLY LABRHR	1.0	0.0	0.0	HR	0.000	24.38	0.00	0.00	USD
UWU3 H103		1,000	0	0	PC	0.000	189.03	0.00	0.00	USD
300105	PACK SETUP	10	0	0	MIN	0.000	9.54	0.00	0.00	USD
300105	PACK MACHHR	0.486	0.0	0.0	HR	0.000	8.84	0.00	0.00	USD
300105	PACK LABRHR	0.972	0.0	0.0	HR	0.000	25.03	0.00	0.00	USD
UWU3 V500		1,000	0	0	PC	0.000	230.00	0.00	0.00	USD

Figure 1.22: Cost estimate with operation scrap for the BOM item

Material	F302			White Pen Blue Ink Grp.Count:4										
Sequence:	0													

Operation Overview

	Ope...	Work cen...	Plant	"C...	Description	Base...	Un...	Se...	Unit	Activit...	M...	Unit	Activit...	La...	Unit	Activit...	Scrap	Use
☐	0010	INJECT	UWU3	YBP1	Inject Ink	1,000	PC	50	MIN	SETUP	45	MIN	MACHHR	45	MIN	LABRHR		
☐	0020	ASSEMBLY	UWU3	YBP2	Assemble pen	1,000	PC	25	MIN	SETUP	60	MIN	MACHHR	60	MIN	LABRHR		
☐	0030	PACK	UWU3	YBP3	Packaging	100	OZ	10	MIN	SETUP	35	MIN	MACHHR	70	MIN	LABRHR	10.000	

Figure 1.23: Operation scrap at operation 0030

Figure 1.24 shows the effect of putting 10% scrap on the cost estimate. There are several impacts of assigning operation scrap to one operation. First, note that the quantity in the costing structure has been reduced from 1,000 (in Figure 1.22) to 900. Second, the quantities remain the same for activities and materials as they were in the previous cost estimate. However, these quantities are now associated with a lot size of 900 instead of 1,000. The effect of this is an increase of 11.111% to these quantities (1 divided by 0.90 expressed as a percentage). Therefore, 10% operation scrap impacts the resulting cost estimate by 11.111%. Component H100 previously had a scrap quantity of 2.1 L using the operation scrap assigned to the BOM component. The 10% operation scrap is based on the original material quantity and not the quantity calculated after the BOM scrap was assigned. This is applied to the original BOM quantity, so the total scrap quantity is 2.1 L (BOM) plus 2.1 L (operation). Finally, the fixed SETUP activities do not have an associated scrap component. The scrap portion can only be calculated for the activity type quantities that are associated with the base quantity of the operation.

Resource		Quantity	Co...	Scrap...	U...	Scrap...	Total va...	Comp.S...	Scrap	Cur...
UWU3 F302		900	0	0	PC	0.000	1,326.15	0.00	0.00	USD
300104	INJECT SETUP	0.833	0.0	0.0	HR	0.000	45.76	0.00	0.00	USD
300104	INJECT MACHHR	0.750	0.0	0.075	HR	0.000	19.31	0.00	1.93	USD
300104	INJECT LABRHR	0.750	0.0	0.075	HR	0.000	18.28	0.00	1.83	USD
UWU3 H107		1.000	0	100	PC	0.000	668.34	0.00	66.83	USD
UWU3 H100		24.255	1.155	4.200	L	5.000	38.99	1.86	6.75	USD
300104	ASSEMBLY SETUP	0.417	0.0	0.0	HR	0.000	22.91	0.00	0.00	USD
300104	ASSEMBLY MACHHR	1.0	0.0	0.1	HR	0.000	25.75	0.00	2.58	USD
300104	ASSEMBLY LABRHR	1.0	0.0	0.1	HR	0.000	24.38	0.00	2.44	USD
UWU3 H103		1.000	0	100	PC	0.000	189.03	0.00	18.90	USD
300105	PACK SETUP	10	0	0	MIN	10.000	9.54	0.00	0.00	USD
300105	PACK MACHHR	0.486	0.0	0.049	HR	0.000	8.84	0.00	0.89	USD
300105	PACK LABRHR	0.972	0.0	0.097	HR	0.000	25.03	0.00	2.50	USD
UWU3 V500		1.000	0	100	PC	0.000	230.00	0.00	23.00	USD

Reduced lot size → Quantity column (900)
Operation scrap cumulatively applied to component → Total val column
Quantities as if for 1,000
Scrap applied to components and variable activities

Figure 1.24: Cost estimate with operation scrap on last operation

Figure 1.25 shows what happens when 10% operation scrap is assigned to the last operation of the route. To make the comparison easier, the itemization display has been changed from COSTING LOT SIZE to USER ENTRY. The quantity entered is 1,000, and the full impact is evident by comparing this with Figure 1.22.

Activity costs are affected for all operations up to and including the operation for which the scrap was assigned. Material costs are impacted by the reduction in lot size based on the scrap percentage. In the previous example, the 10% scrap reduced the costing lot size from 1,000 PC to 900 PC. The quantities of each of the materials consumed remain the same as for the 1,000 quantity. Therefore, this accounts for the increase in the quantities of components that are required in manufacturing. Using both BOM operation scrap and routing operation scrap together can cause the component quantity to be overstated in the final cost, as is the case for component H100 in this example.

BOM AND ROUTING ADVANCED FEATURES

Resource			Quantity	Co...	Scrap ...	U...	Scrap...	Total val...	Comp.S...	Scrap	Cur...
UWU3 F302			1.000	0	0	PC	0.000	1,473.50	0.00	0.00	USD
300104	INJECT	SETUP	0.926	0.0	0.0	HR	0.000	50.84	0.00	0.00	USD
300104	INJECT	MACHHR	0.833	0.0	0.083	HR	0.000	21.46	0.00	2.14	USD
300104	INJECT	LABRHR	0.833	0.0	0.083	HR	0.000	20.31	0.00	2.02	USD
UWU3 H107			1.111.111	0	111.111	PC	0.000	742.60	0.00	74.26	USD
UWU3 H100			26.950	1.283	4.667	L	5.000	43.33	2.06	7.50	USD
300104	ASSEMBLY	SETUP	0.463	0.0	0.0	HR	0.000	25.46	0.00	0.00	USD
300104	ASSEMBLY	MACHHR	1.111	0.0	0.111	HR	0.000	28.61	0.00	2.86	USD
300104	ASSEMBLY	LABRHR	1.111	0.0	0.111	HR	0.000	27.09	0.00	2.71	USD
UWU3 H103			1.111.111	0	111.111	PC	0.000	210.03	0.00	21.00	USD
300105	PACK	SETUP	11.111	0	0	MIN	10.000	10.60	0.00	0.00	USD
300105	PACK	MACHHR	0.540	0.0	0.054	HR	0.000	9.82	0.00	0.98	USD
300105	PACK	LABRHR	1.080	0.0	0.108	HR	0.000	27.81	0.00	2.78	USD
UWU3 V500			1.111.111	0	111.111	PC	0.000	255.56	0.00	25.56	USD

Figure 1.25: Cost estimate adjusted to 1,000 PC

> **Operation scrap in recipes**
>
> Operation scrap is not available for recipes.

1.5.3 Assembly scrap

Assembly scrap is defined in the MRP 1 tab of the material master. The effect of this type of scrap is an increase in the quantities of activities and material components by the percentage defined in the material master. Figure 1.26 shows assembly scrap of 10% assigned to the material in the LOT SIZE DATA section of the MRP 1 tab.

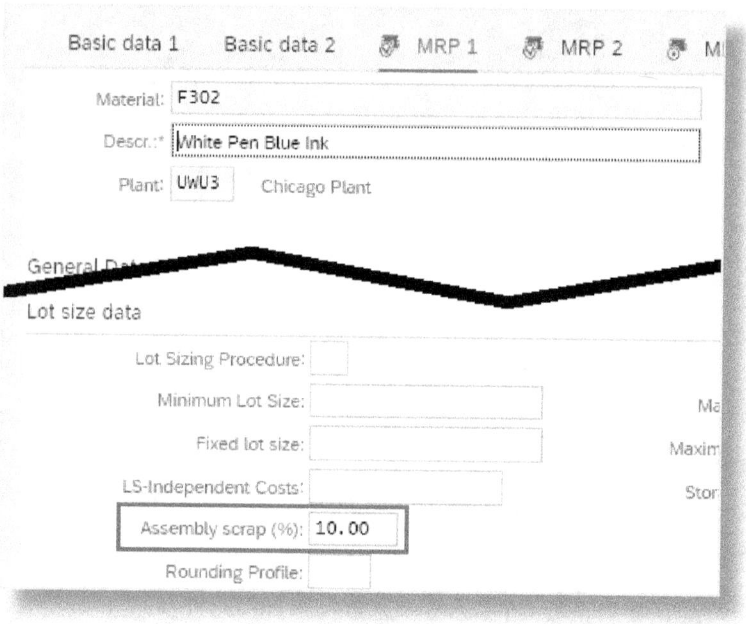

Figure 1.26: Assembly scrap assignment in MRP 1

All operation scrap from the previous examples has been removed. Looking at the resulting cost estimate in Figure 1.27, the 10% scrap has been applied to all components and all activities whose quantities are based on the operation base quantity. The SETUP activities, which don't rely on base quantity, are unaffected. This makes sense, because setting up the equipment should not be affected by scrap associated with the production process. Another thing to note is that the lot size is unaffected and remains at 1,000.

The component scrap for material H100 was also raised by 10%. This is because the NET SCRAP INDICATOR for that component was not selected. Figure 1.28 shows the impact of selecting NET SCRAP INDICATOR for the component in the BOM. When this checkbox is selected, the assembly scrap factor has no impact on the quantity of the component in the final cost estimate. In this case, only the 5% component scrap is assigned. Other scrap is set to 0. Compare this with Figure 1.27.

Figure 1.27: Cost estimate with assembly scrap

Normal lot size → (Quantity column)
Component scrap based on assembly scrap-adjusted quantity → (Scrap Total val... column)

Resource			Quantity	Co...	Scrap...	U...	Scrap...	Total val...	Comp.S...	Scrap	Cur...
UWU3 F302			1,000	0	0	PC	0.000	1,447.05	0.00	0.00	USD
300104	INJECT	SETUP	0.833	0.0	0.0	HR	0.000	45.76	0.00	0.00	USD
300104	INJECT	MACHHR	0.825	0.0	0.075	HR	0.000	21.24	0.00	1.93	USD
300104	INJECT	LABRHR	0.825	0.0	0.075	HR	0.000	20.11	0.00	1.83	USD
UWU3 H107			1.100	0	100	PC	0.000	735.17	0.00	66.83	USD
UWU3 H100			24.255	1.155	2.100	L	5.000	38.99	1.86	3.38	USD
300104	ASSEMBLY SETUP		0.417	0.0	0.0	HR	0.000	22.91	0.00	0.00	USD
300104	ASSEMBLY MACHHR		1.1	0.0	0.1	HR	0.000	28.33	0.00	2.58	USD
300104	ASSEMBLY LABRHR		1.1	0.0	0.1	HR	0.000	26.81	0.00	2.44	USD
UWU3 H103			1.100	0	100	PC	0.000	207.93	0.00	18.90	USD
300105	PACK	SETUP	10	0	0	MIN	0.000	9.54	0.00	0.00	USD
300105	PACK	MACHHR	0.535	0.0	0.049	HR	0.000	9.73	0.00	0.89	USD
300105	PACK	LABRHR	1.069	0.0	0.097	HR	0.000	27.53	0.00	2.50	USD
UWU3 V500			1.100	0	100	PC	0.000	253.00	0.00	23.00	USD

Variable quantities increased by applying assembly scrap %
Scrap applied to components and variable activities

Figure 1.27: Cost estimate with assembly scrap

Resource			Quantity	Co...	Scrap...	U...	Scrap...	Total val...	Comp.S...	Scrap	Cur...
UWU3 F302			1.000	0	0	PC	0.000	1,443.53	0.00	0.00	USD
300104	INJECT	SETUP	0.833	0.0	0.0	HR	0.000	45.76	0.00	0.00	USD
300104	INJECT	MACHHR	0.825	0.0	0.075	HR	0.000	21.24	0.00	1.93	USD
300104	INJECT	LABRHR	0.825	0.0	0.075	HR	0.000	20.11	0.00	1.83	USD
UWU3 H107			1.100	0	100	PC	0.000	735.17	0.00	66.83	USD
UWU3 H100			22.050	1.050	0	L	5.000	35.45	1.69	0.00	USD
300104	ASSEMBLY SETUP		0.417	0.0	0.0	HR	0.000	22.91	0.00	0.00	USD
300104	ASSEMBLY MACHHR		1.1	0.0	0.1	HR	0.000	28.33	0.00	2.58	USD
300104	ASSEMBLY LABRHR		1.1	0.0	0.1	HR	0.000	26.81	0.00	2.44	USD
UWU3 H103			1.100	0	100	PC	0.000	207.93	0.00	18.90	USD
300105	PACK	SETUP	10	0	0	MIN	0.000	9.54	0.00	0.00	USD
300105	PACK	MACHHR	0.535	0.0	0.049	HR	0.000	9.73	0.00	0.89	USD
300105	PACK	LABRHR	1.069	0.0	0.097	HR	0.000	27.53	0.00	2.50	USD
UWU3 V500			1.100	0	100	PC	0.000	253.00	0.00	23.00	USD

Figure 1.28: Cost estimate with Net Scrap Indicator set

Assembly scrap and operation scrap also interact with each other. However, if the operation scrap is assigned to the BOM component, the NET SCRAP INDICATOR must be selected, and only the operation scrap is applied to that component. The example in Figure 1.29 shows a cost estimate with mixed assembly and operation scrap.

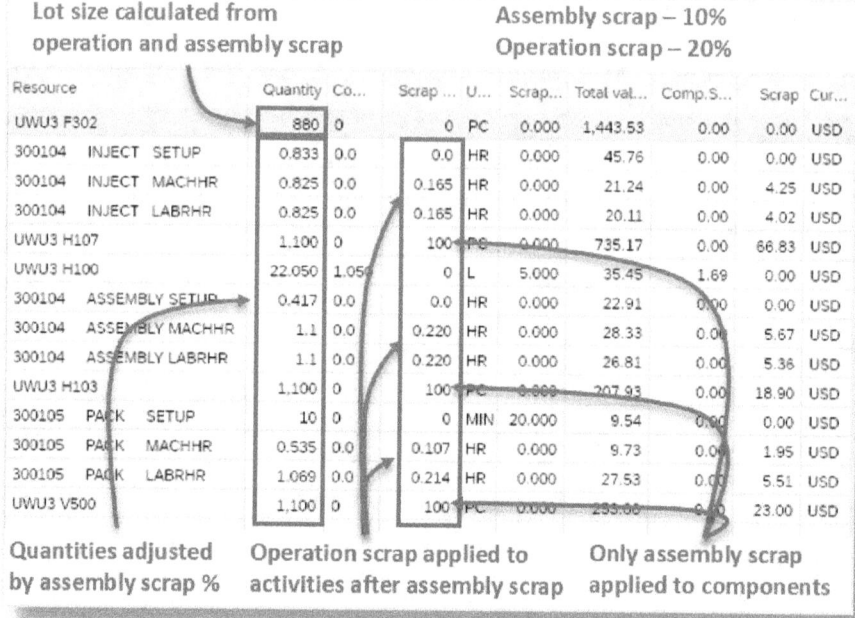

Figure 1.29: Cost estimate with assembly and operation scrap

Operation 0030 has scrap set at 20%. Assembly scrap is set to 10%. The costing lot size is calculated based on a combination of the two scrap values. First, the operation scrap is applied to reduce the output quantity. This is 20%, so the result is 800 PC. Next, the assembly scrap percentage is applied to the result. 10% of 800 is 80. These are added together to arrive at the final lot size of 880 PC. Next, the assembly scrap percentage is applied to the variable quantities for the activities and the components that don't have the NET SCRAP INDICATOR checkbox selected in the BOM. The scrap associated with the variable activities is calculated from the operation scrap in the route using the updated activity quantities. The scrap quantity calculated is based on the 20% value shown in Figure 1.29. If the NET SCRAP INDICATOR checkbox is not selected for the components, the scrap quantity is calculated using the assembly scrap percentage (10% in this case). If the checkbox is selected in the BOM, then the scrap is determined by the BOM operation scrap value.

The above example was designed to show the impact when the two different types of scrap are used together. If the implementation requires the use of both assembly and operation scrap, the values selected should complement one another. For example, if the operation scrap is set at 20%, the assembly scrap should be 25%. When the operation scrap reduces the lot quantity to 80% of the original, then multiplying the result by 1.25 to represent the 25% assembly scrap provides a consistent scrap quantity calculation for both variable activities and components.

1.5.4 Component allocation and scrap calculations

The routing for the example material has three operations. Previously, operation scrap was only assigned to one operation in the routing. However, scrap can be assigned to any or all the operations. When scrap is assigned to an operation, it has a cost impact on that operation and any operation that occurred before it. When multiple operations have scrap assigned to them, the calculation of total scrap is cumulative. To see the effect, each of the three operations is assigned 10% operation scrap (see Figure 1.30). Assembly scrap is set to 0, and the costing lot size is 1,000 PC.

Ope...	Work cen...	Plant	°C...	Description	Base	Un...	Se...	Unit	Activit...	M...	Unit	Activit...	La...	Unit	Activit...	Scrap	U
0010	INJECT	UWU3	YBP1	Inject ink	1,000	PC	50	MIN	SETUP	45	MIN	MACHHR	45	MIN	LABRHR	10.000	
0020	ASSEMBLY	UWU3	YBP1	Assemble pen	1,000	PC	25	MIN	SETUP	60	MIN	MACHHR	60	MIN	LABRHR	10.000	
0030	PACK	UWU3	YBP3	Packaging	100	DZ	10	MIN	SETUP	35	MIN	MACHHR	70	MIN	LABRHR	10.000	

Figure 1.30: Operation scrap on all operations

Because this is operation scrap, the output of each operation is reduced by the specified percentage. Starting with 1,000, the output of operation 0010 becomes 900 (1,000 minus 1,000 multiplied by 0.10). The output of operation 0020 is then 810 (900 minus 900 multiplied by 0.10), and the output from 0030 is 729 (810 minus 810 multiplied by 0.10). Therefore, the final costing lot size should be 729, as shown in Figure 1.31. The quantities superimposed on the figure are from a cost estimate with no operation scrap.

BOM AND ROUTING ADVANCED FEATURES

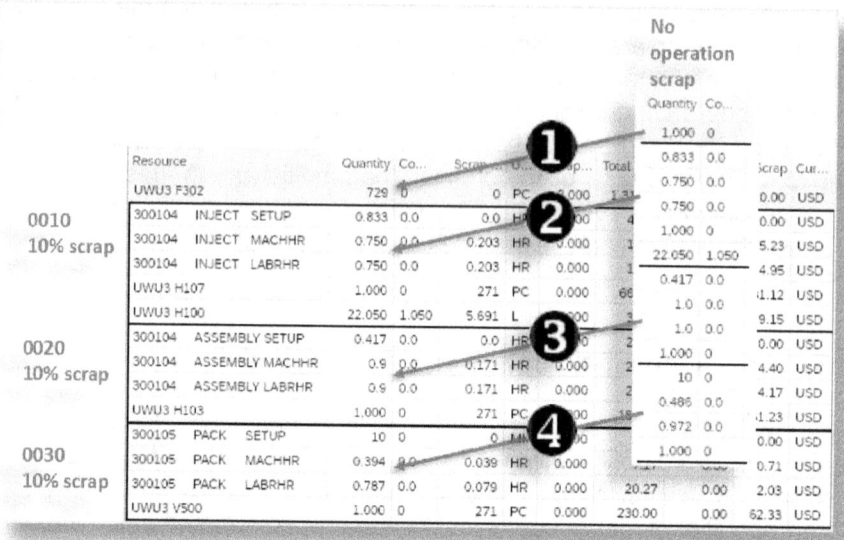

Figure 1.31: Cost estimate activity quantities with operation scrap

Section ❶ shows the reduction of the lot size from 1,000 to 729 as explained above. Section ❷ indicates the activity quantities for MACHHR and LABRHR for operation 0010. Because the full effect of the accumulated scrap for all operations impacts the variable activities for this operation, the quantities are the same. This repeats the behavior that was seen in the cost estimates where only one operation had scrap assigned (see Section 1.5.2). The behavior changes when looking at operation 0020 (section ❸). Note that the quantities for MACHHR and LABRHR have been reduced from 1.0 to 0.9. This is because the output of operation 0010 is 10% less than the input quantity. If the operation started with 1,000, then only 900 go into operation 0020. The quantity of activity needs to reflect this, and 10% of the 1.0 HR allocated in the route is not used in operation 0020. Therefore, the number of hours for MACHHR and LABRHR will be 0.9 for the same lot size. Section ❹ shows a further reduction. Again, there is a 10% reduction in quantity in operation 0020, so only 810 of the original 1,000 are processed in operation 0030. The original 0.486 HR of MACHHR and 0.972 HR of LABRHR must be reduced by 19%. This leaves 0.394 HR of MACHHR and 0.787 HR of LABRHR. The final output of operation 0030 is 729 PC, and this becomes the final lot size for costing.

Figure 1.32 shows the component allocation for material F302 at plant UWU3. Components H107 and H100 are allocated to operation 0010. Component H103 is allocated to operation 0020, and component V500 is allocated to operation 0030. Because these components are allocated to specific operations in the routing, the scrap quantity calculations are expected to follow the same logic as the activity quantities. H107 and H100 are issued into the first operation. Therefore, the full quantities (1,000 PC and 22.050 L) should be accounted for in the cost estimate. The next operation is for 900 PC because of the scrap in the first operation, and 900 PC of H103 is used in operation 0020. For operation 0030, the quantity is reduced to 810 PC based on the accumulated scrap totals, and only 810 PC of material V500 is included in the cost estimate.

Material:	F302							White Pen Blue Ink	
Plant:	UWU3								
Group:	50000044			Sequence:	0			White Pen Blue Ink in-house	
BOM:	00000234			Alt. BOM:	2				

Path	Ite...	Component	Quantity	So...	Un...	It...	Ba...	Activity	...	...	Material Description
0	0010	H107	100		PC	L	✓	0010	0		Ink Reservoir
0	0020	H100	2.100		L	L	✓	0010	0		Blue Ink
0	0030	H103	100		PC	L	✓	0020	0		White Barrel
0	0040	V500	100		PC	L	✓	0030	0		Pen Packaging

Figure 1.32: Component allocation for material F302

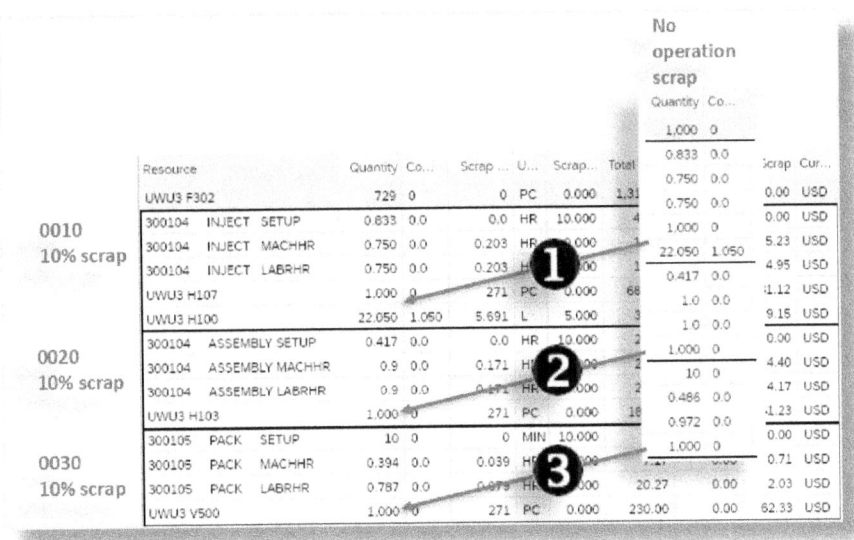

Figure 1.33: Components in cost estimate with operation scrap

Figure 1.33 is the resulting cost estimate. Section ❶ shows the expected quantities of 1,000 PC and 22.050 L for components H107 and H100. However, sections ❷ and ❸ show 1,000 PC for components H103 and V500 instead of the expected 900 PC and 810 PC respectively. This is because the operation scrap calculations only work for costs associated directly with the operation and not for BOM components. Had there been no component allocation, or if all components been allocated to the first operation, then this cost estimate would be correct.

There are two possible remedies for this situation. The first is to adjust the BOM quantities to account for the scrap associated with each operation. In this case, material H103 would have a quantity of 90 PC per the BOM base quantity of 100, and V500 would have a quantity of 81 PC. Figure 1.34 shows the adjusted quantities.

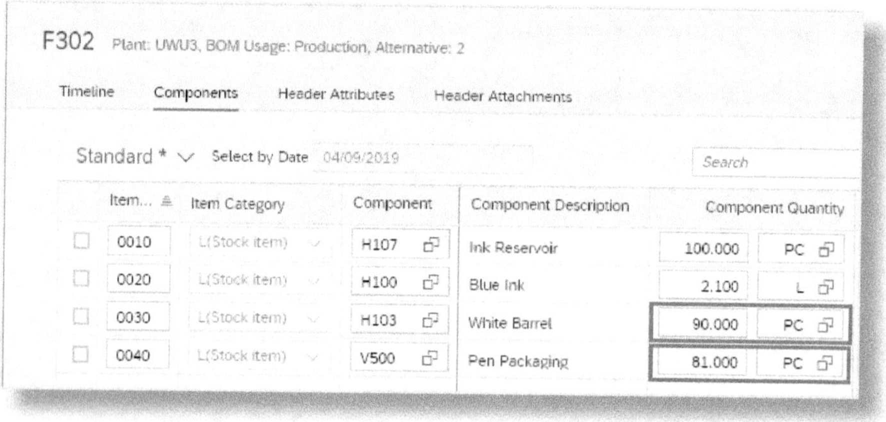

Item...	Item Category	Component	Component Description	Component Quantity	
0010	L(Stock item)	H107	Ink Reservoir	100.000	PC
0020	L(Stock item)	H100	Blue Ink	2.100	L
0030	L(Stock item)	H103	White Barrel	90.000	PC
0040	L(Stock item)	V500	Pen Packaging	81.000	PC

Figure 1.34: Adjusted component quantities

Figure 1.35 is the resulting cost estimate. Section ❶ shows a value of 1,248.59 USD per 729 PC. Section ❷ shows the proper quantity for material H103 (900 PC), but the accompanying calculated scrap quantity and corresponding cost is high. Section ❸ shows the same thing for component V500. The correct quantity is included in the cost, but the scrap quantity and amount appear high. With a 10% loss at operation 0030, 81 PC of V500 should be accounted for as scrap.

BOM AND ROUTING ADVANCED FEATURES

Resource			Quantity	Co...	Scrap...	U...	Scrap...	Total val...	Comp.S...	Scrap	Cur...
UWU3 F302			729	0	0	PC	❶	1,248.59	0.00	0.00	USD
300104	INJECT	SETUP	0.833	0.0	0.0	HR	10.000	45.76	0.00	0.00	USD
300104	INJECT	MACHHR	0.750	0.0	0.203	HR	0.000	19.31	0.00	5.23	USD
300104	INJECT	LABRHR	0.750	0.0	0.203	HR	0.000	18.28	0.00	4.95	USD
UWU3 H107			1.000	0	271	PC	0.000	668.34	0.00	181.12	USD
UWU3 H100			22.050	1.050	5.691	L	5.000	35.45	1.69	9.15	USD
300104	ASSEMBLY	SETUP	0.417	0.0	0.0	HR	10.000	22.91	0.00	0.00	USD
300104	ASSEMBLY	MACHHR	0.9	0.0	0.171	HR	0.000	23.18	0.00	4.40	USD
300104	ASSEMBLY	LABRHR	0.9	0.0	0.171	HR	0.000	21.94	0.00	4.17	USD
UWU3 H103		❷	900	0	243.900	PC	0.000	170.13	0.00	46.11	USD
300105	PACK	SETUP	10	0	0	MIN	10.000	9.54	0.00	0.00	USD
300105	PACK	MACHHR	0.394	0.0	0.039	HR	0.000	7.17	0.00	0.71	USD
300105	PACK	LABRHR	0.787	0.0	0.079	HR	0.000	20.27	0.00	2.03	USD
UWU3 V500		❸	810	0	219.510	PC	0.000	186.30	0.00	50.49	USD

Figure 1.35: Cost estimate with adjusted BOM quantities

The second option to adjust the BOM quantities is to load a negative operations scrap quantity for the last two components. This is shown in Figure 1.36. Component H103 shows operation scrap of -10.00 to account for the 900 PC per 1,000 that should be consumed at this operation. The quantity needs to be reduced from the BOM quantity, so a negative scrap is required. Component 0040 (material V500) shows a scrap value of -19% to reduce its quantity to 810.

F302	Plant: UWU3, BOM Usage: Production, Alternative: 2							
Timeline	Components	Header Attributes	Header Attachments					
Standard * ∨	Select by Date 04/08/2019				Search			
Item...	Item Category		Component	Component Description	Component Quantity		N...	Operation Scrap...
0010	L(Stock item)		H107	Ink Reservoir	100.000	PC	☐	0.00
0020	L(Stock item)		H100	Blue Ink	2.100	L	☐	0.00
0030	L(Stock item)		H103	White Barrel	100.000	PC	☑	-10.00
0040	L(Stock item)		V500	Pen Packaging	100.000	PC	☑	-19.00

Figure 1.36: BOM showing negative operation scrap

Figure 1.37 is the resulting cost estimate. The value at ❶ matches the cost from the previous example: 1,248.59 USD per 729 PC. The cells at ❷ and ❸ show quantities of 900 and 810 for those components, as expected. The scrap quantities are now correct for each of those components.

Resource			Quantity	Co...	Scrap...	U...	Scrap...	Total val...	Comp.S...	Scrap	Cur...
UWU3 F302			729	0	0	PC	❶ 00	1,248.59	0.00	0.00	USD
300104	INJECT	SETUP	0.833	0.0	0.0	HR	10.000	45.76	0.00	0.00	USD
300104	INJECT	MACHHR	0.750	0.0	0.203	HR	0.000	19.31	0.00	5.23	USD
300104	INJECT	LABRHR	0.750	0.0	0.203	HR	0.000	18.28	0.00	4.95	USD
UWU3 H107			1.000	0	271	PC	0.000	668.34	0.00	181.12	USD
UWU3 H100			22.050	1.050	5.691	L	5.000	35.45	1.69	9.15	USD
300104	ASSEMBLY	SETUP	0.417	0.0	0.0	HR	10.000	22.91	0.00	0.00	USD
300104	ASSEMBLY	MACHHR	0.9	0.0	0.171	HR	0.000	23.18	0.00	4.40	USD
300104	ASSEMBLY	LABRHR	0.9	0.0	0.171	HR	0.000	21.94	0.00	4.17	USD
UWU3 H103		❷	900	0	171	PC	0.000	170.13	0.00	32.32	USD
300105	PACK	SETUP	10	0	0	MIN	10.000	9.54	0.00	0.00	USD
300105	PACK	MACHHR	0.394	0.0	0.039	HR	0.000	7.17	0.00	0.71	USD
300105	PACK	LABRHR	0.787	0.0	0.079	HR	0.000	20.27	0.00	2.03	USD
UWU3 V500		❸	810	0	81	PC	0.000	186.30	0.00	18.63	USD

Figure 1.37: Cost estimate with negative operation scrap

Although it seems counter-intuitive, the use of negative operation scrap for the BOM components provides the correct costing result.

1.6 Recursion

Recursion is a process by which a manufactured material consumes itself in the production process. Often in the process industry, the product is used as a base which helps the other components to combine to create more of the product material. Recursion can occur at any level of the exploded BOM. The final product can be used in one of the earlier manufacturing processes, and this also represents a recursive component.

Cost estimates are processed iteratively, and the cost estimate for the recursive item must converge until the cost of the incoming component is equal to the cost of the outgoing material. The cost estimate is successful if the solution successfully converges, the solution is positive, the component usage is less than the product yield, and the yield is significantly higher than the usage. The dividing line for successful completion based on consumption and yield is approximately 0.95 (a component quantity of 0.95 yields a product quantity of 1.00). If no solution exists or the costing result does not converge, the cost estimate ends in error.

Material H102 (black ink) at the Los Angeles plant (UWU2) has an alternative BOM 3 that includes 90 L of H102 as a component of itself based on manufacturing 100 L of material. Figure 1.38 shows the resulting cost estimate. Arrow ❶ shows that H102 is a component of itself. Arrow ❷ shows that the component quantity ratio to the yield quantity is 0.90; this is less than the 0.95 cutoff, and the costs converge. Section ❸ shows that no error messages were generated.

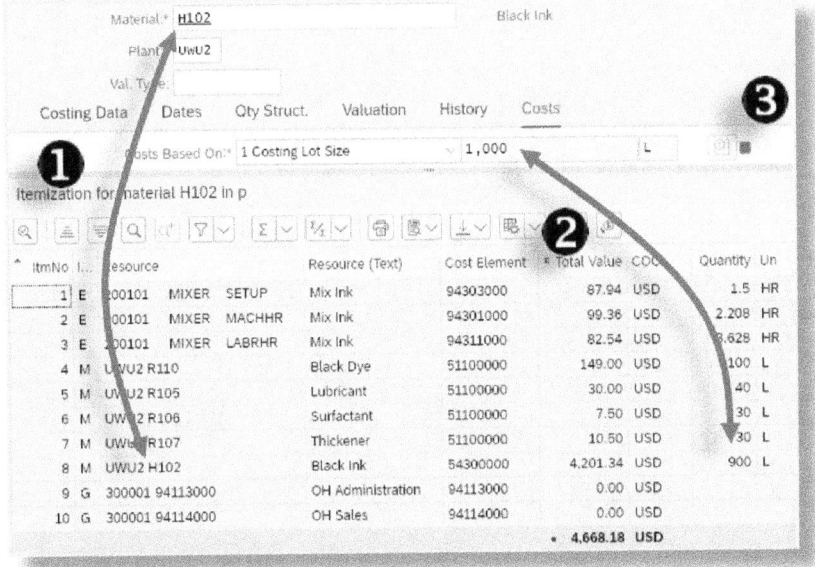

Figure 1.38: Successful cost estimate with recursion

The component quantity is now changed to 98 L of H102 for 100 L of product. The resulting cost estimate fails, and error messages are generated, as in Figure 1.39.

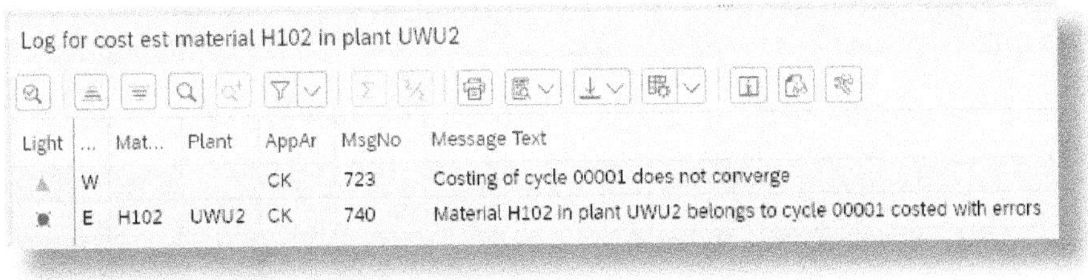

Figure 1.39: Recursion errors from the revised cost estimate

Message CK723 (COSTING OF CYCLE 00001 DOES NOT CONVERGE) is a warning, but because convergence failed, message CK740 is generated as an error. The cost estimate has failed because the ratio is now 0.98, which exceeds the error threshold.

2 Costing with special procurement

Special procurement keys are used in SAP Production Planning to denote the standard method for procuring a material. Keys are used in conjunction with the procurement type to denote processes such as internal manufacturing, subcontracting, stock transfers from another plant, withdrawal of goods from another plant, and manufacturing in another plant. CO-PC-PCP uses many of the special procurement keys in product costing with quantity structure. Costing requirements can differ from those of planning, and both can be accommodated when assigning special procurement keys to materials.

2.1 Special procurement keys

Special procurement keys are part of the SAP Production Planning (PP) module. These are used to direct the standard behavior of material procurement in Material Resource Planning (MRP). PROCUREMENT TYPE is used to determine whether a material is manufactured in-house, procured externally, or procured both ways. The PROCUREMENT TYPE is defined on the MRP 2 tab of the material master (see Figure 2.1, section ❶).

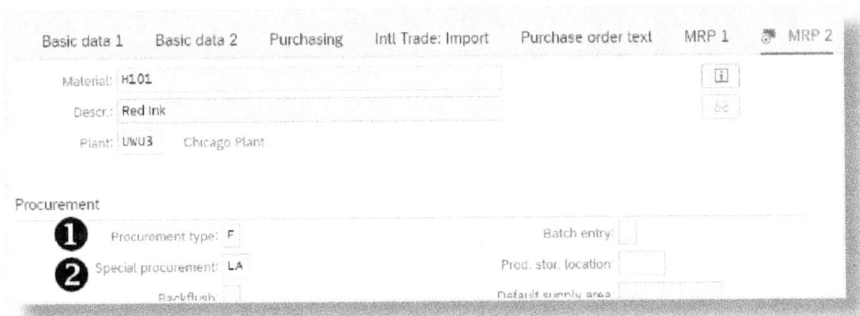

Figure 2.1: Procurement definition on MRP 2 tab

There are three values that can be assigned:

- ▶ E—the material is produced within the plant. When the material is costed, the system looks for a BOM and routing to determine the cost.

41

- ▶ F—the material is procured from a source external to the plant. SPECIAL PROCUREMENT determines the source. If this is blank, the material is assumed to be purchased from an outside vendor.
- ▶ X—procurement can either be internal to the plant or external. When the material is costed, the system looks for a BOM and routing first. If these are not found, it then searches for purchasing information for the material.

The SPECIAL PROCUREMENT key defines a specific behavior for the procurement type and can be assigned to a material in two different sections of the material master. In the MRP 2 tab (see Figure 2.1, section ❷), it defines the default planning behavior of procurement. Because there are times that the requirements for costing a material can differ from those of planning, a separate definition can be made in the COSTING 1 tab of the material master (see Figure 2.2, section ❶).

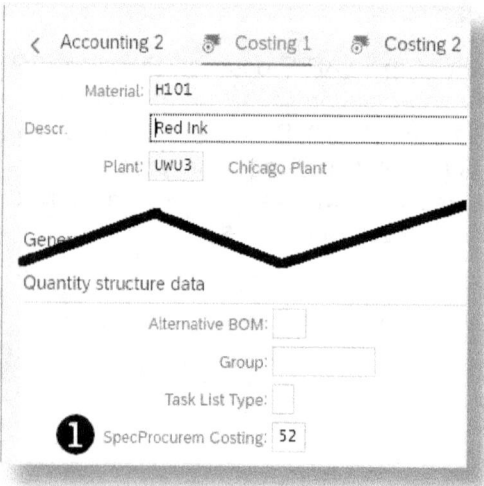

Figure 2.2: Special procurement key for costing

When a cost estimate is created for a material, the system first searches to see if a special procurement key is defined in the SPECPROCUREM COSTING field of the COSTING 1 tab. If one is found, the system uses that key in the cost estimate calculations. If no key is defined in COSTING 1, then the system looks to the MRP 2 tab to determine processing. This search strategy ensures that planning requirements and costing requirements do not have to coincide with each other. For material H101 definitions, shown in Figure 2.1 and Figure 2.2, the resulting cost estimate uses the special procurement key 52 (in-house processing) from the COSTING 1 tab (Figure 2.2) to generate the cost estimate. For MRP purposes, special procurement key LA (transfer from Los Angeles plant) is used to generate a stock transport order to satisfy demand. If the special procurement key for costing for the material is blank, then the system uses the one defined on the MRP 2 tab.

Special procurement key configuration is found under IMG menu path CONTROLLING • PRODUCT COST CONTROLLING • PRODUCT COST PLANNING • MATERIAL COST ESTIMATE WITH QUANTITY STRUCTURE • SETTINGS FOR QUANTITY STRUCTURE CONTROL • MATERIAL DATA • CHECK SPECIAL PROCUREMENT TYPES, and it can also be found under production planning configuration menus. Figure 2.3 shows the initial window for the special procurement key configuration.

Change View "Special Procurement": Overview

Plnt	Name 1	Sp.Pr.Type	Description of Special Procurement Type
UWU2	Los Angeles Plant	52	Direct production / collective order
UWU2	Los Angeles Plant	60	Phantom in planning
UWU3	Chicago Plant	10	Consignment
UWU3	Chicago Plant	20	External procurement
UWU3	Chicago Plant	30	Subcontracting
UWU3	Chicago Plant	50	Phantom assembly
UWU3	Chicago Plant	52	Direct production / collective order
UWU3	Chicago Plant	60	Phantom in planning
UWU3	Chicago Plant	7L	Withdrawal from Los Angeles
UWU3	Chicago Plant	8L	Manufactured in Los Angeles
UWU3	Chicago Plant	LA	Transfer from Los Angeles

Figure 2.3: Special procurement key configuration

Configuration of a key is plant dependent, and the same key IDs can be assigned to multiple plants. The definition of an ID at one plant can be different than the definition of the same ID assigned to another plant, which could lead to confusion. If the implementation has multiple plants, a well-thought-out, standard process for defining keys should be used to prevent confusion over the meaning of each key.

Figure 2.4 shows the configuration of special procurement key (SP.PR.TYPE) 20 at plant UWU3. The definition of this key duplicates the behavior of PROCUREMENT TYPE F (external) with the SPECIAL PROCUREMENT field left blank on the MRP 2 tab of the material master. It is normally used as the special procurement key for costing on the COSTING 1 tab to override the setting on the MRP 2 tab for costing purposes. Leaving the SPECIAL PROCUREMENT key for costing blank on the COSTING 1 tab indicates to the system that the special procurement key on MRP 2 should be used for costing purposes.

Therefore, a specific definition needs to be made for outside purchases if used on COSTING 1.

```
Plant           UWU3  Chicago Plant
Sp.Pr.Type      20    External procurement

Procurement type      F      External procurement

Special Procurement
Special procurement         Init.value: external
Plant

As BOM Component
☐ Phantom item
☐ Direct Production
☐ Direct Procurement
☐ Withdr.altern.plant    Issuing Plant
☐ Multil. Subcontr.
```

Figure 2.4: Special procurement key details

There are three sections associated with the configuration. The top section defines the name and procurement type relating to this special procurement configuration. PROCUREMENT TYPE can either be F (external) or E (internal). The SPECIAL PROCUREMENT section determines a category of procurement. There are six possible values:

- ▶ Blank—indicates that the procurement is from an outside source, such as a vendor. This is only used with procurement type F.

- ▶ E—indicates that this is used for in-house production. This is only used with procurement type E.

- ▶ K—indicates consignment stock. This is only used with procurement type F and has no impact on costing.

- ▶ L—indicates that this is for subcontracting. This is only used with procurement type F. Subcontracting is covered in Chapter 3.

- ▶ P—indicates production in a different plant. The plant is entered in the PLANT field. This is only used with procurement type E.

- ▶ U—indicates a stock transfer from another plant. The source plant is entered in the PLANT field. This is only used with procurement type F.

The As BOM COMPONENT section further defines the behavior of the special procurement key when the material is used as a component of another material. PHANTOM ITEM and WITHDR.ALTERN.PLANT impact costing when they are defined along with the configuration in the SPECIAL PROCUREMENT section. The specific behaviors are covered in the next sections.

Special procurement type 20 in Figure 2.4 has no special modifiers. Any material with this key assigned to it follows the standard raw material pricing procedures defined in the valuation variant to generate the cost estimate for the material.

2.2 Plant to plant transfers

A common use of special procurement keys is to indicate a plant-to-plant stock transfer. Figure 2.5 shows the definition of a stock transfer from plant UWU2 (Los Angeles) to plant UWU3 (Chicago).

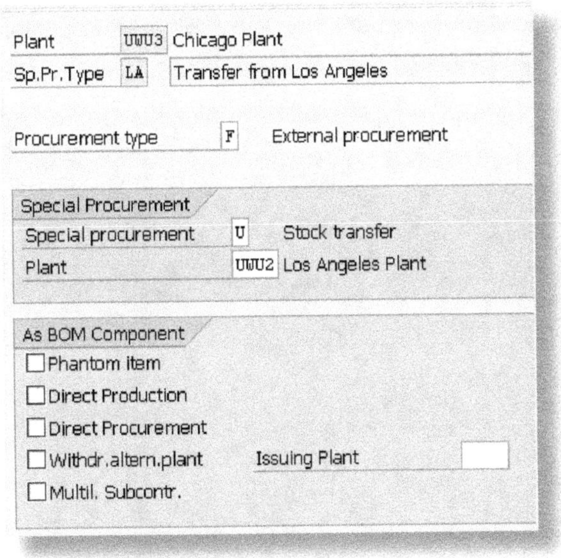

Figure 2.5: Special procurement key stock transfer

Material H101 is transferred from plant UWU2 to UWU3. SPECIAL PROCUREMENT type LA is used to represent this. Figure 2.6 shows no special procurement key for costing defined in the COSTING 1 tab, but PROCUREMENT TYPE F and SPECIAL PROCUREMENT LA defined in the MRP 2 tab.

Costing with Special Procurement

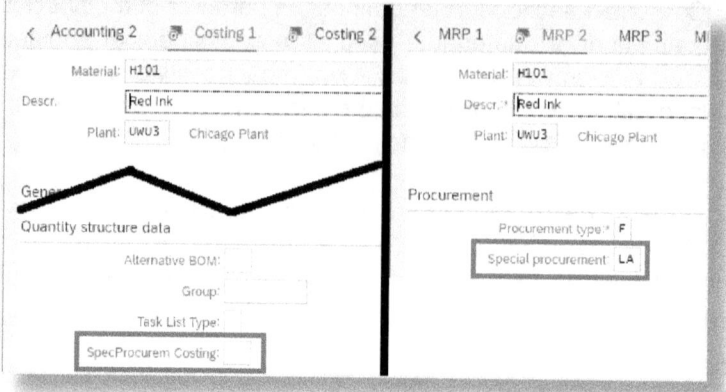

Figure 2.6: Special procurement key LA in material master

The resulting cost estimate is shown in Figure 2.7. At the bottom of the screenshot, the line item type shows M for material, and the resource indicates material H101 at plant UWU2 (the source plant). This image also shows the QTY STRUCT. tab of the cost estimate. The SPECIAL PROCUREMENT DATA section shows the special procurement key and the type of special procurement used in calculating the cost.

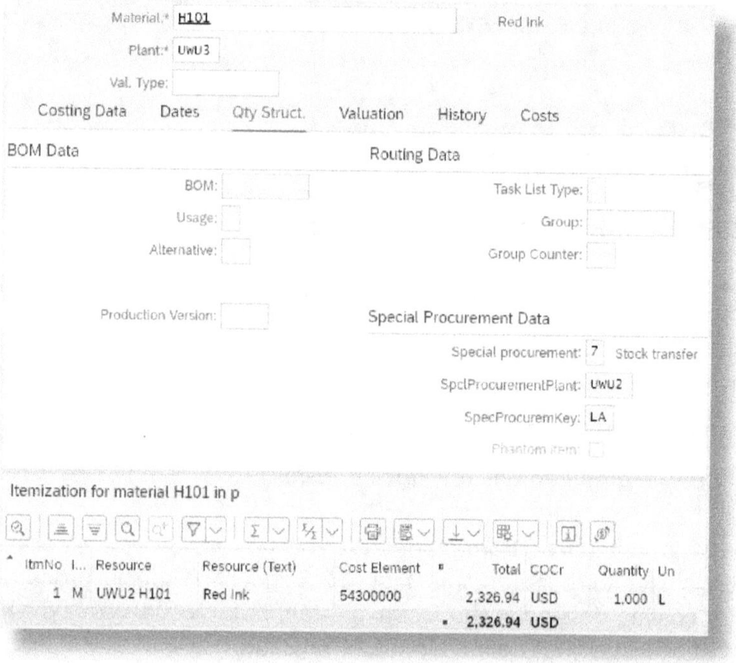

Figure 2.7: Itemization for stock transfer costing

2.3 Withdrawal from another plant

Certain manufacturing situations require materials to be withdrawn from a different plant to the one in which the production is being processed. This can happen when the plants are close together or, in subcontracting situations, where the components are shipped from one plant to the vendor, and the resulting product is returned to a different plant. Special procurement keys can be defined to account for this practice. A feature of the special procurement key for withdrawal from another plant is the costing behaviors associated with the SPECIAL PROCUREMENT and AS BOM COMPONENT sections of the configuration.

```
Plant          UUU3  Chicago Plant
Sp.Pr.Type     7L    Withdrawal from Los Angeles

Procurement type      F    External procurement

Special Procurement
  Special procurement       Init.value: external
  Plant

As BOM Component
  ☐ Phantom item
  ☐ Direct Production
  ☐ Direct Procurement
  ☑ Withdr.altern.plant    Issuing Plant       UUU2  Los Angeles Plant
  ☐ Multil. Subcontr.
```

Figure 2.8: Special procurement key—withdrawal from another plant

Figure 2.8 shows the definition of the special procurement key, indicating withdrawal from an alternative plant if the material is a BOM component. For type 7L, PROCUREMENT TYPE is set to F (external), and SPECIAL PROCUREMENT is blank, indicating an outside purchase. Compare this with the definition in Figure 2.4. The normal method for procuring the item is from a vendor. However, the AS BOM COMPONENT modifier defines a different behavior when the item is used in a BOM. Material R105 is used in mixing ink at the Chicago plant. There are two areas of master data where this special procurement key comes into play for both planning and costing. The first place is in the material master. Figure 2.9 shows a material master setup where SPECIAL PROCUREMENT key 7L is assigned to the MRP 2 tab. It can also be assigned to the COSTING 1 tab for costing purposes only, but this would be a rare occurrence because the main purpose for using this is in planning.

Costing with Special Procurement

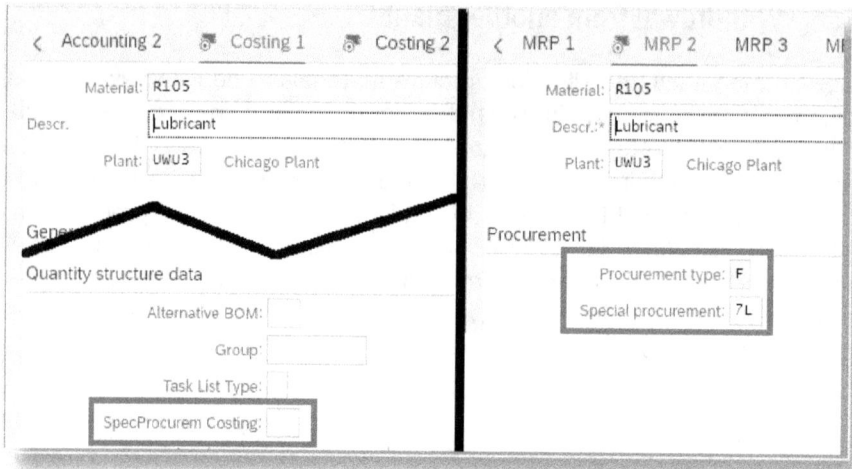

Figure 2.9: Material settings for withdrawal from another plant

The second area of master data where this key can be assigned is in the BOM. The special procurement key can be assigned to a specific component without regard to how the material is defined. For example, in most cases a component material is purchased from a vendor and has no special procurement key defined in the MRP 2 tab of the material master. However, in certain manufacturing situations, the material should be issued directly from the Los Angeles plant. SPECIAL PROCUREMENT key 7L is assigned that component on the BOM.

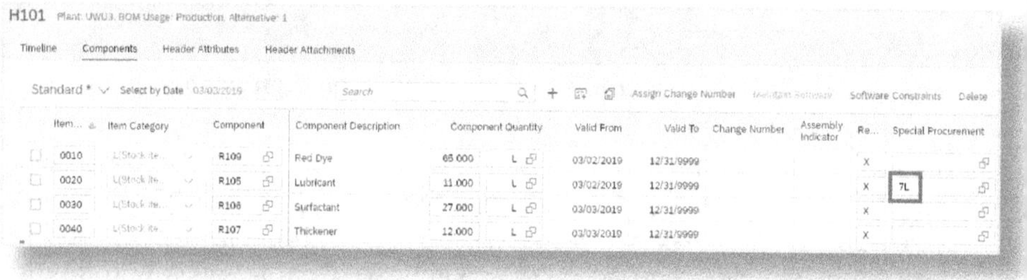

Figure 2.10: Bom showing component with special procurement

Figure 2.10 highlights the assignment of a special procurement key for component R105 in the BOM in the Maintain Bill of Materials Fiori app. For SAPGUI transactions CS01 and CS02, this is available by drilling into the component number. The setting is at the bottom of the BASIC DATA tab in the MRP DATA section. The costing behavior is the same regardless of where the system finds the special procurement key. The BOM setting overrides the material settings.

48

Itemization for material H100 in p

ItmNo	I...	Resource			Resource (Text)	Cost Element	∎	Total	COCr	Quantity	Un
1	E	300101	MIXER	SETUP	Mix Ink	94303000		63.13	USD	1.0	HR
2	E	300101	MIXER	MACHHR	Mix Ink	94301000		246.88	USD	5.0	HR
3	E	300101	MIXER	LABRHR	Mix Ink	94311000		192.98	USD	7.917	HR
4	M	UWU3 R108			Blue Dye	51100000		913.98	USD	600	L
5	M	UWU2 R105			Lubricant	51100000		82.50	USD	110	L
6	M	UWU3 R106			Surfactant	51100000		65.69	USD	270	L
7	M	UWU3 R107			Thickener	51100000		42.60	USD	120	L
							∎	1,607.76	USD		

Figure 2.11: Itemization with material withdrawn from other plant

The resulting cost estimate is shown in Figure 2.11. Item 5 shows that the resource is UWU2 R105, instead of UWU3 R105 which is associated with the other components of item type M. The cost is pulled in directly from plant UWU2 (Los Angeles). This is the behavior of the cost estimate that uses R105 as a component and is dictated by the configuration in the As BOM COMPONENT section of the key. However, the cost estimate of R105 itself in plant UWU3 is based on the SPECIAL PROCUREMENT section of the configuration alone. For key 7L (see Figure 2.8), all fields are blank, indicating purchase from an external vendor.

Material:* R105   Lubricant
Plant:* UWU3
Val. Type:

Costing Data   Dates   Qty Struct.   Valuation   History   Costs

Valuation View: 0 Legal Valuation
Currency: USD
Material Valuation: 4 Planned Price 1
Costing Sheet:

Itemization for material R105 in p

ItmNo	I...	Resource	Resource (Text)	Cost Element	∎	Total	COCr	Quantity	Un
1	I	UWU3 R105	Lubricant	51100000		780.00	USD	1,000	L
					∎	780.00	USD		

Figure 2.12: Cost estimate for R105 at plant UWU3

Figure 2.12 shows the cost estimate of the raw material R105 at plant UWU3. The lone item in the itemization has the item type I, indicating purchasing. To demonstrate an alternative method of configuring the special procurement key, a new key, 7G, is defined for withdrawal from the Gent plant (UWU1). This configuration is shown in Figure 2.13. The difference between this and the configuration for 7L is that the SPECIAL PROCUREMENT section is defined for a stock transfer from plant UWU2.

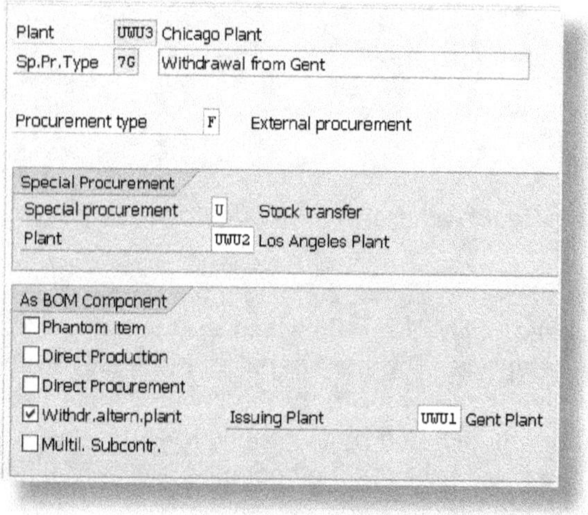

```
Plant           UWU3  Chicago Plant
Sp.Pr.Type  7G    Withdrawal from Gent

Procurement type      F    External procurement

Special Procurement
Special procurement   U    Stock transfer
Plant                 UWU2 Los Angeles Plant

As BOM Component
☐ Phantom item
☐ Direct Production
☐ Direct Procurement
☑ Withdr.altern.plant    Issuing Plant    UWU1 Gent Plant
☐ Multil. Subcontr.
```

Figure 2.13: Withdrawal from another plant with stock transfer

When this is loaded as the SPECIAL PROCUREMENT key on the MRP 2 tab of the R105 material master (see Figure 2.14), the behavior of the cost estimate for material H101, for which R105 is used as a BOM component, is similar to what occurred when 7L was used.

```
Material:  R105
Descr.:*   Lubricant
Plant:     UWU3    Chicago Plant

Procurement
            Procurement type:  F
            Special procurement:  7G
```

Figure 2.14: Special procurement for R105 set to 7G

The cost of R105 in the cost estimate for H100 now comes from the cost at the Gent plant UWU1 (see Figure 2.15).

Itemization for material H100 in p							
ItmNo I...	Resource			Resource (Text)	Cost Element	Total COCr	Quantity Un
1 E	300101	MIXER	SETUP	Mix Ink	94303000	63.13 USD	1.0 HR
2 E	300101	MIXER	MACHHR	Mix Ink	94301000	246.88 USD	5.0 HR
3 E	300101	MIXER	LABRHR	Mix Ink	94311000	192.98 USD	7.917 HR
4 M	UWU3 R108			Blue Dye	51100000	913.98 USD	600 L
5 M	UWU1 R105			Lubricant	51100000	948.75 USD	110 L
6 M	UWU3 R106			Surfactant	51100000	65.69 USD	270 L
7 M	UWU3 R107			Thickener	51100000	42.60 USD	120 L
						• 2,474.01 USD	

Figure 2.15: R105 source with special procurement key 7G

However, when material R105 is costed by itself, the cost is determined based on stock transfer from UWU2 (Los Angeles), as shown in Figure 2.16. The item type is M for material and the resource is UWU2 R105, indicating that the material cost comes from material R105 at plant UWU2.

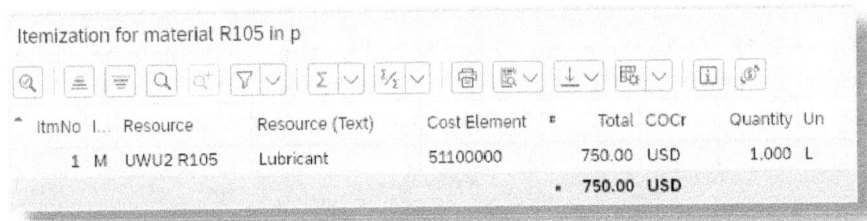

Itemization for material R105 in p					
ItmNo I...	Resource	Resource (Text)	Cost Element	Total COCr	Quantity Un
1 M	UWU2 R105	Lubricant	51100000	750.00 USD	1,000 L
				• 750.00 USD	

Figure 2.16: Itemization for R105 with special procurement key 7G

To ensure that the individual component cost estimates are correct for items that are normally withdrawn from another plant, the SPECIAL PROCUREMENT section should be defined for stock transfer (U) and the plant assigned here should match the plant in the AS BOM COMPONENT section. This provides the proper costing consistency.

2.4 Manufactured in another plant

One form of procurement involving manufacturing is to execute the production in a separate plant from the planning plant. An example of this would be a combination manufacturing plant and warehouse. Each entity is represented by a separate plant, and planning is performed in the warehouse.

Production is handled in the manufacturing plant, but the end product is delivered into the warehouse.

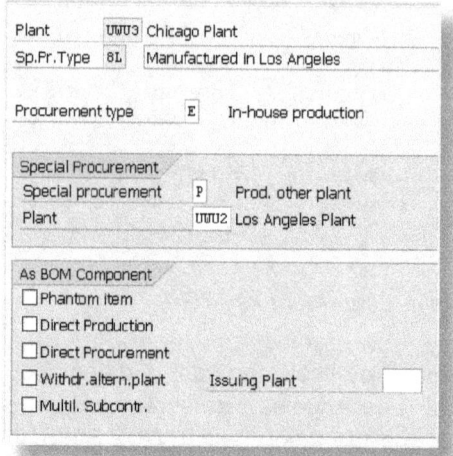

Figure 2.17: Special procurement key manufactured in other plant

Figure 2.17 shows the setup for key 8L to be used to indicate manufacturing in an alternative plant. Figure 2.18 shows material H101 at plant UWU3 defined for manufacturing in the Los Angeles plant (UWU2).

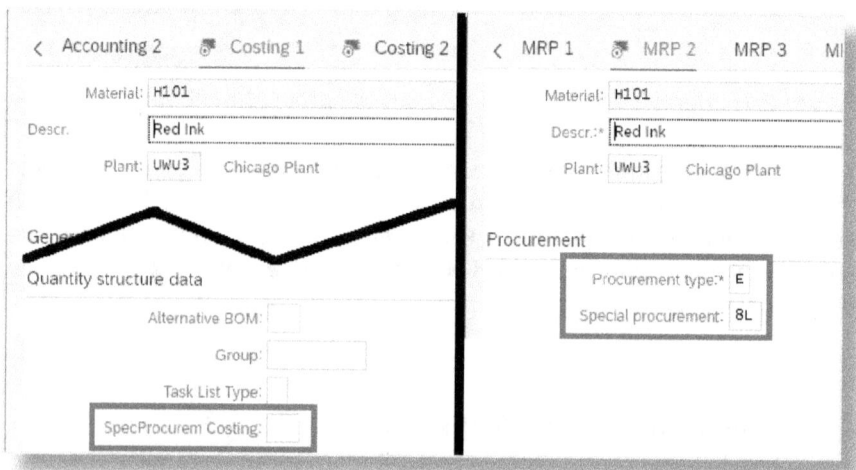

Figure 2.18: Material master settings for manufacture in other plant

Figure 2.19 shows the resulting cost estimate. The cost at the top level uses the resulting cost of H101 from the Los Angeles plant (UWU2).

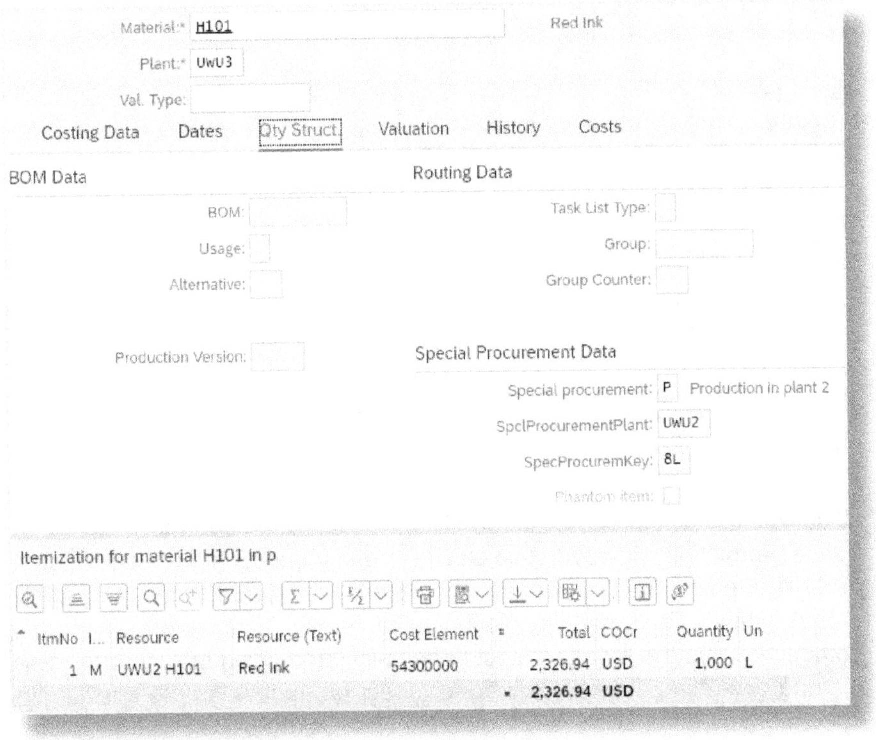

Figure 2.19: Cost estimate for manufacture in alternative plant

For costing purposes, the result is the same as it would be for stock transfers. For planning purposes, no stock transport order is issued, and the material is delivered directly into the receiving plant. The SPECIAL PROCUREMENT DATA section on the QTY STRUCT. tab shows the origin of the costs.

2.5 In-house manufacturing

Setting up a special procurement key for in-house manufacturing duplicates the behavior of a material that is defined as procurement type E (internal) with no special procurement key.

Figure 2.20 shows the configuration. The DIRECT PRODUCTION setting in the AS BOM COMPONENT section has no impact on how the cost is calculated.

```
Plant         UWU3  Chicago Plant
Sp.Pr.Type    52    Direct production / collective order

Procurement type    E    In-house production

Special Procurement
 Special procurement   E    In-house production
 Plant

As BOM Component
 ☐ Phantom item
 ☑ Direct Production
 ☐ Direct Procurement
 ☐ Withdr.altern.plant    Issuing Plant
 ☐ Multil. Subcontr.
```

Figure 2.20: Special procurement key for in-house production

Usually, there would be no need to have a special procurement key for in-house production. However, this can be useful for costing purposes. Material H101 at plant UWU3 (Chicago) is normally transferred from plant UWU2 (Los Angeles). The capability exists in Chicago to manufacture it, and the company wants the standard cost to be calculated using that method. This is done by setting the key defined for direct production as the special procurement key for costing (see Figure 2.21).

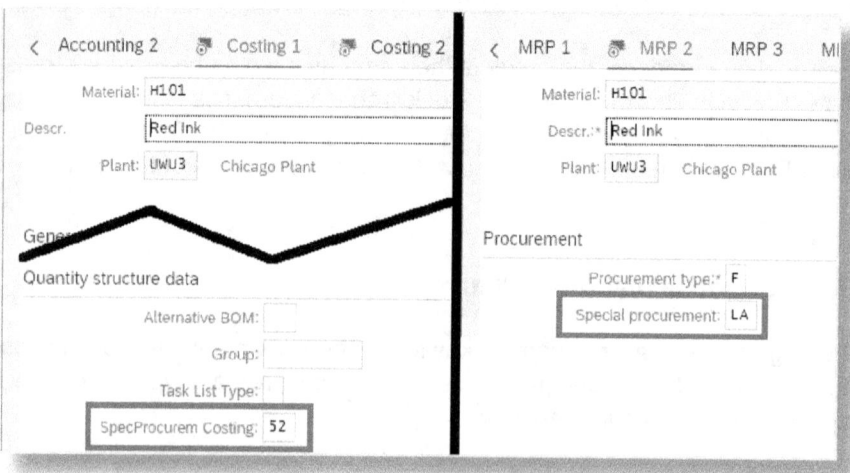

Figure 2.21: Manufacturing override for costing

The resulting cost estimate uses the manufacturing BOM and routing in Chicago to generate the cost estimate. Figure 2.22 shows the resulting cost estimate with the SPECIALPROCUREMKEY field displayed on the QTY STRUCT. tab. The key assigned to the SPECPROCUREM COSTING field on the COSTING 1 tab overrides the key assigned to the SPECIAL PROCUREMENT field on the MRP 2 tab.

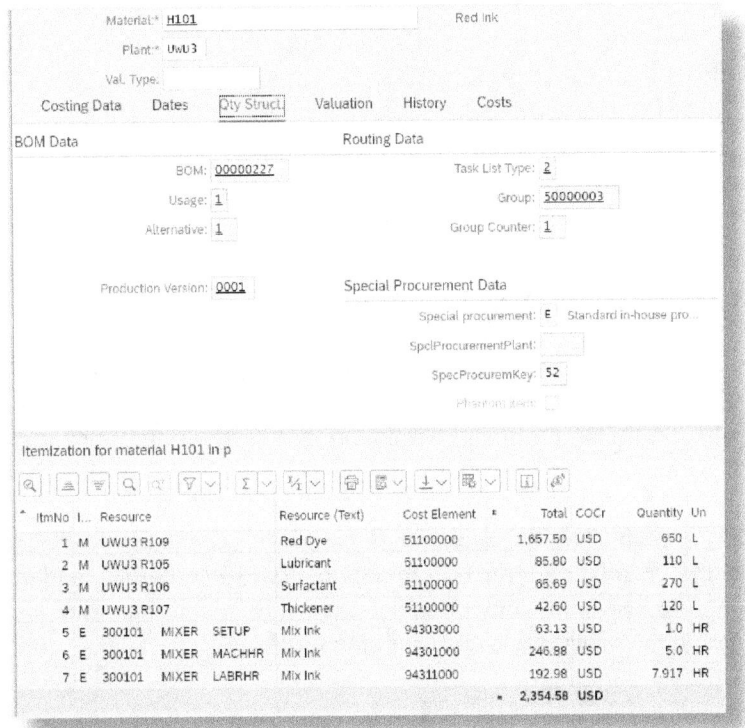

Figure 2.22: Cost estimate using in-house production override

2.6 Phantom assemblies

A *phantom assembly* is a material with a BOM that never exists in inventory. It represents a group of components that are always issued to a manufacturing order together with set quantities. A phantom material is used as a single component in a product's BOM with an associated quantity. However, when used in production, the phantom's BOM components are exploded, and the individual components must be issued out of inventory. The phantom can never be issued directly. Only its components can be issued.

55

```
Plant          UWU3  Chicago Plant
Sp.Pr.Type     50    Phantom assembly

Procurement type      E    In-house production

Special Procurement
Special procurement   E    In-house production
Plant

As BOM Component
☑ Phantom Item
☐ Direct Production
☐ Direct Procurement
☐ Withdr.altern.plant   Issuing Plant
☐ Multil. Subcontr.
```

Figure 2.23: Special procurement key—phantom assembly

Figure 2.23 shows the configuration for the special procurement type of a phantom material. PROCUREMENT TYPE and SPECIAL PROCUREMENT are both set to 'E', indicating in-house production. PHANTOM ITEM in the AS BOM COMPONENT section is selected.

Material H221 at plant UWU3 is a phantom material that contains the base chemicals of the ink mixture. This is common to most ink materials, and instead of using the individual components in the ink BOMs, the phantom is used. The material definition is shown in Figure 2.24.

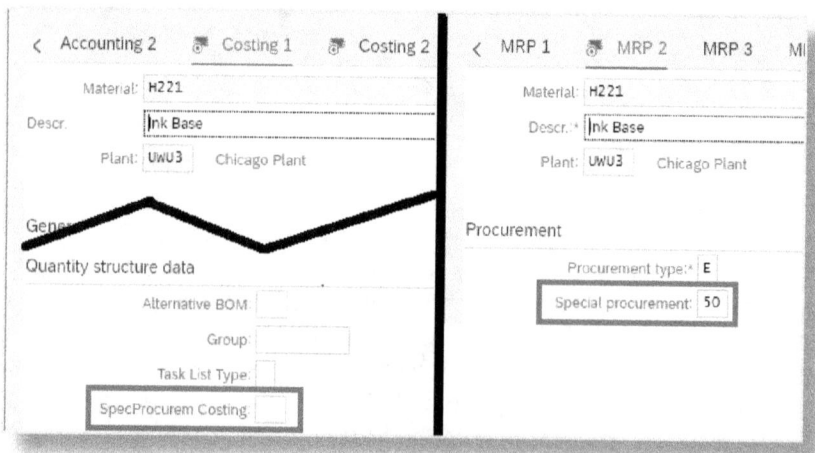

Figure 2.24: Material master settings for phantom material

The phantom material must have a BOM associated with it. Figure 2.25 shows the BOM components for material H221. The base quantity of the BOM is 100 L.

H221 Plant: UWU3, BOM Usage: Production, Alternative: 1

Timeline	Components	Header Attributes	Header Attachments		

Standard * ∨ Select by Date 03/02/2019   Search

Item...	Item Category	Component	Component Description	Component Quantity	
0010	L(Stock it...	R105	Lubricant	22.000	L
0020	L(Stock it...	R106	Surfactant	54.000	L
0030	L(Stock it...	R107	Thickener	24.000	L

Figure 2.25: BOM for phantom material H221

This phantom material is included in the BOM for material H101 (red ink) at plant UWU3. The box in Figure 2.26 highlights the phantom material H221 as a component, using 50 L for the base quantity of 100 L.

H101 Plant: UWU3, BOM Usage: Production, Alternative: 1

Timeline	Components	Header Attributes	Header Attachments		

Standard ∨ Select by Date 03/03/2019   Search

Item...	Item Category	Component	Component Description	Component Quantity	
0010	L(Stoc...	R109	Red Dye	65.000	L
0020	L(Stoc...	H221	Ink Base	50.000	L

Figure 2.26: Material BOM with phantom H221 as a component

Figure 2.27 shows the itemization for the cost estimate for material H101 at plant UWU3. The box shows the expanded components of phantom H221. H221 does not show up in the quantity structure. The quantities calculated for the phantom's components are based on the BOM of H221. In the BOM, the quantity 22H221 of component R105 is 22 L for the base quantity of 100 L of H221. The component quantity of H221 in the red ink material H101 is 50 L per 100 L. The resulting quantity in the cost estimate for 1,000 L is then 110 L (22 divided by 100 multiplied by 50 divided by 100 multiplied by 1,000).

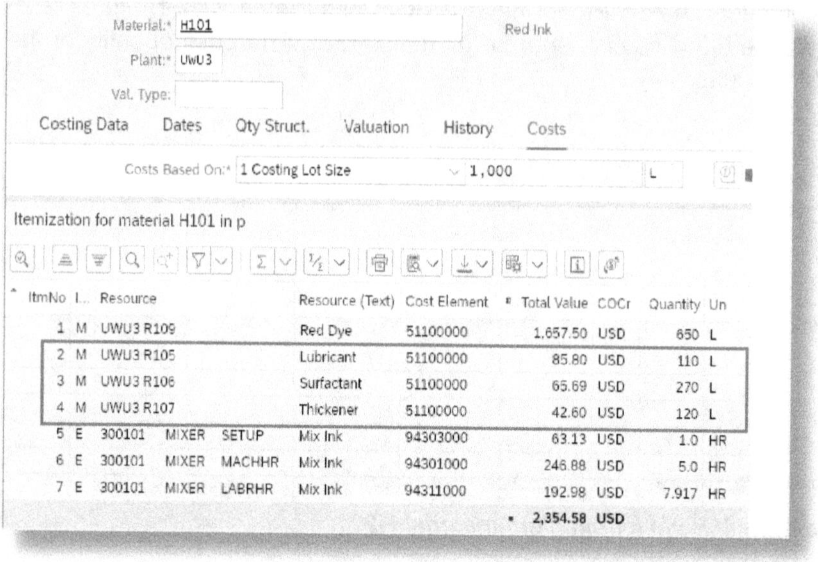

Figure 2.27: Itemization with phantom material in BOM

Even though the phantom material cannot have inventory, a cost estimate can be generated for it independently. The behavior of the special procurement key when the material is not a BOM component is the same as an in-house procured material (see Figure 2.20—SPECIAL PROCUREMENT section). A cost estimate at this level is useful as information only. It can be suppressed by selecting the DO NOT COST checkbox on the COSTING 1 tab of the phantom material definition (see Figure 2.28). This prevents a cost estimate from being created for the phantom material but does not impact costing when the phantom is used in a BOM of another material.

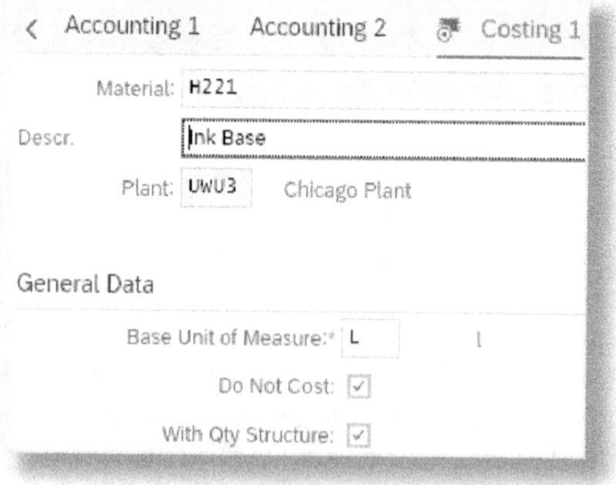

Figure 2.28: Do Not Cost setting for phantom material

3 Subcontracting and external processing

A company often needs to outsource some of its manufacturing processes. Reasons for this include lack of capacity, lack of the right equipment, and even lack of expertise. Subcontracting and external processing are two forms of outside manufacturing. These manufacturing models differ from a straight purchase of the goods in that the company supplies the components or work in process to the external partner who then provides the necessary services to manufacture the goods. CO-PC-PCP has special procedures defined for obtaining the cost of these services in order to include them in the material cost estimate.

3.1 Subcontracting description

Subcontracting is a process by which a company provides components to a business partner so that the partner can manufacture the finished or semi-finished goods. There are various reasons why this process is used. For example, the business partner has expertise in a specific manufacturing process that does not exist within the company. Other reasons include: lower cost at the business partner, faster response time, or lack of capacity within the company. The physical process comprises sending component materials to the subcontractor. When the subcontractor signals that the manufacturing process has been completed, and the goods have been shipped, the quantity is received back into the requesting plant. It is then either used in further manufacturing or shipped to a customer. The service that the subcontractor provides has a cost associated with it. The resulting cost for material includes the cost of the components plus the cost of the service.

3.2 Subcontracting master data

Three areas of master data have to be set up in order to properly cost a subcontracted material. These include: the material master, the bill of materials (BOM), and subcontracting purchasing information.

3.2.1 Material master setup

A subcontracting special procurement key must be assigned to the material. As for any other material with a special procurement key, the system first searches in the COSTING 1 tab of the material master, and if that is blank, it uses the setting in the MRP 2 tab of the material master. In Figure 3.1, material H100 in plant UWU3 has key 30 assigned to the SPECIAL PROCUREMENT field in the MRP 2 tab. The special procurement key for costing in the COSTING 1 tab is blank.

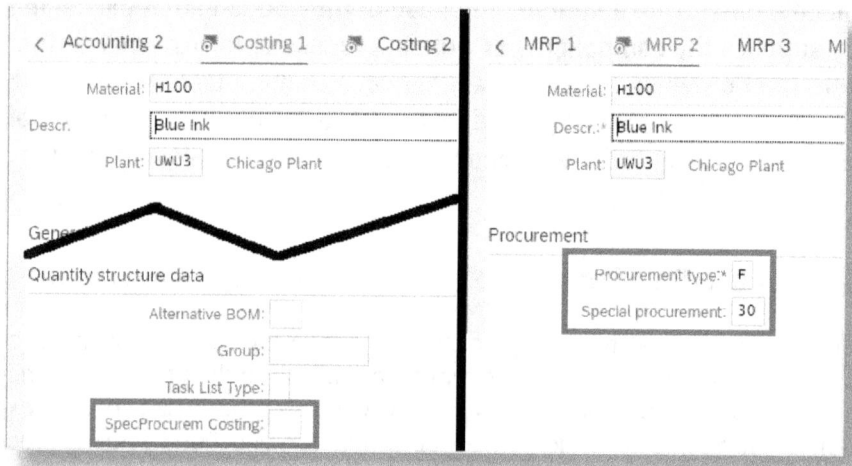

Figure 3.1: Material setup for subcontracting

Special procurement key configuration is found under IMG menu path CONTROLLING • PRODUCT COST CONTROLLING • PRODUCT COST PLANNING • MATERIAL COST ESTIMATE WITH QUANTITY STRUCTURE • SETTINGS FOR QUANTITY STRUCTURE CONTROL • MATERIAL DATA • CHECK SPECIAL PROCUREMENT TYPES. The specific settings for subcontracting are shown in Figure 3.2. PROCUREMENT TYPE must be set to F, and SPECIAL PROCUREMENT is set to L. No plant is required because this is always processed by an outside business partner. The normal code used for subcontracting is 30, but any two-character ID can be used.

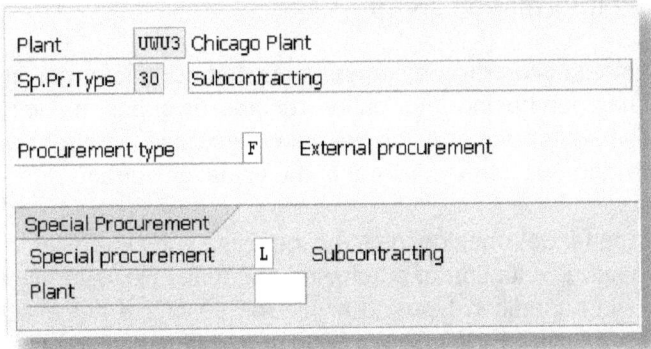

Figure 3.2: Special procurement key definition for subcontracting

3.2.2 BOM setup

No special settings are required for the BOM. The component quantities should reflect the contracted yield of the manufacturing process for the business partner. The BOM defines the default quantity consumed for each component when the product is received into inventory. Figure 3.3 shows the BOM for material H100 at plant UWU3.

Item	Item Category	Component	Component Des...	Component Quantity	
0010	L(Stock item)	R108	Blue Dye	60.000	L
0020	L(Stock item)	R105	Lubricant	11.000	L
0030	L(Stock item)	R106	Surfactant	27.000	L
0040	L(Stock item)	R107	Thickener	12.000	L

Figure 3.3: BOM for a subcontracted material

3.2.3 Purchasing information setup

The processing cost for subcontracting comes from purchasing information associated with either purchasing information records or subcontracting purchase orders. The source depends on the price determination strategy sequence defined on the SUBCONTRACTING tab of the valuation variant.

The strategy sequence for determining the subcontracting price is similar to the sequence for material valuation of purchased materials. However, the two strategies for using condition types to divide the costs are not available for subcontracting, which means that it is not possible to split subcontracting costs in the same way that raw material costs can be split. In addition, specifying planned prices for subcontracting in the material master as is done for raw material costing is not allowed for subcontracting. This is because the material cost is developed from a combination of the subcontracting price plus the components in the BOM. The subcontracting cost must be derived from either a purchasing information record or from purchase order information. The valuation variant configuration is found via IMG menu path CONTROLLING • PRODUCT COST CONTROLLING • MATERIAL COST ESTIMATE WITH QUANTITY STRUCTURE • COSTING VARIANT: COMPONENTS • DEFINE VALUATION VARIANTS or by using transaction OKK4. Figure 3.4 shows the configuration of the strategy sequence.

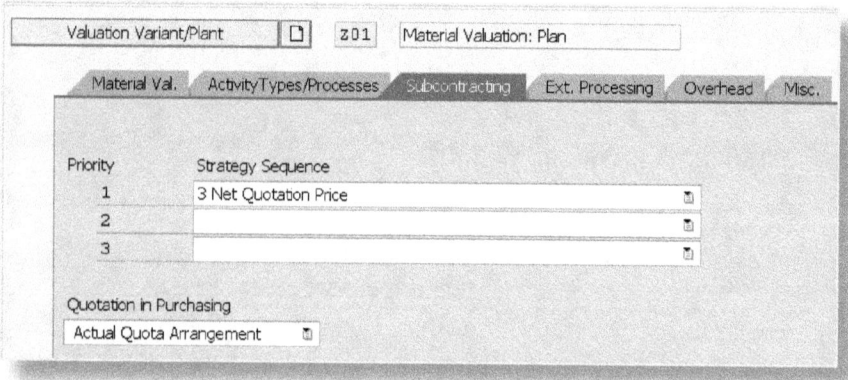

Figure 3.4: Subcontracting price determination

Strategies based on purchasing information records are:

- 3 NET QUOTATION PRICE—This is based on active conditions from the pricing procedure (calculation schema) up to subtotal type 7 (rebate basis 1).

- 4 GROSS QUOTATION PRICE—This is based on active conditions from the pricing procedure up to and including the first subtotal type 9 (gross value).

- 5 EFFECTIVE PRICE FROM QUOTATION—This is based on active conditions from the pricing procedure up to subtotal type S (effective value).

- 2 EFFECTIVE PRICE FROM QUOTATION WITHOUT FIXED COST—This is the same as EFFECTIVE PRICE FROM QUOTATION, but no fixed condition values are included except tax.

Strategies based on the latest purchase order information are:

- 7 NET PURCHASE ORDER PRICE—This is based on active conditions from the pricing procedure (calculation schema) up to subtotal type 7 (rebate basis 1).

- 8 GROSS PURCHASE ORDER PRICE—This is based on active conditions from the pricing procedure up to and including the first subtotal type 9 (gross value).

- 9 EFFECTIVE PRICE FROM PURCHASE ORDER—This is based on active conditions from the pricing procedure up to subtotal type S (effective value).

- 6 EFFECTIVE PRICE FROM PURCHASE ORDER WITHOUT FIXED COST—This is the same as EFFECTIVE PRICE FROM PURCHASE ORDER, but no fixed condition values are included except tax.

Pricing conditions are used to calculate the purchasing price of goods and services. These conditions are assigned to a pricing procedure or calculation schema which define the order in which the conditions are processed and the behavior of the conditions. Conditions can specify a price per quantity, a fixed price regardless of quantity, or a percentage to apply to a calculation of costs for conditions assigned earlier in the procedure.

Pricing Schema RM0000 (Partial)					
Step	Counter	Condition	Name	Subtotal	Calculation
1	1	PB00	Gross Price	9	Quantity
1	2	PBXX	Gross Price	9	Quantity
2	0	VA00	Variants/Quantity		Quantity
10	1	RB00	Absolute discount		Fixed
10	2	RC00	Discount/Quantity		Quantity
10	6	ZB00	Surcharge (Value)		Fixed
10	7	ZC00	Surcharge/Quantity		Quantity
20	0			7	
21	1	NAVS	Non-Deductible Tax		Fixed
21	2	NAVM	Non-Deductible Tax		Fixed
22	0				
31	1	FRA1	Freight %		Percentage
31	2	FRB1	Freight (Value)		Fixed
31	3	FRC1	Freight/Quantity		Quantity
35	1	SKTO	Cash Discount		Percentage
37	0	A001	Rebate		Percentage
38	0	A002	Material Rebate		Quantity
40	0			S	
60	0	WOTB	OTB Procurement		Quantity
79	0			C	

Figure 3.5: Purchasing calculation schema RM0000

Figure 3.5 shows a partial list of conditions assigned to the main purchasing calculation schema RM0000. Note the SUBTOTAL column. This column contains indicators that help group together certain types of conditions to identify gross price, net price, and effective price. Subtotal type 9 is assigned to GROSS PRICE and does not include any surcharges or deductions. Typically, only one gross price condition is active at any time. Net price includes conditions representing surcharges and deductions. At the end of the list of these conditions is an empty row with subtotal type 7 assigned to it. The values of all active conditions up to this point are included in the net price calculation. This includes the top two shaded sections of Figure 3.5. All these costs are associated with agreements with the vendor business partner. Effective price is net price minus any cash discounts plus delivery costs. These costs are included in subtotal type S, which is represented in the third shaded area. These costs are not directly related to the vendor (e.g. freight, which is usually handled by a third party).

Pricing conditions are used by purchasing information records and purchase orders to determine the cost to be paid to the vendor, and any other miscellaneous costs associated with the purchase. Conditions assigned to the purchasing information record are used when a purchase order is created. Conditions can also be defined separately from the purchasing information record and automatically pulled into the pricing procedure when creating a purchase order or when creating a cost estimate.

Multiple alternative vendors can be used in the subcontracting process, and there is a specific search strategy that is used to determine which vendor to use in the cost estimate. This strategy is the same as for standard purchases:

1. **Check if the source list is required.** The system first searches to see if there is a source list requirement in place. A source list requirement can be defined at the plant level using configuration (MATERIALS MANAGEMENT • PURCHASING • SOURCE LIST • DEFINE SOURCE LIST REQUIREMENT AT PLANT LEVEL), or it can be assigned directly to the material in the PURCHASING tab of the material master. The source list defines the valid suppliers for a material. If the source list is required and no source list is found, then the process for determining the vendor stops.

2. **Check for a quota arrangement.** Next, if the source list is found, or if the source list is not required, the system checks to see if there is a quota arrangement defined for sourcing the material. A quota arrangement specifies that a certain percentage of the material is to be purchased from one vendor and other percentages are assigned to other vendors. If a valid quota arrangement is found, the system checks for permitted vendors in the list. The vendor with the highest plan quota or lowest actual quota is chosen. The option selected in the QUOTATION IN PURCHASING field in the valuation variant configuration (see Figure 3.4) defines whether the planned or actual quota arrangement is used. The purchasing information for that vendor is used in the cost estimate. If neither a quota arrangement nor a permitted vendor is found, the system goes to step 3 of the process.

3. **Check for vendors from the source list.** This step looks for a source list associated with the plant and material. If the source list exists, then the system checks if one of the vendors has been set as a fixed source of supply. If such a vendor is found, the system uses the subcontracting purchasing information for that vendor. If no fixed source of supply is found, the system next checks to see if the plant uses a regular vendor. If a regular vendor is found in the source list for the

material, the purchasing information for that vendor is used for the cost. If a regular vendor is not permitted, or one is not found in the source list, the system goes through the purchasing information for all vendors on the list and determines the cheapest vendor using all active conditions through to subtotal type 7. This includes any discounts and surcharges that are defined. If, after these checks, a vendor is not found, the system makes one last set of checks in step 4.

4. **Check for regular vendor allowed, regardless of source list.** If a regular vendor is allowed at the plant level, the system checks through all the purchasing information records for the plant to see if a match is found for the regular vendor. If such a match is found, the purchasing information record is used for the cost. If a regular vendor is not allowed or the above search has failed, then a general search of the purchasing information records for that plant and material is performed. The record for the cheapest vendor including discounts and surcharges provides the values for the cost estimate.

If after a complete search is done and no valid purchasing information record is found, the main valuation strategy will have failed, and the system tries to find a cost using the next available valuation strategy. If no valid source of supply is found after exhausting the defined strategies, an error message appears: CK380 – NO VALID SOURCE OF SUPPLY COULD BE FOUND. This is a hard error and causes the cost estimate to fail.

Only purchasing information records used for subcontracting (type 3) are allowed. Purchase orders must also be specific to subcontracting in order for costs to be used in product costing. The item category assigned to a purchasing line on the purchase order must be set to L.

The examples in Section 3.3 use strategies associated with the purchasing information records. The purchasing information record used for the examples is shown in Figure 3.6. Section ❶ indicates that this is for subcontracting (category 3). Section ❷ shows the conditions that are used. PB00 represents the gross price. ZA01 is a percentage surcharge based on the gross price. FRC1 is the cost of freight per 1,000 L of the ink.

Figure 3.6: Subcontracting purchasing information record

3.3 Subcontracting cost estimate

Material H100 (blue ink) at the Chicago plant (UWU3) is currently being manufactured by the vendor Ink Supply Company, using materials supplied by the plant. Referring to Figure 3.6, we see that the current price for the service is 540.00 USD per 1,000 L. However, due to a requirement for quick processing and delivery, Ink Supply Company has included a 1.5% surcharge for the processing. Freight costs are not included in the price and amount to 0.05 USD per L.

The pricing strategy currently selected for costing is Net Quotation Price (strategy 3). Based on the pricing procedure from Figure 3.5, the price associated with subcontracting should include the values assigned to conditions PB00 and ZA01. Because ZA01 is a percentage based on the value of PB00, this must be calculated to determine the value. 1.5% of 540.00

is 8.10. The value for the costing lot size of 1,000L in the cost estimate is therefore 548.10 USD. Figure 3.7 shows the cost estimate. Section ❶, in the QTY STRUCT tab, indicates that the cost was derived from subcontracting. Section ❷ shows the itemization for the four components from the BOM. These all have item type M in the cost estimate. In section ❸, we see the itemization line for the subcontracting cost derived from the purchasing information record. It uses item category L. The resulting cost per 1,000 L is 548.10 USD as predicted.

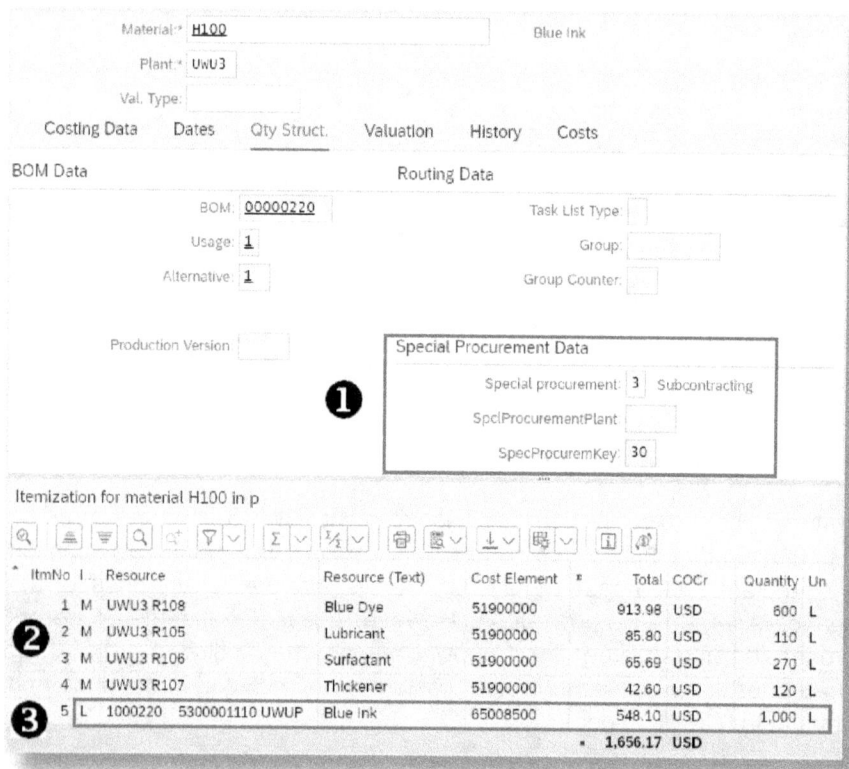

Figure 3.7: Subcontracting cost estimate using net price strategy

Figure 3.8 shows that the subcontracting costs are assigned to cost component 130 – 3RD PARTY COSTS. Cost element 65008500 is used for the subcontracting cost based on the automatic account assignment configuration for transaction event key FRL (External Activity) in transaction OBYC. This cost element is in turn assigned to the 3RD PARTY COSTS cost component.

Cost Components for Material H100

CC...	Name of Cost Comp.	Overall	Fixed	Variable	Crcy
100	Direct Material				USD
101	Ink	1,108.07		1,108.07	USD
105	Packaging				USD
110	Labor				USD
120	Utilities				USD
130	3rd Party Costs	548.10		548.10	USD
140	Supplies				USD
150	Depreciation				USD
160	Freight				USD
170	Transfer Surcharge				USD
999	Other				USD
		1,656.17		1,656.17	USD

Figure 3.8: Cost component split for subcontracting cost estimate

If the valuation strategy for subcontracting is changed from 3 NET QUOTATION PRICE to 4 GROSS QUOTATION PRICE, the only condition from the purchasing information record to be used in the cost estimate is PB00, or 540.00 USD per 1,000 L. This is shown in Figure 3.9.

Itemization for material H100 in p

ItmNo	I...	Resource	Resource (Text)	Cost Element	Total	COCr	Quantity	Un
1	M	UWU3 R108	Blue Dye	51900000	913.98	USD	600	L
2	M	UWU3 R105	Lubricant	51900000	85.80	USD	110	L
3	M	UWU3 R106	Surfactant	51900000	66.69	USD	270	L
4	M	UWU3 R107	Thickener	51900000	42.60	USD	120	L
5	L	1000220 5300001110 UWUP	Blue Ink	65008500	540.00	USD	1,000	L
					1,648.07	USD		

Figure 3.9: Itemization using gross price strategy

Finally, when using strategy 5 EFFECTIVE PRICE FROM QUOTATION, the resulting value includes not only the surcharge condition, but also the freight condition. The effective price is 540.00 USD (gross price) plus 8.10 USD (calculated surcharge) plus 50.00 USD (freight at .05 per L), which equates to 598.10 USD per 1,000 L (see Figure 3.10).

ItmNo	I...	Resource		Resource (Text)	Cost Element	r	Total	COCr	Quantity	Un
1	M	UWU3 R108		Blue Dye	51900000		913.98	USD	600	L
2	M	UWU3 R105		Lubricant	51900000		85.80	USD	110	L
3	M	UWU3 R106		Surfactant	51900000		65.69	USD	270	L
4	M	UWU3 R107		Thickener	51900000		42.60	USD	120	L
5	L	1000220	5300001110 UWUP	Blue Ink	65008500		598.10	USD	1,000	L
							1,706.17	USD		

Figure 3.10: Itemization using effective price strategy

There are no fixed price conditions associated with this, therefore strategy 2 EFFECTIVE PRICE FROM QUOTATION WITHOUT FIXED COSTS returns the same value as the cost estimate using strategy 5.

3.4 External processing description

External processing differs from subcontracting in that instead of shipping components to a vendor to return a new product, work in process is sent as part of a manufacturing order to execute a specific operation, and is then returned to complete processing in the sending plant. External processing is defined as an operation within a routing.

There are two methods for handling external processing operations. A standard purchase order can be sent to the vendor to perform a service. Work in process is sent to the vendor and when the processing is complete, the work in process with added value is returned. At this point, the operation is confirmed for the quantity that is returned. Any purchasing information record that is created for this must be a standard type record (type 0).

The second method requires components to be sent, along with any work in process, to the vendor. This requires a subcontracting purchase order (item type L) so that the components can be consumed when the operation is confirmed. Any components must be allocated directly to the operation for the goods issue to occur as part of the confirmation. Even though this is not a straightforward subcontracting situation, the purchasing information record associated with this must use type 3 for subcontracting.

3.5 External processing master data

No special material master data is required to use external processing. External processing is defined solely within an operation of a routing or recipe. First, a special control key must be assigned to the operation.

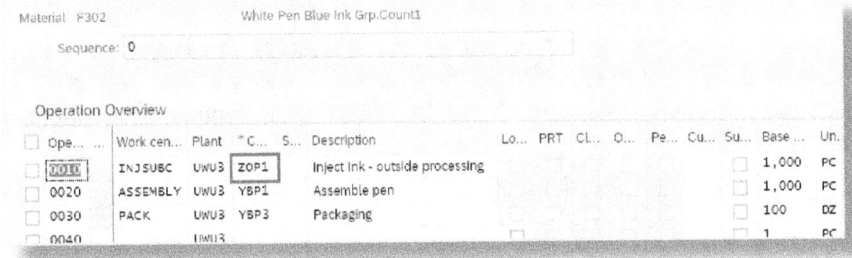

Figure 3.11: Control key assignment for external operation

Figure 3.11 shows operation 0010 of a routing for material F302 at plant UWU3, using control key ZOP1. Figure 3.12 shows the configuration for ZOP1. This is part of the Production Planning module configuration and is processed using transaction OPJ8 or via IMG menu path PRODUCTION • SHOP FLOOR CONTROL • MASTER DATA • ROUTING DATA • DEFINE CONTROL KEY.

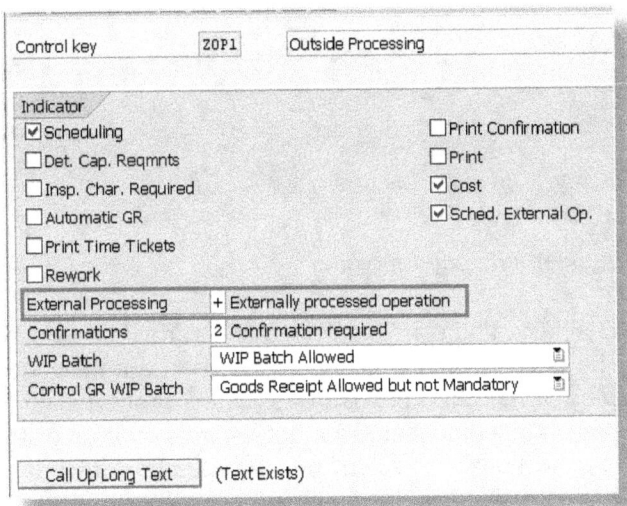

Figure 3.12: Operation control key for external processing

If EXTERNAL PROCESSING is set to ' ' (blank space), then the operation cannot be processed externally and the key denotes an in-house manufacturing step. '+' indicates that the operation is always processed externally. 'X' means that the operation could be either internally or externally processed. For costing purposes, this last setting is regarded as in-house manufacturing.

Information required for the execution of an external processing operation is entered by double-clicking on the operation to get to the details. The EXTERNAL PROCESSING section, shown in Figure 3.13, contains the required master data for generating purchasing requisitions and costing for the process.

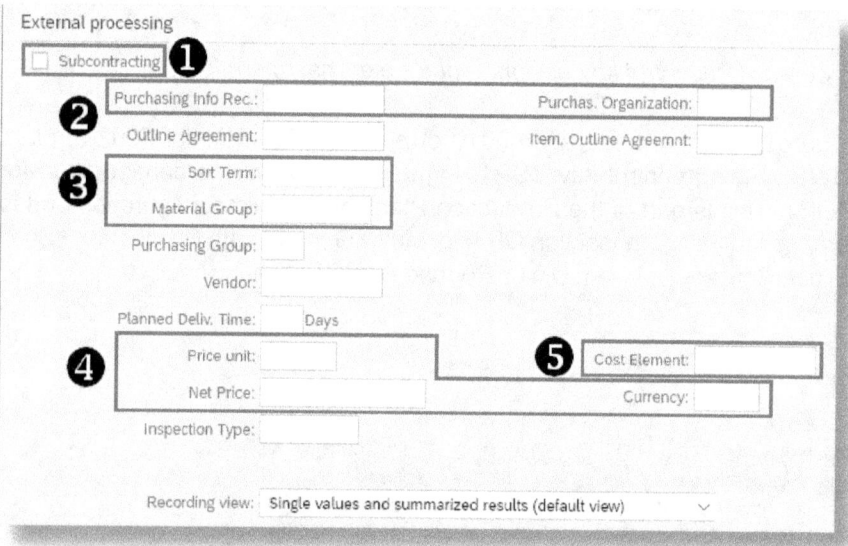

Figure 3.13: Operation external processing data

Section ❶ shows a checkbox that can be selected to determine how purchase orders should be defined, and whether components are included with the work in process. If the checkbox is not selected, then standard purchase orders are used, and components are not issued as part of operation confirmation. If the checkbox is selected, then the operation purchase orders are handled in a normal subcontracting manner, with components provided to the vendor. Any component to be handled in this way must be allocated to the specific external processing operation. These components and any work in process are then provided to the vendor to perform the service. When the service is complete, and the work in process is shipped back, confirmation of the operation is performed. At this point, the component quantities are issued to the manufacturing order and taken out of inventory. This checkbox selection determines which types of purchasing information records or purchase orders are used to calculate the cost.

Purchasing information is selected by directly assigning a purchasing information record to the operation (section ❷) or by specifying a material group and sort term for selecting purchasing information (section ❸). If the latter approach is taken, a price can be entered directly in the operation in section ❹. This price can be used to calculate the cost of the process. Finally, enter a cost element (section ❺) to represent the external processing associated with the operation.

Selecting the cost element for external processing

A default cost element can be assigned depending on configuration, but this is not necessarily the cost element that should be used. The cost element is derived from the automatic account assignment definition of transaction/event key GBB using modifier VBR with no valuation class assignment (transaction OBYC). The VBR modifier is assigned in other purchasing configuration for account assignment via IMG menu path MATERIALS MANAGEMENT • PURCHASING • ACCOUNT ASSIGNMENT (MAINTAIN ACCOUNT ASSIGNMENT CATEGORIES) and DEFINE COMBINATION OF ITEM CATEGORIES/ACCOUNT ASSIGNMENT CATEGORIES). Always make sure the cost element is reviewed and the proper cost element is entered manually, if necessary.

External processing in recipes

Setting up external processing in a recipe is similar to setting it up in a routing. Double-click into the phase of the operation and update the fields in the EXTERNAL PROCESSING section of the GENERAL DATA tab. This information is only available at the phase level and not at the higher-level operation.

3.6 External processing cost estimate

3.6.1 Price determination strategies

Price determination for external processing costs follows a similar strategy sequence to the one used by subcontracting. The external processing strategy sequence is found on the EXT. PROCESSING tab of the valuation variant configuration. Figure 3.14 shows the strategy sequence, which contains three alternatives.

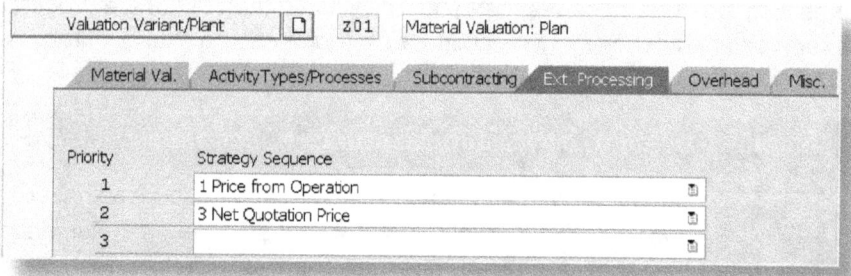

Figure 3.14: External processing price determination

The strategies used are the same as for subcontracting (see Section 3.2.3), with one addition. Strategy 1 PRICE FROM OPERATION allows for a price to be specifically loaded in the NET PRICE field on the operation to be used for determining the processing cost. This is analogous to selecting one of the material master prices which can be used for raw material costing. This option is only possible when SORT TERM and MATERIAL GROUP are used to determine the purchasing information. If PURCHASING INFO REC. and PURCHAS. ORGANIZATION are used, the net price is calculated from the purchasing information record, and costing must use one of the other strategies to determine the cost. This strategy should be used in conjunction with one or more of the other strategies to ensure that a cost estimate is properly generated.

3.6.2 Cost estimate using price from operation

Figure 3.15 shows the external processing details of operation 0010 (from Figure 3.11) when the price is to be derived from the operation itself. Section ❶ shows that SORT TERM and MATERIAL GROUP have been filled in. Section ❷ shows the rest of the information required for costing. NET PRICE is the price of the operation. This is divided by the PRICE UNIT to get the actual unit price. The CURRENCY field defines the payment currency. Finally, COST ELEMENT is set for outside manufacturing.

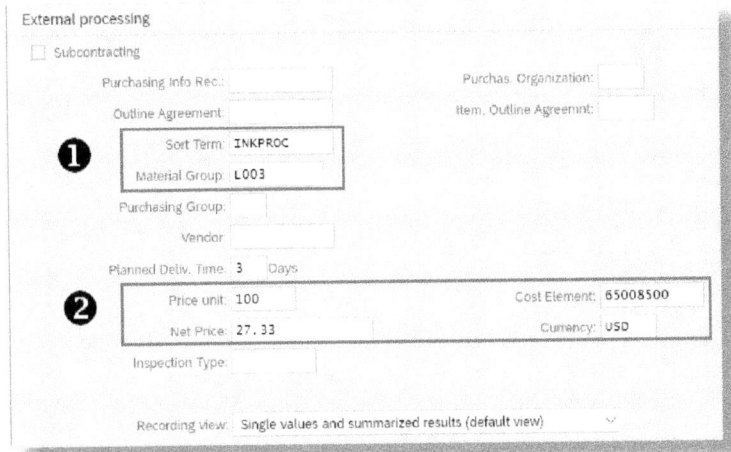

Figure 3.15: External processing details—price from operation

The resulting cost estimate itemization using a costing lot size of 1,000 PC is shown in Figure 3.16. Item 1 represents the cost of external processing. The item category is F (external activity), and the value is 273.30 USD per 1,000 PC, which matches the cost from the operation.

ItmNo	I...	Resource			Resource (Text)	Cost Element	* Total Value	COCr	Quantity	Un
1	F				Inject ink - outside processing	65008500	273.30	USD	1,000	PC
2	M	UWU3 H107			Ink Reservoir	54300000	668.34	USD	1,000	PC
3	M	UWU3 H100			Blue Ink	54300000	33.76	USD	21	L
4	E	300104	ASSEMBLY	SETUP	Assemble pen	94303000	22.91	USD	0.417	HR
5	E	300104	ASSEMBLY	MACHHR	Assemble pen	94301000	25.75	USD	1.0	HR
6	E	300104	ASSEMBLY	LABRHR	Assemble pen	94311000	24.38	USD	1.0	HR
7	M	UWU3 H103			White Barrel	54300000	189.03	USD	1,000	PC
8	E	300105	PACK	SETUP	Packaging	94303000	9.54	USD	10	MIN
9	E	300105	PACK	MACHHR	Packaging	94301000	8.84	USD	0.486	HR
10	E	300105	PACK	LABRHR	Packaging	94311000	25.03	USD	0.972	HR
							* 1,280.88	USD		

Figure 3.16: Itemization with price from operation

3.6.3 Cost estimate using standard purchasing

Figure 3.17 shows the external processing details for operation 0010 set up to use information directly associated with the purchasing information record.

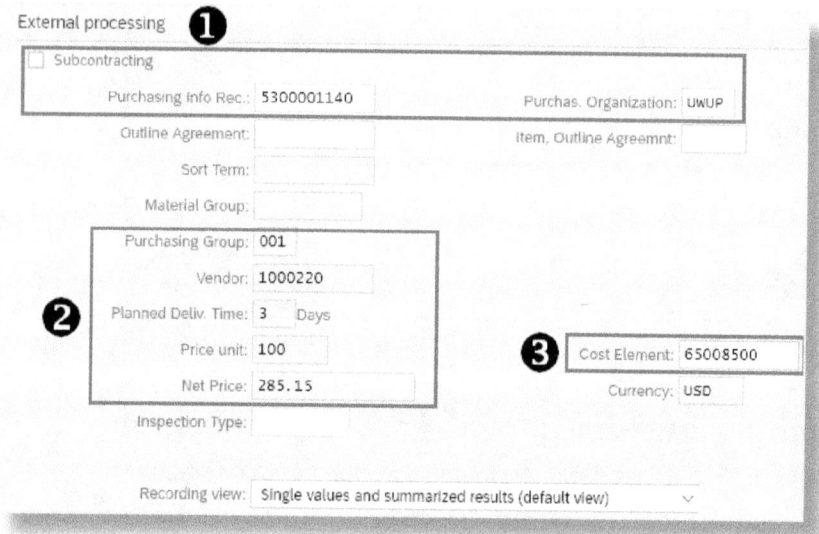

Figure 3.17: External processing details—standard purchasing

Section ❶ shows the purchasing information record and purchasing organization entries. The data in section ❷ shows the information that is derived directly from the purchasing information record. This includes purchasing group, vendor, planned delivery time, and net price. The net price is calculated using the values loaded in the purchasing information, which includes a standard order quantity.

Figure 3.18 shows the purchasing conditions assigned to the standard purchasing information record. Conditions ZB00 and ZC00 both belong in the net price calculation range. ZB00 represents a setup charge for the ink injection. It is a fixed condition, and the 30.00 USD is the same regardless of costing lot size. The FRC1 freight condition is only used if effective price is chosen for the calculation. The configuration from Figure 3.14 indicates that if a price is not manually entered into the operation, the next source of costing information uses the NET QUOTATION PRICE strategy. With this strategy and a costing lot size of 1,000 PC, the total value for the outside processing should be 2,750.00 USD (PB00) plus 100.00 USD (ZC00) plus 30.00 USD (ZB00 – fixed), which equals 2,880.00 USD.

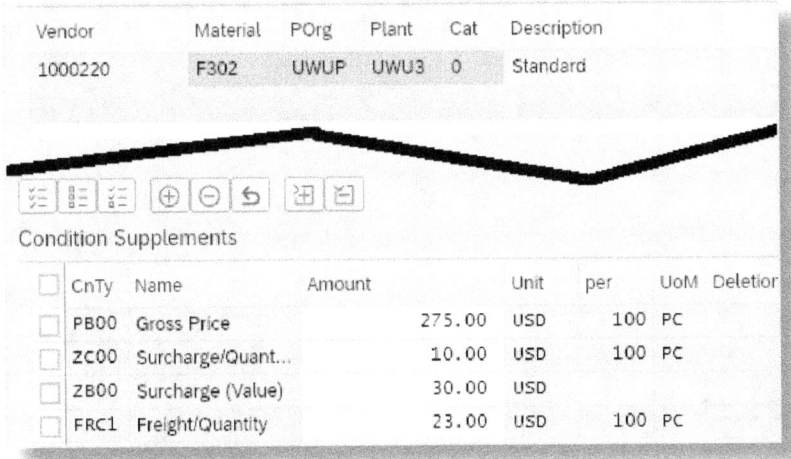

Figure 3.18: Conditions for standard purchasing information record

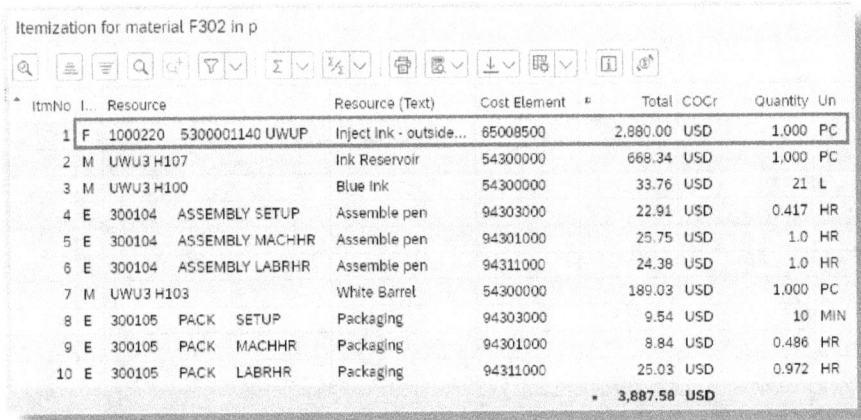

Figure 3.19: Itemization using net price with standard purchasing

Figure 3.19 shows the resulting cost estimate. The item category remains F for external activity, and the total value is 2,880 USD as expected. The freight cost is not included in the calculation because its condition is associated with effective price, not net price.

3.6.4 Cost estimate using subcontracting

The final example uses subcontracting with the effective price strategy with no fixed costs other than taxes. This configuration change is shown in Figure 3.20.

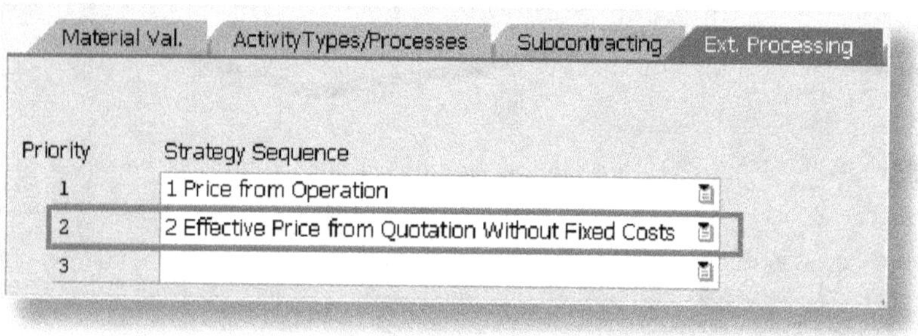

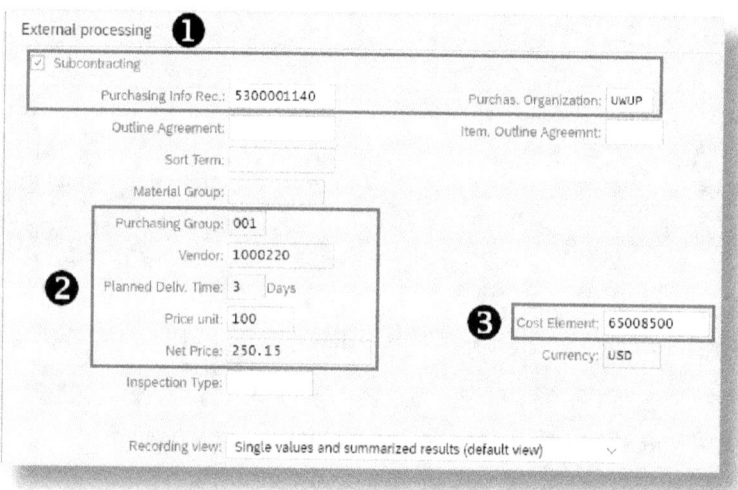

Figure 3.20: Strategy using effective price with no fixed costs

The intent of using this strategy is to see if the fixed setup costs associated with condition ZB00 can be excluded from the cost. Figure 3.21 shows the EXTERNAL PROCESSING section of route operation 0010.

Figure 3.21: External processing details—subcontracting

Section ❶ shows that the purchasing information record is defined for subcontracting. Section ❷ shows the defaults loaded from the purchasing information record. Section ❸ shows the selected cost element. Figure 3.22 shows the conditions for the subcontracting purchasing information record. The ZB00 condition represents the setup surcharge and FRC1 represents the freight. ZB00 is included as part of the net price calculation, and FRC1 is included in the effective price calculation (refer to Figure 3.5).

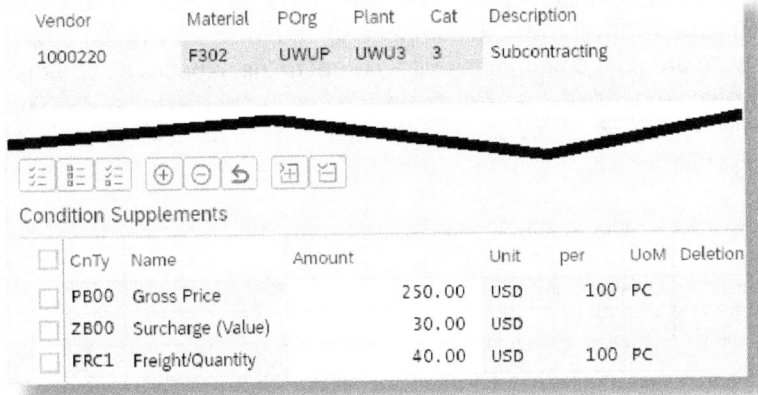

Figure 3.22: Conditions for subcontracting purchasing information record

If the fixed price ZB00 condition is not included in the effective price without fixed costs, the price of the operation is 2,500.00 USD (PB00) plus 400.00 USD (FRC1), or 2,900.00 USD. Figure 3.23 shows the resulting cost estimate.

ItmNo	I...	Resource			Resource (Text)	Cost Element	Total	COCr	Quantity	Un
❶ 1	L	1000220	5300001140	UWUP	Inject Ink - outside...	65008500	2,930.00	USD	1.000	PC
❷ 2	M	UWU3 H107			Ink Reservoir	54300000	668.34	USD	1.000	PC
3	M	UWU3 H100			Blue Ink	54300000	33.76	USD	21	L
4	E	300104	ASSEMBLY SETUP		Assemble pen	94303000	22.91	USD	0.417	HR
5	E	300104	ASSEMBLY MACHHR		Assemble pen	94301000	25.75	USD	1.0	HR
6	E	300104	ASSEMBLY LABRHR		Assemble pen	94311000	24.38	USD	1.0	HR
7	M	UWU3 H103			White Barrel	54300000	189.03	USD	1.000	PC
8	E	300105	PACK	SETUP	Packaging	94303000	9.54	USD	10	MIN
9	E	300105	PACK	MACHHR	Packaging	94301000	8.84	USD	0.486	HR
10	E	300105	PACK	LABRHR	Packaging	94311000	25.03	USD	0.972	HR
							3,937.58	USD		

Figure 3.23: Itemization using effective price with subcontracting

Section ❶ shows the item for the operation cost. Note that the item category is L (subcontracting) and not F (external activity). That is because subcontracting was selected for the operation. Note also that the resulting price is 2,930.00 USD and not 2,900.00 USD. This is because ZB00 is part of the calculation for effective price, and the fixed price exclusion only affects those conditions that come into play when effective price calculations are used. Any fixed price condition that is associated with the net price is always included when using one of the "effective price without fixed costs" strategies. Section ❷ shows the components that are allocated to operation 10. These are the components that are sent to the subcontractor along with any work in process to be used in the service. Item 7 (material H103) is only consumed as part of the order at the plant and is not issued into subcontracting stock.

4 Costing and variant configuration

The items in certain classes of materials can be so similar to one another that they only vary based on particular sets of characteristics that are common to the specific class. Master data maintenance and customer service needs would become burdensome if separate materials, BOMs, and routings were required for each unique set of characteristics. Configurable materials have been created to help simplify this. In its purest form, a configurable material cannot be assigned a standard cost because each set of characteristics assigned to it could provide a different cost. Certain configurations are considered standard and can be kept in inventory. Special variant materials are created which are based on the configurable material, with the characteristics assigned at the material level. Standard material cost estimates are created for these items.

4.1 Configurable materials

Certain products, such as cars and computers, are sold with varying arrays of options, accessories, and colors. Usually, these variations are determined at the time a sales order is taken for the product. Accounting for all the different combinations of the various characteristics would require many thousands of materials to be created. To avoid this unnecessary creation of materials, many of which would never be produced, SAP created the *configurable material*. A configurable material is assigned characteristics that can be filled in at the time a sales order is taken. The values of these characteristics drive both the components that are used in the manufacture of the product and the steps needed to build the product. A few examples of these characteristics for an automobile include color, transmission type, engine size, and optional accessories. Each of these characteristics are used to drive cost as well as the manufacturing process.

Since the individual components and production operations can vary based on the values of the characteristics, special BOMs and routings are required. These so-called super BOMs and super routes contain links to all possible components and routing operations that can be used in the manufacture of the material. Special object dependencies, which reference the characteristics assigned when the order is taken, control which components and operations to use. Only those components and operations that match the characteristics are used in the manufacturing process.

Material cost estimates cannot be generated for configurable materials. A MATERIAL IS CONFIGURABLE checkbox is selected on the BASIC DATA 2 tab of the material master to denote a configurable material (see Figure 4.1).

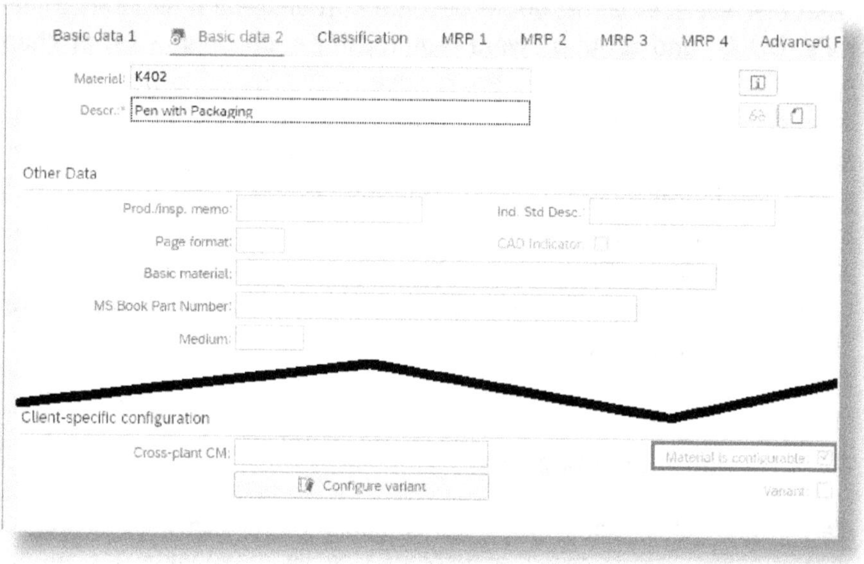

Figure 4.1: Defining a material as configurable

Characteristics are assigned to the configurable material on the CLASSIFICATION tab of the material master (see Figure 4.2). The characteristics are assigned to a class, and the class is assigned to the material. Section ❶ shows CLASS TYPE 300, which is used for configurable materials. Section ❷ shows where the class is assigned. Multiple classes, each with its own set of characteristics, can be assigned to the material. Section ❸ shows the characteristics associated with the class or classes assigned. No values are loaded at this point because they are loaded when the sales order is taken.

Although a special material type is not required to allow a material to be configurable, it is usual practice to use a separate material type, such as KMAT, to segregate the configurable materials from other more standard materials. Selecting MATERIAL IS CONFIGURABLE prevents these materials from being costed using standard procedures. Instead, a special cost estimate that is tied to a sales order line item is created. This ties directly to the characteristics that are associated with the line item. Sales order cost estimates are part of Cost Object Controlling for sales orders and are not covered in this book.

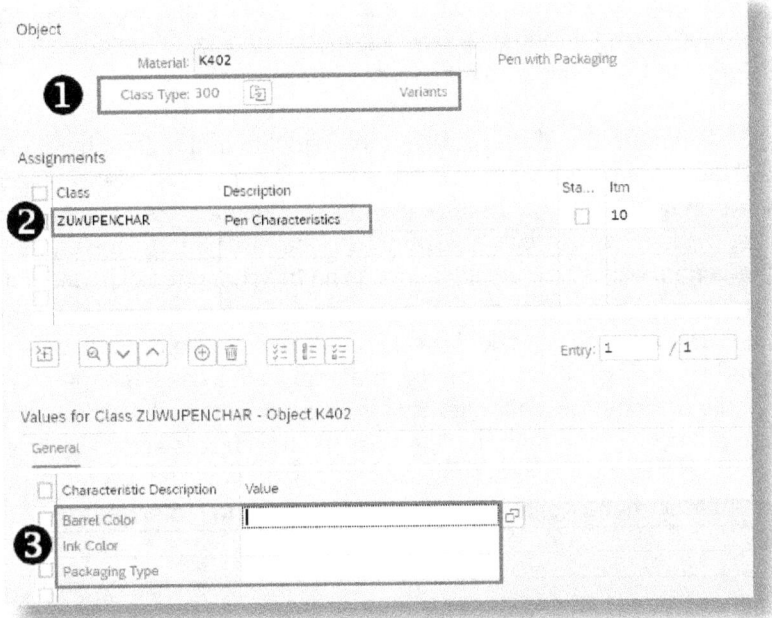

Figure 4.2: Assignment of characteristics to a configurable material

4.2 Variants

Certain sets of characteristics for a configurable material can be commonly selected when an order is taken. Because these configurations are frequently ordered, they are often kept in stock for quicker delivery to the customer. This presents a problem, because stock associated with a configurable material should be allocated directly to a specific sales order. The *material variant* was created to combine the flexibility of a configurable material with the stability of a standard material. A variant is a material based on a configurable material where the characteristics are assigned at the material level. A variant uses the same super BOM and super route as the configurable material to which it is linked.

Universal Writing Utensils sells its pens in different types of packaging. The manufacturing line at the Chicago plant can handle multiple different ink colors and pen barrel colors. Two different types of packaging have been defined. Usually, when an order is placed, the ink color, barrel color, and packaging are selected at that time for material K402. This material is manufactured as a make-to-order item that is shipped directly to the customer. Over time, the company determined that a few combinations were regularly ordered, and lead time for production was reduced if these were kept in stock. Therefore, variant materials were created that access the characteristics assigned to the configurable material K402.

Figure 4.3 shows the definition of one of the variants at the plant level on the MRP 3 tab of the material master. There is a corresponding client-based assignment on the BASIC DATA 2 tab of the material master, but this is used to copy the global characteristic assignment to the MRP 3 tab. This can be used if the variant exists in multiple plants using the characteristics defined at the client level. The variant should be defined at the plant level for connection to BOMs and routes. The CONFIGURABLEMATERIAL field is used to connect the variant to a specific configurable material. In this case, the material is K402. This assigns the characteristics to the variant. If characteristics have been entered for the material, the VARIANT checkbox is selected. This tells the system that the material is a variant. Click on the CONFIGURE VARIANT button to enter or change characteristics assigned to the materials.

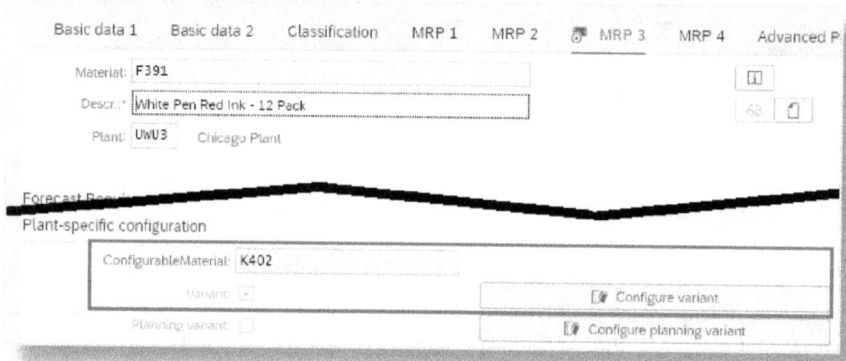

Figure 4.3: Variant definition on MRP 3

Figure 4.4 shows the characteristics assigned to material F391, which is a white pen using red ink, sold as a pack of 12. Note the connection to material K402, which provides the list of characteristics to be filled in.

```
Material: F391
          White Pen Red Ink - 12 Pack
   Plant: UWU3                Chicago Plant
   ConfigurableMaterial: K402

Characteristic Value Assignment

   Char. description        Char. Value              Inf...
   Barrel Color             White Barrel
   Ink Color                Red Ink
   Packaging Type           Dozen
```

Figure 4.4: Material F391 variant characteristics

These characteristics are used to drive behavior when selecting components from the super BOM and operations from the super route. Additional materials can be set up as variants using the same base configurable material. Figure 4.5 shows the variant characteristics assigned to material F394, representing a white pen with blue ink that is sold in boxes of 100.

```
Material: F394
          White Pen Blue Ink - 100 Box
   Plant: UWU3                Chicago Plant
   ConfigurableMaterial: K402

Characteristic Value Assignment

   Char. description        Char. Value              Inf...
   Barrel Color             White Barrel
   Ink Color                Blue Ink
   Packaging Type           Box
```

Figure 4.5: Material F394 variant characteristics

> **Short dump when creating a material variant**
>
>  Between ECC 6 and S/4HANA the internal object numbering scheme for configurable materials and material variants has changed and can cause a short dump to occur when trying to configure a variant. Refer to SAP Note 2641050 – "Saving the variant configuration leads to a short dump", and make sure the number ranges for object CU_INOB are set up correctly using transaction CUNR. There should be three ranges: 01 from 000000000000000001 to 899899999999999999, 02 from 899900000000000001 to 899999999999999999, and 03 from 999900000000000001 to 999999999999999999.

4.3 Super BOMs

The purpose of using a configurable material is mainly to allow for optional components to be used to make a product, and this must be represented when creating a BOM. This type of BOM is known as a *super BOM*. A super BOM contains links to all possible components that can be used in the manufacture of a configurable material. The components that are actually used for a specific configuration are determined based on *object dependencies* that are assigned to the components in the BOM. An object dependency is a procedure that references the values of the characteristics used to drive selection logic for BOMs, routes, configuration profiles, and characteristics. When assigned to a BOM, an object dependency is used for component selection.

Super BOMs are maintained using the same transactions as regular BOMs (transactions CS01 and CS02), but assignment of object dependency is not yet enabled for the Maintain Bill of Material Fiori tile (S/4HANA release 1809). Super BOMs are only created for the base configurable material. The variant must be connected to the configurable material's BOM separately.

Material	K402			Pen w
Plant	UWU3 Chicago Plant			
Alternative BOM	1			

Position		Effectivity Initial Screen		
Material	Document	Class	General	

Item	ICt	Component	Component description	Quantity	Uo	OD	A
0010	L	H107	Ink Reservoir	1,200	PC	✓	
0020	L	H107	Ink Reservoir	10,000	PC	✓	
0030	L	H100	Blue Ink	25.200	L	✓	
0040	L	H100	Blue Ink	210	L	✓	
0050	L	H101	Red Ink	25.200	L	✓	
0060	L	H101	Red Ink	210	L	✓	
0070	L	H102	Black Ink	25.200	L	✓	
0080	L	H102	Black Ink	210	L	✓	
0090	L	H103	White Barrel	1,200	PC	✓	
0100	L	H103	White Barrel	10,000	PC	✓	
0110	L	H104	Red Barrel	1,200	PC	✓	
0120	L	H104	Red Barrel	10,000	PC	✓	
0130	L	H105	Green Barrel	1,200	PC	✓	
0140	L	H105	Green Barrel	10,000	PC	✓	
0150	L	V500	Pen Packaging	100	PC	✓	
0160	L	V501	Shipping Box	100	PC	✓	

Figure 4.6: Configurable material BOM with object dependencies

Figure 4.6 shows an example of a configurable material BOM with the object dependency checkboxes highlighted. When a checkbox is selected, an object dependency is used to determine if the component is used in the manufacturing order or cost estimate. Note that the same component is used multiple times in the BOM with different quantities. Note also that three different types of ink and three different colors of pen barrel are components of this material. This does not mean that all the components will be used. The object dependency definition mandates which, if any components are to be included. To see or change the object dependency, select one of the items and follow the menu path EXTRAS • OBJECT DEPENDENCIES • EDITOR (see Figure 4.7).

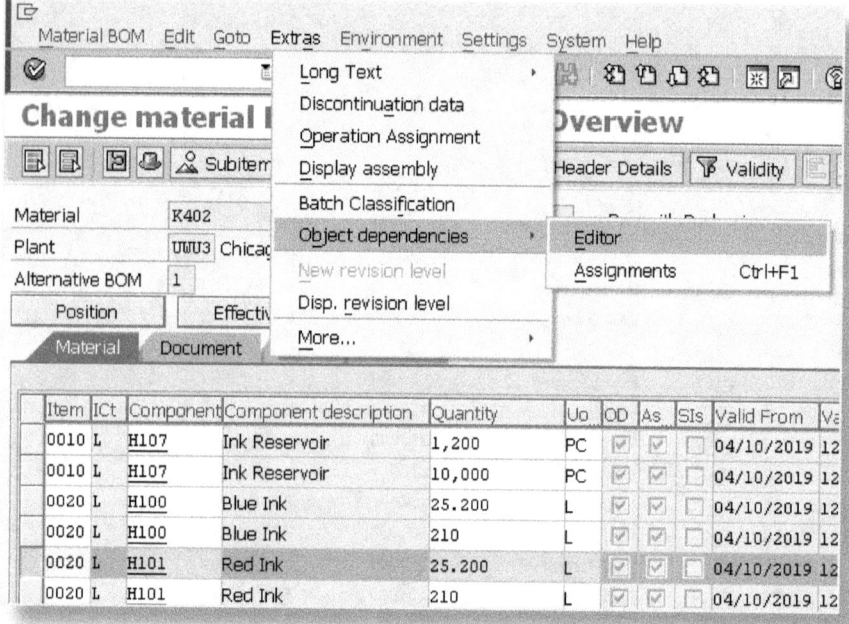

Figure 4.7: Choosing the object dependency editor

The object dependency for this BOM item is a selection condition that indicates that the value for the characteristic representing the ink color ZPENINK must be set to RED (red ink) and the packaging size represented by characteristic ZPENPKG must be set to DOZEN (dozen). This is shown in Figure 4.8.

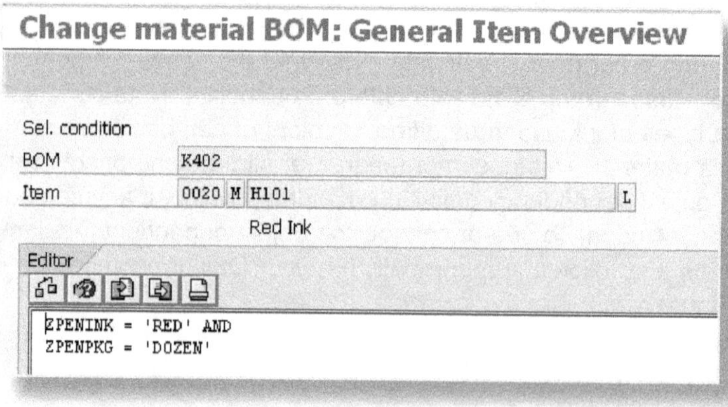

Figure 4.8: Object dependency definition

Each of the components has a similar selection condition using one or more of the characteristics (ZPENBARREL, ZPENINK, and ZPENPKG) to determine whether to use that component in the cost estimate. Although each component has an associated object dependency in this case, it does not have to be the case with all configurable BOMs. If one or more components is common to all configurations, no dependency needs to be defined. The object dependencies used in this example are simple. Much more robust procedures can be written in order to select components by class or to calculate component quantities based on the characteristics assigned.

At this point, the BOM is only associated with the configurable material. For each material variant that is defined, a link must be made for that material to the configurable BOM. Transaction CS41 is used to create the link, and CS42 is used to make any necessary changes. There is a corresponding Create Link to Configurable Material Fiori tile. The link, shown in Figure 4.9, allows the configurable characteristics defined for the variant to be used to determine the BOM components and quantities.

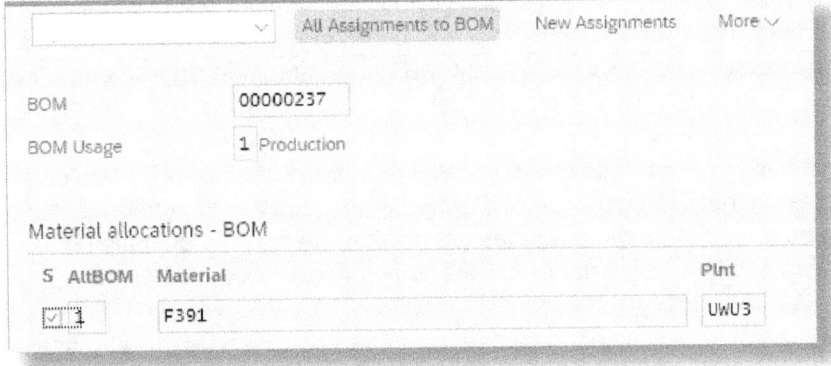

Figure 4.9: Link material to configurable BOM

4.4 Super routes

A *super route* performs the same functions for the manufacturing routings as the super BOM does for the bill of materials. Standard transactions and Fiori tiles are used for this. CA01 and CA02 are used for routings, and C201 and C202 are used for recipes. The corresponding Create Routing, Change Routing, Create Master Recipe, and Change Master Recipe Fiori tiles can also be used.

COSTING AND VARIANT CONFIGURATION

		Previous header	Next header	Header	Select all	Deselect all	Delete	Check	Long text	Refe

Material: K402   Pen with Packaging Grp.Count1
Sequence: 0

Operation Overview

	Ope...	Work cen...	Plant	C...	Description	O...	Base...	Un...	Se...	Unit	Activit...	M...	Unit	Activit...	La...	Unit	Activit...	Scrap
☐	0010	INJECT	UWU3	YBP1	Inject Ink		1,000	PC	50	MIN	SETUP	45	MIN	MACHHR	45	MIN	LABRHR	
☐	0020	ASSEMBLY	UWU3	YBP1	Assemble pen		1,000	PC	25	MIN	SETUP	60	MIN	MACHHR	60	MIN	LABRHR	
☐	0030	PACK	UWU3	YBP3	Packaging		100	DZ	10	MIN	SETUP	35	MIN	MACHHR	70	MIN	LABRHR	
☐	0040	INJECT	UWU3	YBP1	Inject Ink		1,000	PC	50	MIN	SETUP	45	MIN	MACHHR	45	MIN	LABRHR	
☐	0050	ASSEMBLY	UWU3	YBP1	Assemble pen		1,000	PC	25	MIN	SETUP	60	MIN	MACHHR	60	MIN	LABRHR	
☐	0060	PACK	UWU3	YBP3	Packaging		100	DZ	45	MIN	SETUP	20	MIN	MACHHR	20	MIN	LABRHR	
☐	0070		UWU3				1	EA										

Figure 4.10: Routing for configurable material

Figure 4.10 shows the route for configurable material K402. There is an OBJECT DEPENDENCY field for the operations that serves the same function as the one for BOM components. This indicates that an object dependency has been used for the operation. You can find the editor via the EXTRAS • OBJECT DEPENDENCIES • EDITOR dropdown menu after selecting an operation (see Figure 4.11). This is found under the More ⌄ button in the Fiori app.

Figure 4.12 shows the object dependency for operation 0010, which requires the packaging type to be DOZEN. This becomes important because the base unit of measure of material K402 is EA and the operation unit of measure is PC. There needs to be a conversion between PC and EA.

For this route, the object dependencies used are associated with packaging size, and drive the unit of measure conversions as well as standard values assigned to each operation. Note also in Figure 4.10 that operations 0040, 0050, and 0060 basically duplicate operations 0010, 0020, and 0030 respectively. The first three operations are used for packs of 12, and the last three are for boxes of 100. Section ❶ in Figure 4.13 shows the conversion factor for 12 pens per package in operation 0010, and ❷ shows operation 0040 with a conversion factor for 100 pens per box

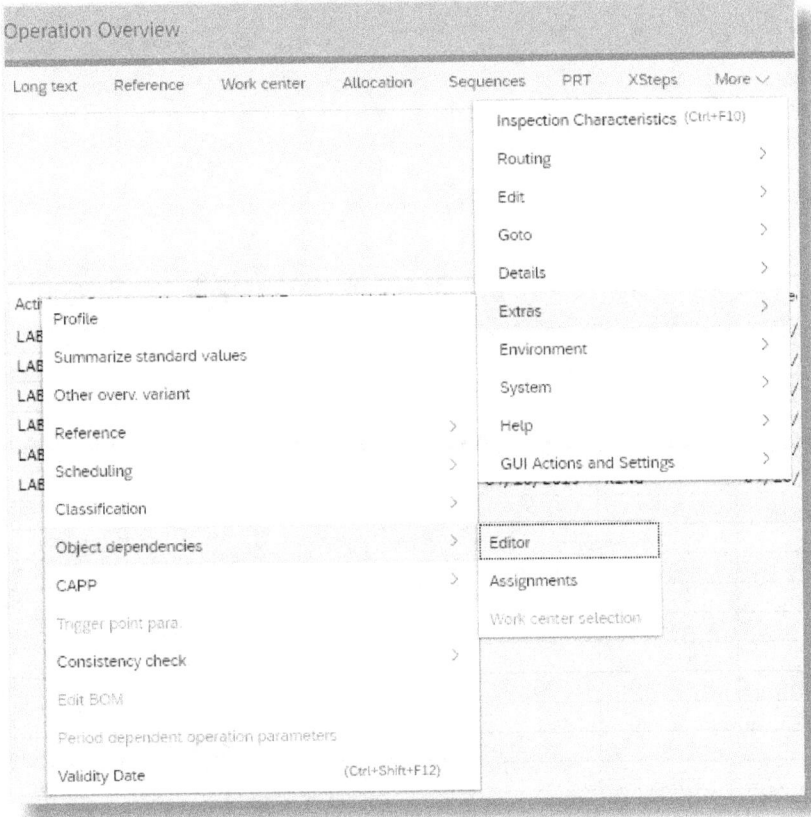

Figure 4.11: Selecting the object dependency editor

Figure 4.12: Object dependency for operation 0010

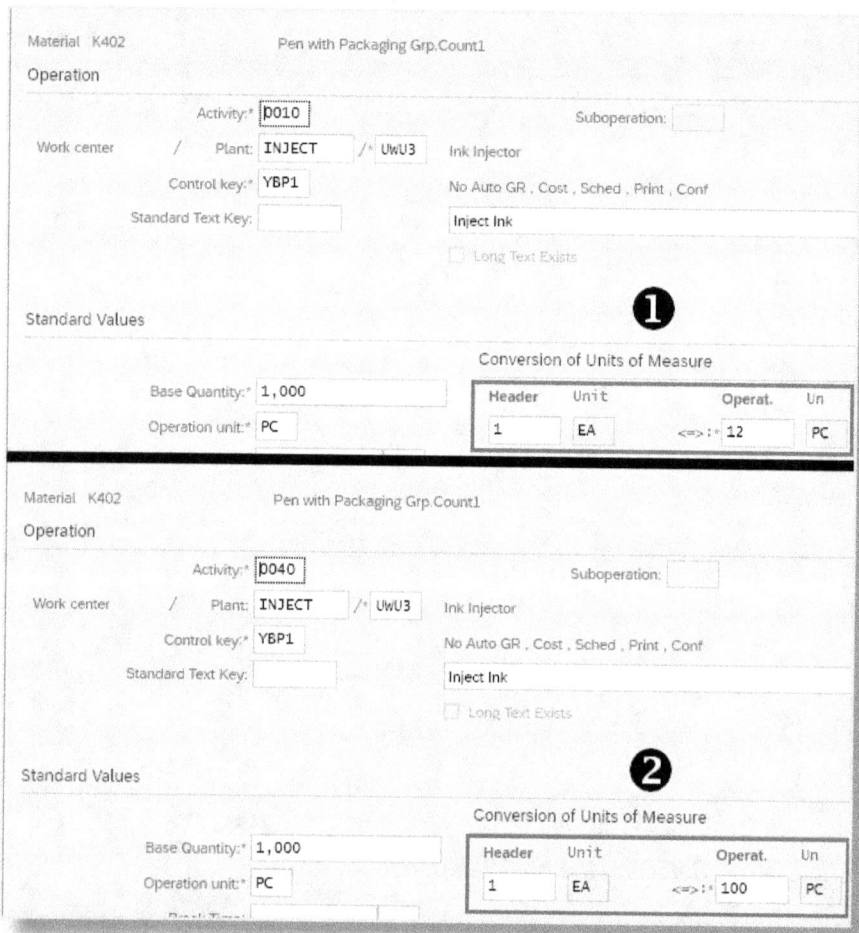

Figure 4.13: Operation comparison

The variant materials must be assigned to the configurable material's route in order to take advantage of the object dependencies. This is done using the material assignment when maintaining the route (see Figure 4.14).

Add the material to the list of materials assigned to the routing shown in Figure 4.15.

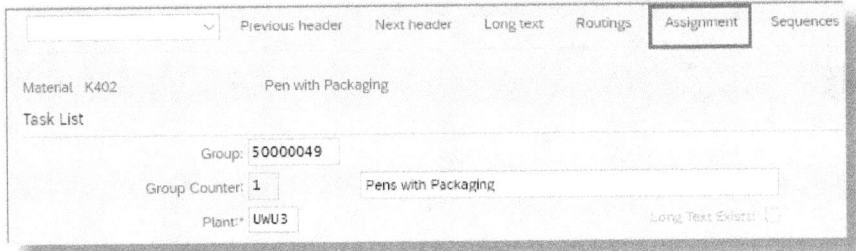

Figure 4.14: Material assignment button on routing header

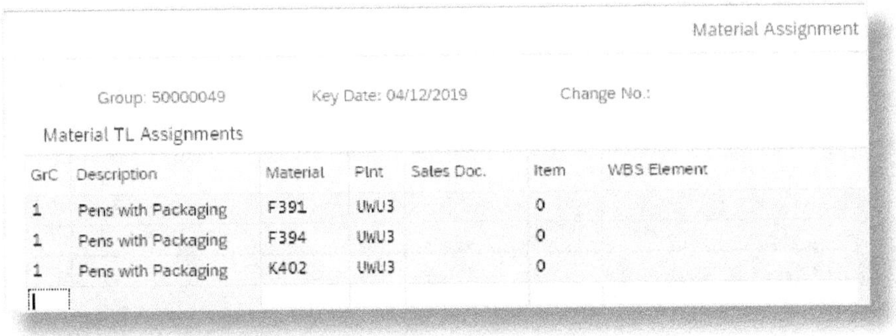

Figure 4.15: Material assignment to a routing

When updating a recipe, the material assignment is found under the drop-down menu GOTO • MATERIAL ASSIGNMENT on the RECIPE HEADER tab. This is found under the More ⌄ button in Fiori.

4.5 Variant cost estimate

Variant cost estimates are created with the same procedures as regular cost estimates. Either transaction CK11N or the Create Material Cost Estimate Fiori app can be used to generate the costs. There are slight differences that show up in the results. Looking at Figure 4.16, section ❶ shows that the cost estimate represents a configured material or variant. The "C" at ❷ indicates that there is a configuration associated with the cost estimate. For this example, two additional columns have been added to the itemization report. The column at ❸ shows the operation numbers from the routing, and at ❹, the BOM item numbers are highlighted.

Costing and Variant Configuration

Figure 4.16: Variant cost estimate for material F391

Note that only the first three operations from the routing in Figure 4.10 are included in the itemization. Only four of the components of the BOM (in Figure 4.6) are referenced. This is because of the object dependencies defined for the routing operations and BOM components. The characteristics of the material can be displayed using the explanation facilities. Click on INFORMATION ON COST ESTIMATE (🛈) when using transaction CK11N) to get to the list of master data that is available to view. Click on CONFIGURATION (see Figure 4.17) to see the list of characteristics associated with the variant.

Figure 4.18 shows that the barrel color is white, the ink color is red, and the packaging size is a dozen (12). These characteristics were used to select the individual items from the BOM and routing.

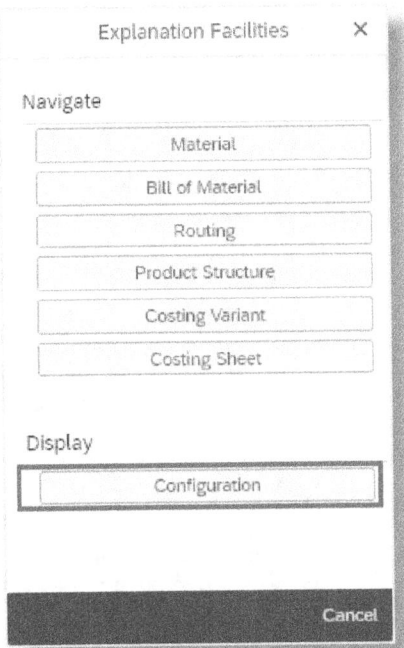

Figure 4.17: Explanation facilities menu with configuration button

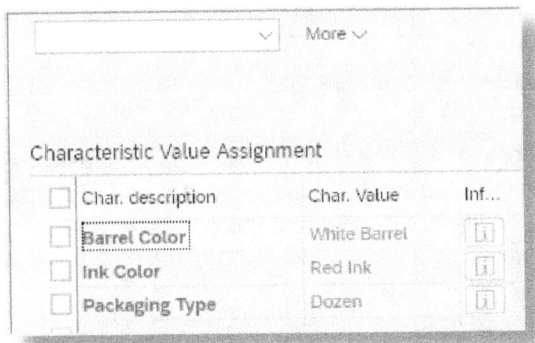

Figure 4.18: Configuration characteristics for material F391

The other variant material is a white pen with blue ink that is packed in a box of 100. Figure 4.19 shows the resulting cost estimate. Compare this with the one for F391 in Figure 4.16.

95

Costing and variant configuration

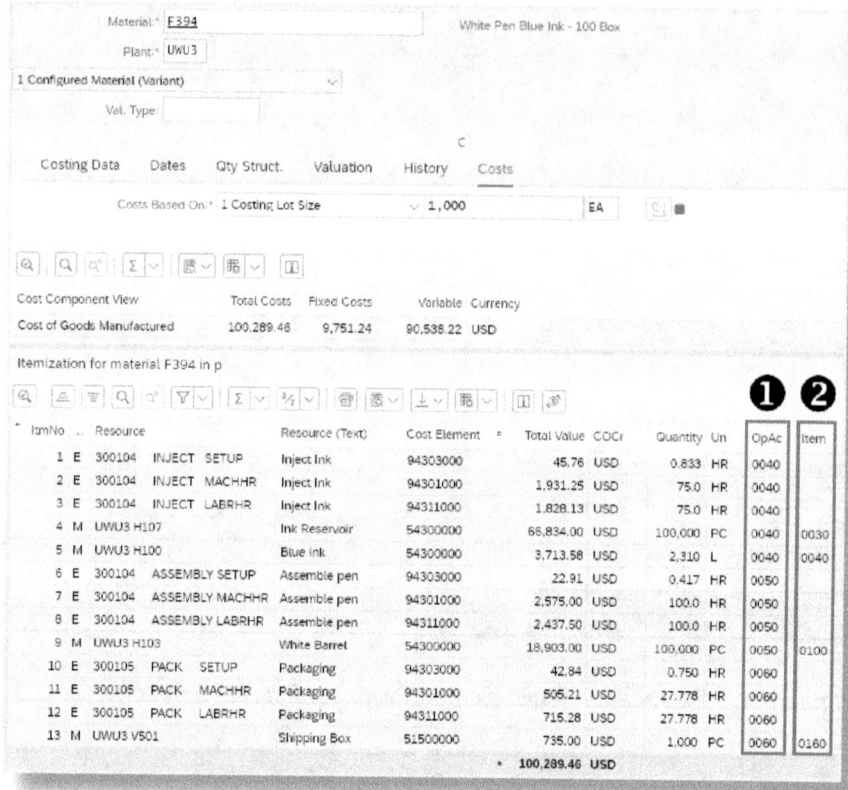

Figure 4.19: Variant cost estimate for material F394

Note that the routing operations at ❶ are different. This is because the packaging type characteristic (see Figure 4.20) indicates the use of a box. The BOM items at ❷ are also different because of the colors and packaging sizes chosen for the variant.

Figure 4.20: Configuration characteristics for material F394

5 Applying overhead to cost estimates

Many types of costs cannot be directly assigned using the standard quantity structures, including BOMs, routings, and special procurement keys. One method for including these costs is to use additive cost estimates, which is covered in Chapter 7. A more consistent way of including these costs is to use overhead costing sheets and template allocation.

5.1 Overhead and cost estimates

The assignment of costs using only component costs and manufacturing costs associated with activity types does not necessarily provide a complete picture of what it takes to manufacture a product. For example, only using vendor pricing for raw materials does not represent the full cost of purchasing a material. Administrative and logistical costs are not easily included in the costing methods previously covered. Some overhead costs associated with manufacturing are also not easily obtainable from BOMs and routings. Costing sheets can be used to allocate these "hard-to-get" costs to a material, and they define the rules for calculating these additional costs. When a costing sheet is connected to a material, these costs are automatically calculated as part of the cost estimate.

Another method used to process overhead and other costs is the CO template. A template contains rules to determine not only the cost to be calculated, but also whether the cost should be calculated based on master data associated with the material and its quantity structures. Templates are associated with Activity Based Costing (ABC) and provide a much more detailed way of allocating costs to a product.

5.2 Overhead costing sheets

Overhead costing sheets are defined using cost bases, overhead rate conditions, and cost object credits. The combination provides the means by which the cost is both calculated and allocated. To use the calculations from the costing sheet, the material must be connected to it. Costing sheets are assigned to the valuation variant and then use pre-defined conditions to determine the costs to be added. The calculations apply to certain ranges of cost elements (bases) used in the cost estimate and can also be assigned to cumulative subtotals of these costs.

5.2.1 Calculation base

The first component of a costing sheet is the calculation base. This defines a grouping of cost elements for which an overhead allocation applies. Each item in the itemization of a cost estimate is assigned a cost element. The base determines which of these cost elements the overhead calculation applies to. Multiple bases can be assigned to a single costing sheet, and overhead can be made to apply to one or more of these groups of cost elements. Configuration is performed via IMG menu path CONTROLLING • PRODUCT COST CONTROLLING • PRODUCT COST PLANNING • BASIC SETTINGS FOR MATERIAL COSTING • OVERHEAD • COSTING SHEET: COMPONENTS • DEFINE CALCULATION BASES or by using transaction KZB2.

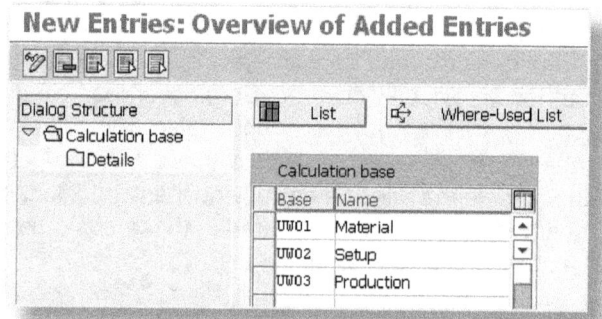

Figure 5.1: Defining costing sheet bases

Figure 5.1 shows that three new costing sheet bases have been defined. UW01 represents cost elements associated with materials, UW02 represents setup costs, and UW03 represents production costs. Select a base to update the cost elements. Enter the CONTROLLING AREA associated with the bases, and enter the cost elements (see Figure 5.2). Ranges and cost element groups can be entered. Origin groups can also be used to more finely identify the source of the cost base. Different bases can be set up for fixed, variable, and total costs associated with the cost elements selected.

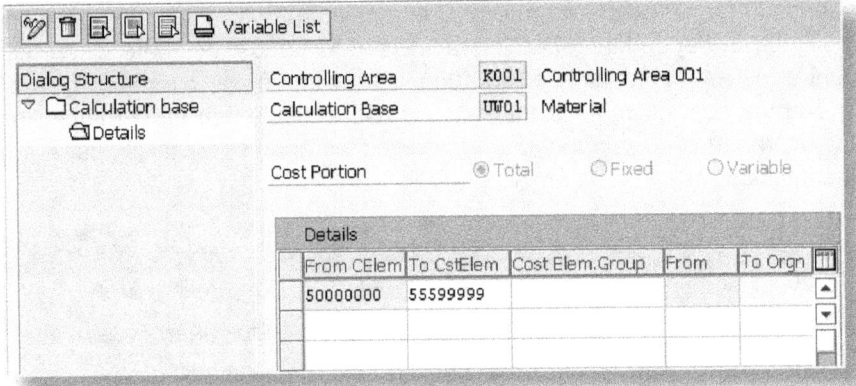

Figure 5.2: Assigning cost elements to the base

5.2.2 Overhead rates

The system uses overhead rates to calculate the amount to be applied to the cost. These are stored in tables determined by the dependency assigned to the overhead rate condition. The dependency defines both a condition table and the fields that are accessible in the cost estimate which are used as keys to the condition table. Condition values are then updated based on the key values and are selected when the proper key combination is found. Several tables come pre-defined with the system, and dependencies are set up using these tables. Should a custom dependency be required, a condition table must first be created via menu path CONTROLLING • COST CENTER ACCOUNTING • ACTUAL POSTINGS • PERIOD-END CLOSING • OVERHEAD • COSTING SHEET: COMPONENTS • EXTRAS: DEPENDENCIES/CONDITION TABLES • DEFINE CONDITION TABLES. The new dependency can then be defined using IMG menu path CONTROLLING • COST CENTER ACCOUNTING • ACTUAL POSTINGS • PERIOD-END CLOSING • OVERHEAD • COSTING SHEET: COMPONENTS • EXTRAS: DEPENDENCIES/ CONDITION TABLES • DEFINE DEPENDENCIES. This new dependency can be assigned to an overhead rate.

Table 5.1 shows a list of the delivered dependencies with the condition table name, description, and key fields. There are three values for overhead type: 1—actual, 2—planned, 3—commitment. Type 2 is applicable for product costing. The key fields determine how the table is accessed when searching for an overhead rate. For example, an overhead rate condition assigned to dependency D020 is accessed for a cost estimate when the controlling area is associated with the cost estimate, the overhead type is 2, and the cost estimate plant matches. Other fields that must match are the overhead key assigned to the material master and the validity dates for the condition.

Dependency	Table	Description	Key Fields
D000	A013	Overhead Type	Controlling Area
			Overhead Type
D010	A014	Overhead Type/	Controlling Area
		Overhead Key	Overhead Type
			Overhead Key
D020	A035	Overhead Type/	Controlling Area
		Plant	Overhead Type
			Plant
D030	A038	Overhead Type/	Controlling Area
		Company Code	Overhead Type
			Company Code
D040	A039	Overhead Type/	Controlling Area
		Business Area	Overhead Type
			Business Area
D050	A036	Overhead Type/	Controlling Area
		Order type	Overhead Type
			Order Type
D060	A037	Overhead Type/	Controlling Area
		Order Category	Overhead Type
			Order Category
D070	A120	Overhead Type/	Controlling Area
		Cost Version	Overhead Type
			Version
D080	A122	Surcharge Type	Controlling Area
		Profit Center	Overhead Type
			Profit Center

Table 5.1: Overhead rate dependencies

The dependencies that are most applicable to product costing are:

- D010—assigns different rates based only on overhead key. These rates are applicable for all plants in the controlling area and differ only based on the overhead key assignment.
- D020—assigns different rates based on plant. These rates can differ for the same overhead key at each plant. The overhead key is assigned to the material.
- D030—assigns different rates based on company code. These rates are the same for all plants within a single company code.

Two different types of rates are used for calculating overhead. The first type is the *percentage rate*, which calculates the amount using the assigned percentage based on the values associated with the cost elements for which it applies. That value is then used for the overhead allocation. The percentage rate conditions are configured via IMG menu path CONTROLLING • PRODUCT COST CONTROLLING • PRODUCT COST PLANNING • BASIC SETTINGS FOR MATERIAL COSTING • OVERHEAD • COSTING SHEET: COMPONENTS • DEFINE PERCENTAGE OVERHEAD RATES or by using transaction KZZ2. Figure 5.3 shows three overhead conditions (UW11, UW22, and UW31) that have been defined using different dependencies. UW11 requires an overhead key to define the condition values. UW22 conditions are plant-wide. All materials include the overhead. UW31 is based on company code, and all materials in all plants within that company code use the same overhead calculation. Overhead rates can be assigned during configuration, but these rates are not included in the transports. Rates should be maintained in the production client.

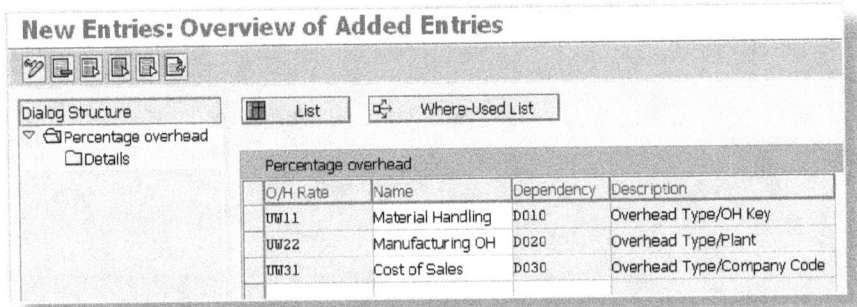

Figure 5.3: Percentage overhead rate conditions

The second type of overhead rate is the *quantity-based rate*. A value per unit of measure is assigned directly to the rate, and this value is allocated to the cost estimate using the costing lot size as the base. These conditions are configured via IMG menu path CONTROLLING • PRODUCT COST CONTROLLING • PRODUCT COST PLANNING • BASIC SETTINGS FOR MATERIAL COSTING • OVERHEAD • COSTING SHEET: COMPONENTS • DEFINE QUANTITY-BASED OVERHEAD RATES or by using transaction KZM2. Figure 5.4 shows the definition. The same dependencies used for percentage rates are also used for quantity-based rates. The UW21 condition also uses dependency D020 and is maintained by plant.

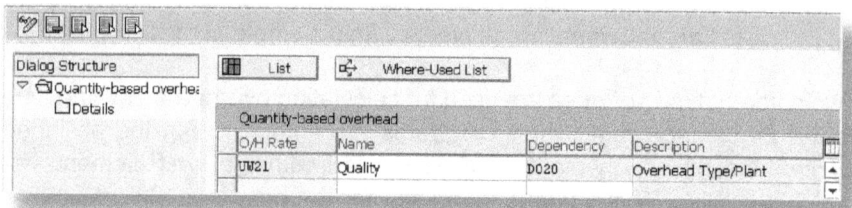

Figure 5.4: Quantity-based rate condition

Conditions of both types are maintained using transaction KK11 (Create Condition) or KK12 (Change Condition). The dependency assigned to the condition determines the maintenance parameters. For example, conditions using dependency D010 require a valid overhead key to be associated with the rate whereas those with dependency D020 require the plant ID. After entering the condition, the screen shown in Figure 5.5 is displayed. The overhead type (2 for cost estimates) and overhead key do not need to be entered at this point. Click on the ⊕ button.

Change Material Handlin (UW11): Selection

Controlling Area	K001	Controlling Area 001
Overhead Type		to
Overhead key		to
Valid On	04/16/2019	

Figure 5.5: Initial window for condition maintenance

Figure 5.6 shows the entries for condition UW11. Because this requires an overhead key, the values are entered for that overhead key. Click on 💾 to save the values.

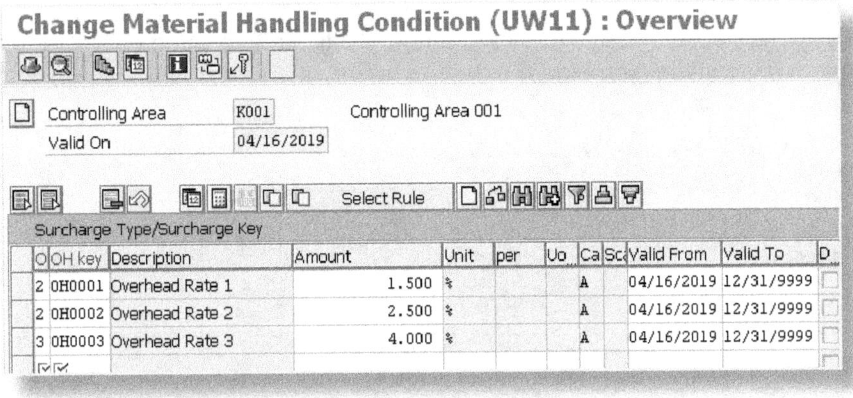

APPLYING OVERHEAD TO COST ESTIMATES

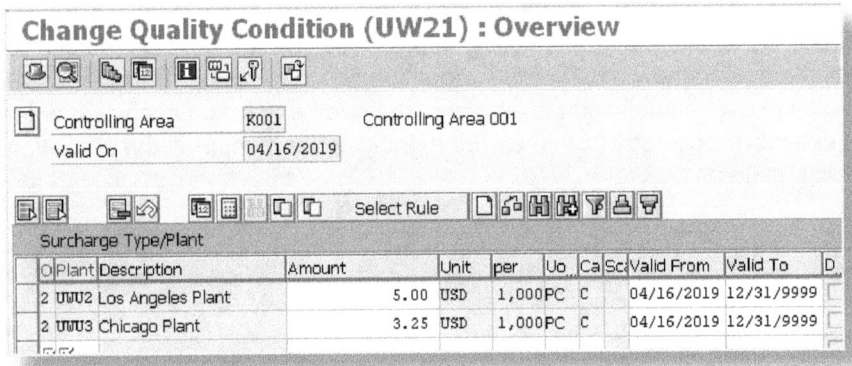

Figure 5.6: Updating the overhead condition rates

Conditions are time dependent, and rate changes can be planned in advance by using a new VALID FROM date. Quantity rates require the amount to refer to a currency per quantity of output (see Figure 5.7). Because this condition is set up using dependency D020, plant is a required field.

Figure 5.7: Quantity condition rate

5.2.3 Credits

Overhead allocations require a source costing object and a special cost element by which the cost object is credited. A secondary cost element defined with category 41 (Overhead Rates), is used to credit the sending object and debit the receiving object. In this case, the object is the cost estimate. Credits are configured via IMG menu path CONTROLLING • PRODUCT COST CONTROLLING • PRODUCT COST PLANNING • BASIC SETTINGS FOR MATERIAL

103

COSTING • OVERHEAD • COSTING SHEET: COMPONENTS • DEFINE CREDITS or by using transaction KZE2. To create a new credit, enter a three-character ID and a description (see Figure 5.8).

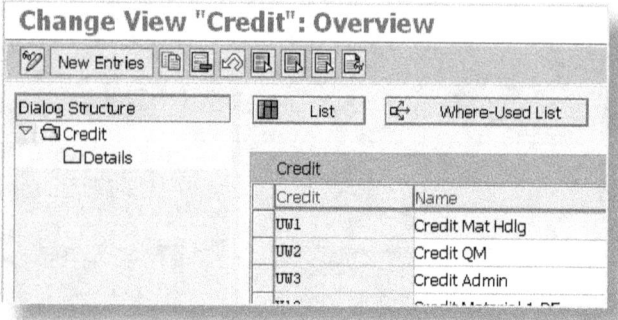

Figure 5.8: Defining the costing sheet credits

Next, select a credit and click on the DETAILS folder. Credits must be assigned a valid-to date, an overhead cost element, and a cost object for the credit, as shown in Figure 5.9. The cost object can be a cost center, a business process, or an internal order. The cost element can be further classified by assigning an origin group as well. The FXD % field is used to tell the system how much of the allocation should be fixed. Enter an asterisk (*) to use the definition assigned to the overhead rate. Otherwise, enter a specific percentage from 0 to 100 to indicate the portion of the allocation that should be fixed.

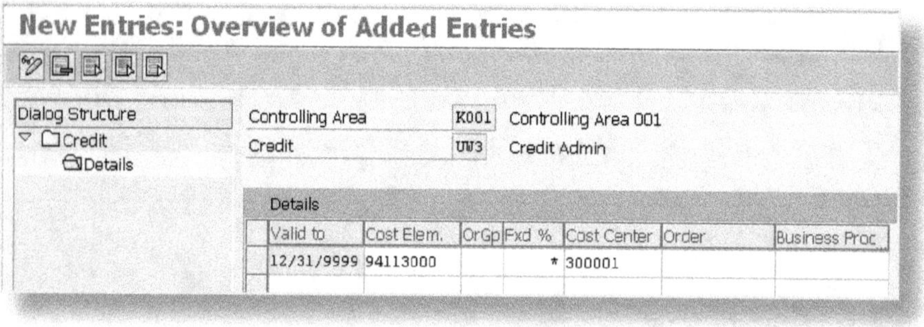

Figure 5.9: Defining the credit allocation information

5.2.4 Defining a costing sheet

The costing sheet defines the rules by which overhead allocation is performed. Bases, rate conditions, credits, and subtotal lines make up the costing sheet. Configuration is performed via IMG menu path CONTROLLING • PRODUCT COST CONTROLLING • PRODUCT COST PLANNING • BASIC SETTINGS FOR MATERIAL COSTING • OVERHEAD • DEFINE COSTING SHEETS or by using transaction KZS2.

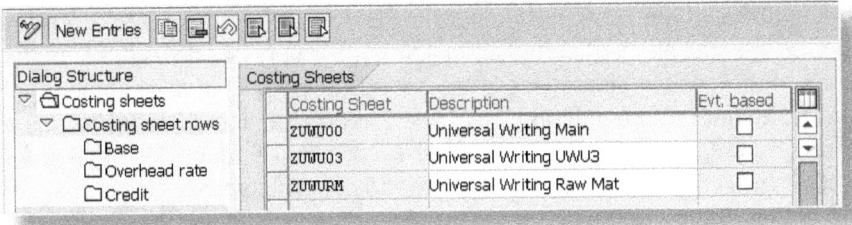

Figure 5.10: Costing sheet configuration

Figure 5.10 shows the list of available costing sheets. Select an existing costing sheet, or create a new one. Click on the COSTING SHEET ROWS folder.

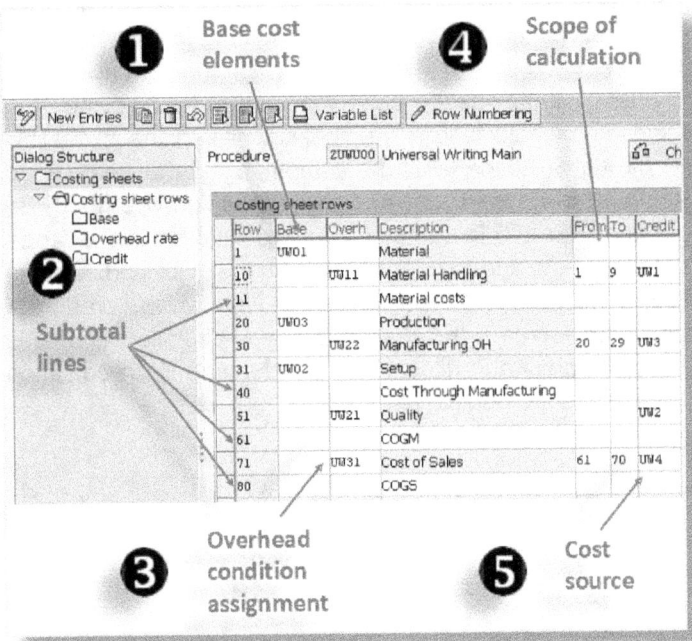

Figure 5.11: Costing sheet row definition

Figure 5.11 shows the definition of the rows of a costing sheet. A row can contain either a base definition, an overhead condition plus a credit, or a blank line indicating a subtotal of costs since the beginning of the sheet. Section ❶ shows the location of the base cost element definition. The line on which the base is defined represents all the costs from the cost estimate associated with the set of cost elements of the base. Base UW01 includes all cost elements from 50000000 to 55999999, which represent the material costs in this implementation. Any overhead calculation referring to that line is only applied to the material costs. UW03 represents the manufacturing activity type costs excluding the SETUP activity, and UW02 only includes the cost element of the setup activity. Section ❷ shows the subtotal lines of the costing sheet. Costs are added together from the beginning of the cost sheet to the subtotal line. Line 11 subtotals the costs from lines 1 through 10. Line 40 subtotals the costs from lines 1 through 31. Section ❸ defines the condition used for the overhead cost calculation. This can either be a percentage condition or a quantity-based condition. The values assigned to the conditions are used in the overhead calculations. Section ❹ shows the scope of a specific calculation. For percentage conditions, this provides the values used in the calculation of the overhead. The calculation in line 10 only applies to lines 1 through 9. In this case, only the material base is used, and the percentage of the UW11 condition is multiplied by the combined material costs. The scope for the calculation for line 30 does not include the subtotal line 11, and so it only applies to the costs for base UW03. Condition UW21, on line 51, has no range of costing sheet lines. This is because it is a quantity-based condition, and it does not need to access specific lines in the calculation. The final calculation line is 71. This includes lines 61 through 70. Line 61 is the subtotal line for all costs up to that point, including all the base costs and any calculated overhead. Be careful defining ranges. If multiple subtotal lines are included in the range, those subtotal costs are also added prior to applying the overhead, and the total overhead costs will be overstated. Section ❺ shows the credit definition which defines the source of the cost for the overhead allocation. This includes both the cost object and allocation cost element. Each condition calculation line must have a credit defined for it.

5.2.5 Overhead keys and overhead groups

Overhead conditions that use overhead keys as part of the dependency definition must have an overhead key assigned to the material master for those conditions to be used in a calculation. Defining overhead keys to use in a plant is a two-step process. The first step is to define the key itself. Overhead keys are 6-character IDs with a description. No other information is required. Configuration is performed via IMG menu path CONTROLLING • PRODUCT COST CONTROLLING • PRODUCT COST PLANNING • BASIC SETTINGS FOR MATERIAL COSTING • OVERHEAD • DEFINE OVERHEAD KEYS or by using transaction OKOG. Figure 5.12 shows three new keys defined. Enough keys need to be defined to be able to account for all the rates that can be used by a single overhead condition. The same overhead key can be used by multiple overhead conditions and associated with different rates based on condition.

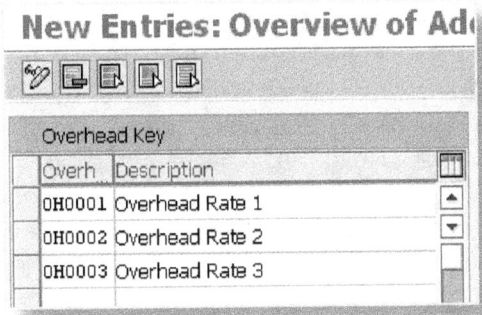

Figure 5.12: Overhead key configuration

The overhead key can only be made available to a plant by assigning it to an overhead group. The overhead group is maintained by valuation area, and the overhead key is assigned to it. The group is then assigned to a material on the COSTING 1 tab of the material master. This connects the overhead key, and the condition values using that key, to the cost estimate. Overhead group configuration is done via IMG menu path CONTROLLING • PRODUCT COST CONTROLLING • PRODUCT COST PLANNING • BASIC SETTINGS FOR MATERIAL COSTING • OVERHEAD • DEFINE OVERHEAD GROUPS or by using transaction OKZ2. Figure 5.13 shows the assignment of overhead keys to the overhead groups of a valuation area or plant.

Applying overhead to cost estimates

Valuation Area	Ovrhd Grp	Overhead Key	Name of Overhead Gr
UWU1	LOW	OH0001	Low Overhead
UWU1	MEDIUM	OH0002	Medium Overhead
UWU1	HIGH	OH0003	High Overhead
UWU2	LOW	OH0001	Low Overhead
UWU2	MEDIUM	OH0002	Medium Overhead
UWU2	HIGH	OH0003	High Overhead
UWU3	LOW	OH0001	Low Overhead
UWU3	MEDIUM	OH0002	Medium Overhead
UWU3	HIGH	OH0003	High Overhead

Figure 5.13: Overhead group definitions

Defining overhead groups

Only one overhead key can be assigned to an overhead group/valuation area combination. Only the overhead group is assigned to a material. Use the same name for the overhead group and the overhead key to make the association of overhead key and material clear.

5.2.6 Connecting a costing sheet to a material

The connection of a costing sheet to a material is made through the valuation variant configuration. Follow IMG menu path CONTROLLING • PRODUCT COST CONTROLLING • PRODUCT COST PLANNING • MATERIAL COST ESTIMATE WITH QUANTITY STRUCTURE • COSTING VARIANT: COMPONENTS • DEFINE VALUATION VARIANTS or use transaction OKK4. Select the OVERHEAD tab (see Figure 5.14).

Two different costing sheets can be assigned to a valuation variant. In section ❶, the costing sheet for finished and semi-finished materials is selected. This is used to calculate overhead for manufactured and transferred materials. Section ❷ shows an additional assignment for purchased materials. Because the overhead needs for manufactured materials and purchased materials can vary greatly, two different costing sheets can be used to serve these needs. Selecting OVERHEAD ON SUBCONTRACTED MATERIALS determines whether overhead is applied to the subcontracting cost calculations. Complex implementations can require that separate overhead calculations be defined for different plant situations. Valuation variant configuration can be made plant dependent. Details are covered in book one "SAP® S/4HANA Product Cost Planning Configuration and Master Data".

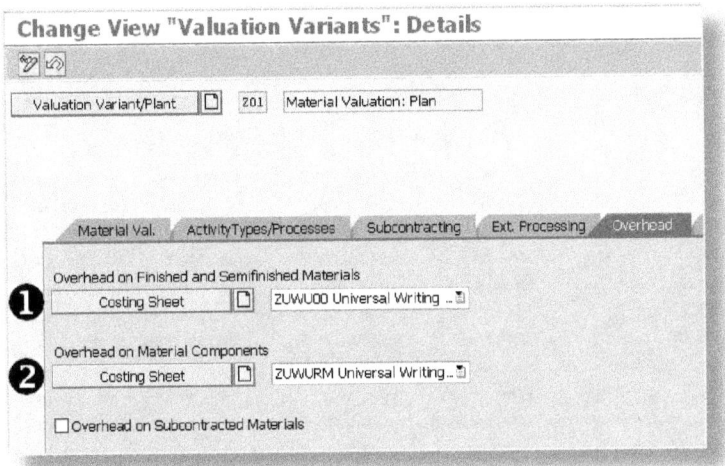

Figure 5.14: Overhead definition in valuation variant

5.2.7 Cost estimate with overhead

Overhead cost items use item type G. Figure 5.15 shows the itemization based on the COST OF GOODS MANUFACTURED (COGM) cost component view. Section ❶ shows the connection to the overhead costing sheet ZUWU00. If the conditions defined in the costing sheet have values, the overhead calculation is processed. The overhead key OH0002 is configured in the MEDIUM overhead group. The MEDIUM group is specified in the COSTING 1 tab of the material master. The overhead items are displayed in section ❷ and they all use item type G to identify them as overhead calculations. The cost center and cost element assignments come from the credit configuration for the costing sheet.

109

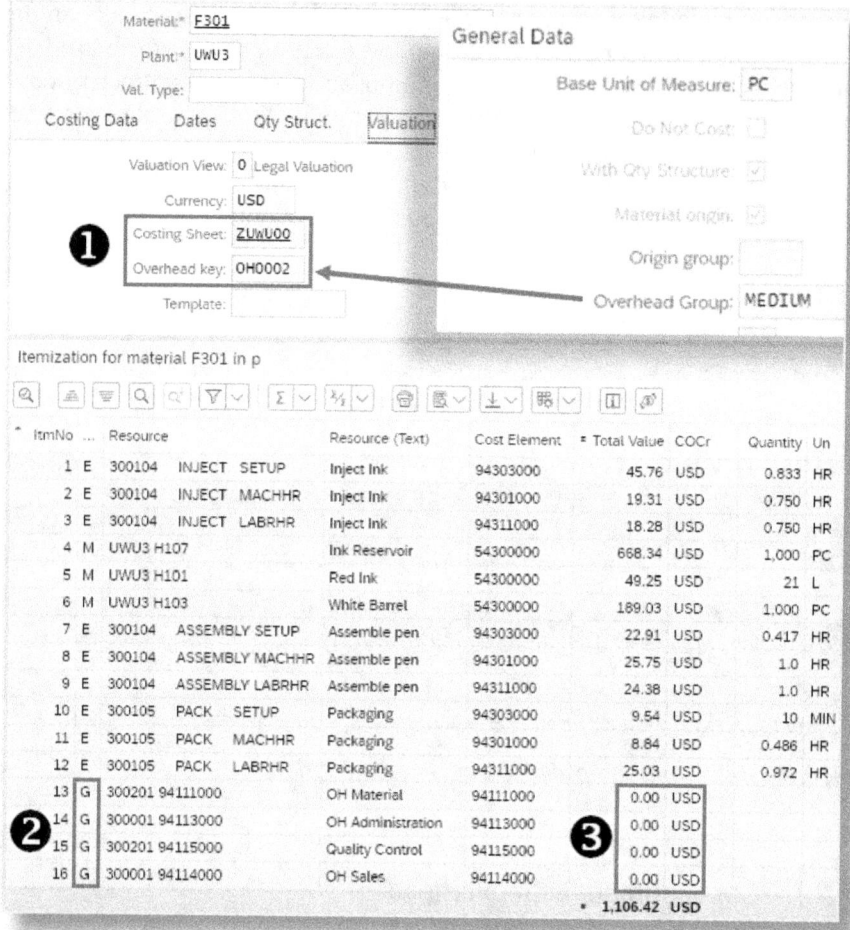

Figure 5.15: COGM itemization with overhead

Section ❸ shows that no value has been calculated in the itemization for these lines. This is because the overhead allocations are made with cost elements which are assigned to cost components that are not included in the COST OF GOODS MANUFACTURED cost component view which was selected for the display. These cost elements belong to cost components 180 and 190 (see Figure 5.16).

In this example, the INVENTORY (COMMERCIAL) view does include these cost components, and Figure 5.17 shows the calculated values in that view.

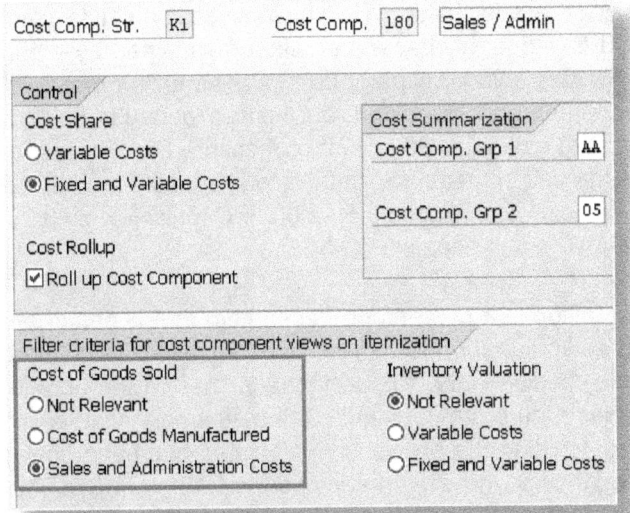

Figure 5.16: Cost component view for Sales / Admin

13	G	300201 94111000	OH Material	94111000	22.67	USD
14	G	300001 94113000	OH Administration	94113000	2.74	USD
15	G	300201 94115000	Quality Control	94115000	6.50	USD
16	G	300001 94114000	OH Sales	94114000	45.53	USD

Figure 5.17: Calculated overhead values for F301

The overhead is calculated based on the cost of goods manufactured item values in the cost estimate, plus any additional overhead calculations from the costing sheet regardless of cost component. Item 13 in the itemization uses condition UW11 from the costing sheet, which only applies to material costs (see Figure 5.11). UW11 uses dependency D010, which calls for an overhead key. The value assigned to overhead key OH0002 is 2.5%. This calculation is based on the material items in the cost estimate (lines 4, 5, and 6). The total value for these three lines is 906.62 USD, and 2.5% of that is 22.67 USD.

Based on the costing sheet in Figure 5.11, item 14 is calculated using the costs associated with the activity types excluding SETUP. The total value in the COGM itemization for those costs elements is 121.59 USD. Condition UW22 is defined for this in the costing sheet, and the value of this condition for plant UWU3 is 2.25%. The overhead value for this is 2.74 USD.

The third condition, UW21, applies to item 15 in the cost estimate. It is used for quality control and is a quantity-based condition maintained by plant. The value for plant UWU3 is 3.25 USD per 1,000 PC. The unit of measure is not based on the material that is costed, but instead depends on any quantity that is in the cost estimate with a unit of measure PC. There are two items with PC as the unit of measure, and the total quantity for both of them is 2,000. The overhead allocation is then 2,000 PC multiplied by 3.25 USD divided by 1,000 PC, which equals 6.50 USD.

The final overhead condition is a percentage-based item that is based on the total COGM cost estimate plus the three overhead values calculated above. This is because condition UW31 is assigned to lines 61 through 70 in the costing sheet (see Figure 5.11). Line 61 is the summary cost for all lines up to that point, including the previously calculated overhead costs. The total value included the first three overhead costs is 1,138.33 USD. The condition value for company code K102 is 4%. This results in an allocation of 45.53 USD.

Overhead on cost estimates

Allocation of overhead does not always use cost elements that are assigned to cost components applicable to cost of goods manufactured. As a result, overhead allocations can appear to be valued at 0 when looking at a cost estimate. Check the applicable cost component views to see the result of the allocation calculations.

5.3 Template allocation

Using overhead costing sheets to allocate costs to a cost estimate provides a systematic approach for cost assignments. However, there are many limitations in using percentage-based and quantity-based calculations for allocation purposes. Costing templates allow for a much more precise calculation using master data available to the cost estimate. The cost sources can be either cost center/activity types or business processes. Business processes were designed to support Activity Based Costing (ABC) and gather together costs from many sources, not just a single cost center/activity type combination. Using template allocation with activity types can also get around the limitation of six activity types assigned to an operation. Templates differ from overhead costing sheets in that they are used to calculate quantities instead of amounts. The calculated quantity of an activity type or business process is then allocated to the receiving cost object.

5.3.1 Business processes and activity types

ABC costing uses entities known as *cost drivers* as building blocks for determining costs. A cost driver identifies the costs associated with a specific activity. Cost drivers can not only identify the cost of performing a specific activity, they can also represent the cost of not performing the activity. Manufacturing costs are normally allocated to a cost estimate using the activity types associated with routing operations. These activity types represent the cost of producing the material at that specific operation. However, costs can also occur when there is no production at that operation. A machine can have a minor breakdown which causes production to cease. There is still cost consumption associated with this stoppage; for example, utilities, maintenance, supplies, etc. This occurs even though there is no production to be reported in order to allocate activity. To account for this, either the activity type price needs to include the cost of expected downtime or another method needs to be found in order to allocate the "machine stopped" activity.

Activity types are simple forms of cost drivers. When planning costs in a cost center, certain costs may be associated with an activity type. This activity type is then used for allocation of those costs to another object, such as a product, production order, or another cost center. Machine run time is a good example of the use of an activity type. Manufacturing costs associated with running the machine are planned for an activity type such as MACHHR in a cost center. Based on the connection of that cost center to a work center, an activity posting is made when production is confirmed at that work center. This consumes the calculated quantity of that machine run time activity.

More complex forms of drivers can be represented by other types of master data called *business processes*. A business process works in a similar fashion to a cost center/activity type combination. Costs are planned and allocated to business processes just as they are with cost center/activity types. Cost allocation from a business process uses a secondary cost element type 43, just like activity types. What sets the business process apart is its independence from the cost center. This allows for a much clearer understanding of the values assigned to a cost driver than if that driver were represented by one of many activity types within a cost center. Costs planned for a business process can be allocated from multiple cost centers or other sources to identify a specific activity. The machine stop can include utility costs associated with one cost center, maintenance labor from another, and so on. Because these are grouped together, the cost performance of a driver represented by a business process is much more evident.

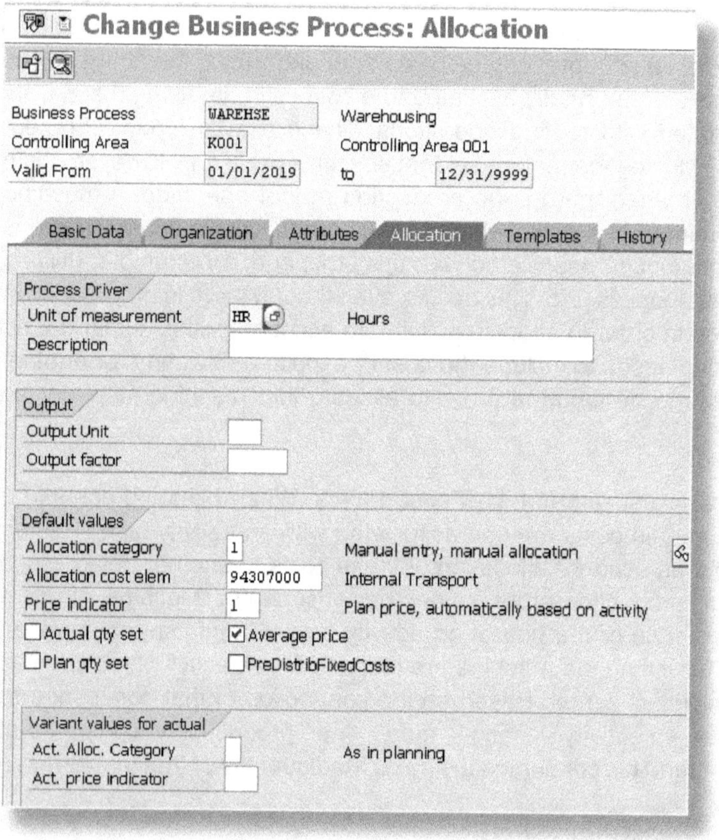

Figure 5.18: Business process allocation definition

Figure 5.18 shows the allocation definition of a business process. This is similar to that of an activity type. Cost element type 43 is used to make the cost allocation.

5.3.2 Template environments

Templates are used for cost allocation for multiple types of cost objects, including manufacturing orders, cost centers, profit centers, and cost estimates. Each cost object has different allocation requirements and master data associated with it. Templates use environments to differentiate between receiver allocation cost objects. The environment dictates how the template is used and what data is available to it. Three environments are associated with Product Cost Planning: 001 for cost estimates with quantity structure, 002 for base planning objects, and 003 for cost estimates without quantity structure. Environment 001 is also used for actual and planned cost allocations for production orders. Base planning objects are obsolete in S/4HANA, so these templates should no longer be used. Each environment has access to a set of data in specific tables for use in calculations. Functions specific to that environment are used for both the access to master data and to process the calculations defined by the formulas. The environment also determines which objects can be used for allocation and what types of allocations can be performed.

5.3.3 Maintaining a template

Transactions CPT1, CPT2, CPT3, and CPT4 are used for maintaining templates. CPT1 is for creation, CPT2 is for modification, CPT3 is for display, and CPT4 is for deletion. Template data is considered configuration, and when saving a template, the system requests a transport be assigned to the changes. As shown in Figure 5.19, there are four sections in the maintenance window:

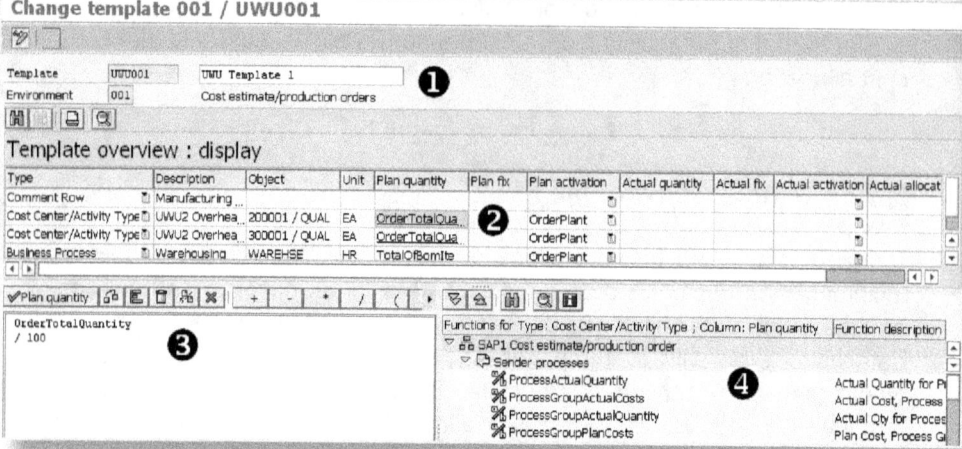

Figure 5.19: Maintaining a template

❶ In this section, a descriptive name is attached to the template.

❷ The template structure is defined in this section. The columns associated with the environment are displayed by default, and rows of various types can be added, modified, or deleted at this point.

❸ The editor section is used for the creation and modification of formulas and methods that are used for object determination, row activation, quantity calculations, and allocation events.

❹ This section contains a list of all template functions that are applicable to the specific row and column that is being edited.

The calculation row is the heart of the template. It is used to connect characteristics of the template environment with functions to form complex formulas which define allocation quantities. In Figure 5.20, section ❶ shows ENVIRONMENT 001 for cost estimates and production orders, and section ❷ shows the rows used for calculation.

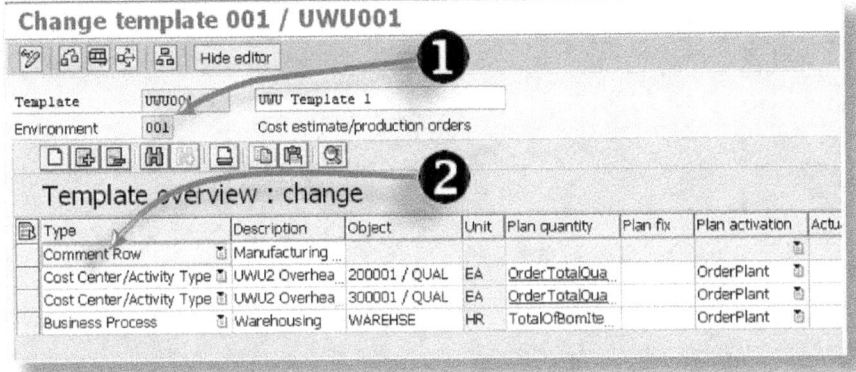

Figure 5.20: Template rows

Environment 001 has the following columns available for each calculation row:

- TYPE—is the object type for the row. This usually identifies the method of allocation to be used, such as cost center/activity type or business process, but it can also represent a comment line or the execution of a sub-template.

- DESCRIPTION—is the description of the object used for allocation.

- OBJECT—identifies the cost object used for the allocation. Section ❶ in Figure 5.21 shows the method used for determining the object. Section ❷ shows a partial list of functions that are available for selecting a specific cost object. These functions can directly refer to the object, or they can use characteristics associated with the object to make the selection. Because this is a cost center/activity type row, the selection returns cost centers and activity types. A business process row returns a business process.

APPLYING OVERHEAD TO COST ESTIMATES

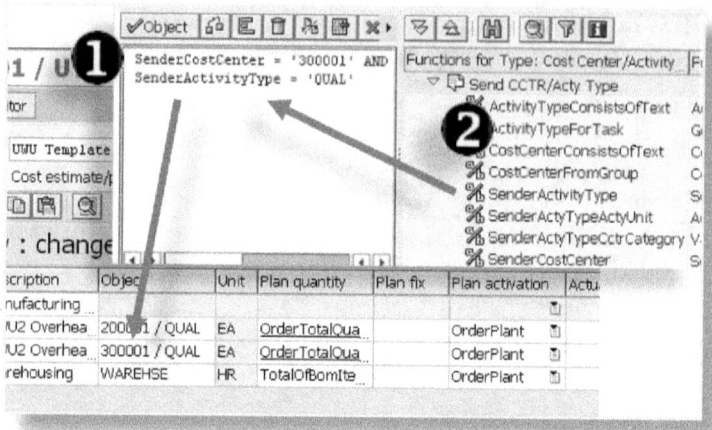

Figure 5.21: Defining the allocation object

- UNIT—is the unit of measure for the allocation determined by the object.

- PLAN QUANTITY—contains a formula to calculate the planned quantity allocated for the cost object. For environment 001, this calculates the quantity for the material cost estimate or preliminary order cost estimate. Section ❶ in Figure 5.22 shows the code representing the formula. Section ❷ shows the listing of available functions that can be used for defining the formula. The result of this formula determines the quantity of activity type QUAL to be allocated to the cost estimate from cost center 300001.

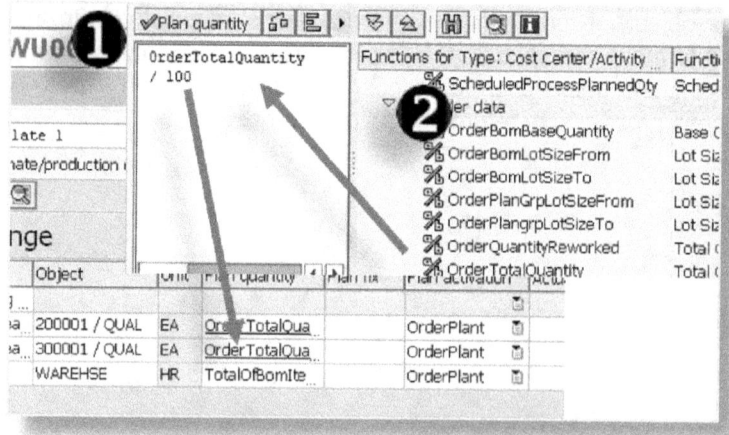

Figure 5.22: Formula for planned allocation quantity

APPLYING OVERHEAD TO COST ESTIMATES

- PLAN FIX—represents a fixed allocation that does not vary by costing lot size or order size. This can contain a formula to calculate that amount.

- PLAN ACTIVATION—determines whether the calculation is executed for the planned allocation. A row can be active or inactive, and environment characteristics and functions can be used to specify if the row is active for this set of circumstances. If the row is active, the accompanying formula is executed. In section ❶ in Figure 5.23, a method is defined using conditions available in the environment. If all the conditions are met, then the row is active, and the allocation is performed. Section ❷ contains a list of available functions to be used in the activation determination. This activation specifies that, for this to be active, the plant must be UWU3, the material type of the product must be FERT, and the unit of measure for the material must be PC.

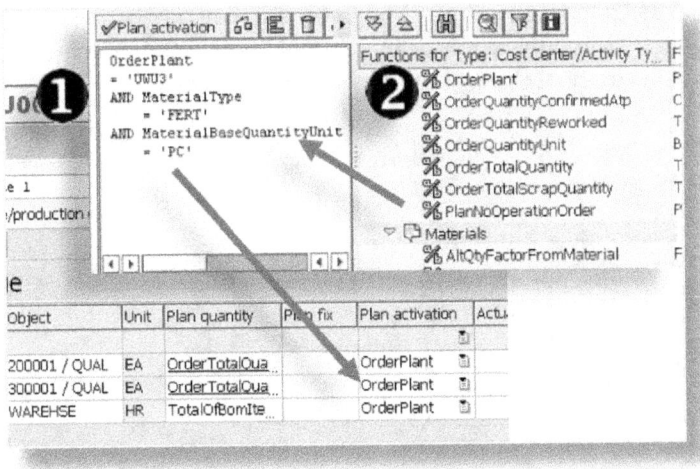

Figure 5.23: Activating the planned allocation

- ACTUAL QUANTITY—is the formula to calculate the quantity for actual allocations to production orders.

- ACTUAL FIX QUANTITY—is the formula to calculate the fixed quantity for actual allocations to production orders.

- ACTUAL ACTIVATION—is the method to determine that a calculation row should be used for actual allocations.

- ACTUAL ALLOCATION EVENT—is the method to determine the specific period for performing the actual allocation.

5.3.4 Connecting a template to the material

To connect a template to a cost estimate requires the template to be associated with an overhead costing sheet in combination with an overhead key. The overhead costing sheet must then be assigned to the valuation variant (see Section 5.2.6). This must be done for both cost estimates with quantity structure (environment 001) and cost estimates without quantity structure (environment 003).

Configuration is found via IMG menu path CONTROLLING • PRODUCT COST CONTROLLING • PRODUCT COST PLANNING • BASIC SETTINGS FOR MATERIAL COSTING • TEMPLATES • ASSIGN TEMPLATES or by using transaction KTPF. Figure 5.24 shows the configuration. The template of a specific environment is assigned to the costing sheet in conjunction with an overhead key. Every overhead key for which the template applies must be configured here. The template is accessed for a cost estimate when the material has that overhead key and uses that costing sheet. The overhead key can be left blank in the configuration. When this occurs, the template is used when the overhead group is blank in the COSTING 1 tab of the material master.

COAr	CostSh	OH key	Environ.	Template	Name
K001	ZUWU00	OH0001	001	UWU001	UWU Template 1
K001	ZUWU00	OH0002	001	UWU001	UWU Template 1
K001	ZUWU00	OH0003	001	UWU001	UWU Template 1

Figure 5.24: Connecting a template to a costing sheet

5.3.5 Cost estimate using a template

Management at plant UWU3 wants to capture warehousing costs to move components in the warehouse to the manufacturing floor. This activity is represented by the business process WAREHSE. Management also wants to capture pen inspection activity. One out of every 100 pens is inspected. Activity type QUAL in cost center 300001 represents the cost of one inspection. Template UWU001, covered in Section 5.3.3, was created to perform the allocations. There are three formula rows in the template. The first row is for inspection at plant UWU2 in Los Angeles. The second row is for inspection at plant UWU3 in Chicago. The third row is for allocating warehouse costs at plant UWU3 based on the component quantity. Only the second and third rows are active because the cost estimate is made for a material in plant UWU3.

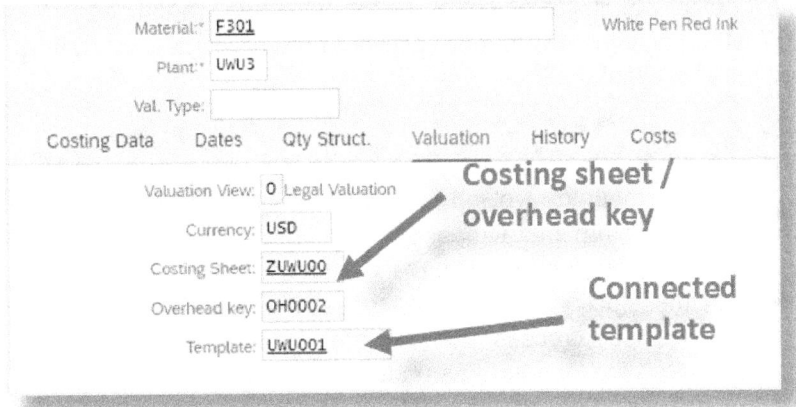

Figure 5.25: Valuation view of the cost estimate

Figure 5.25 shows the resulting valuation view. Cost sheet ZUWU00 is defined in the valuation variant used by the cost estimate. Overhead key OH0002 is assigned to the material master on the COSTING 1 tab. Because overhead key OH0002 is associated with template UWU001 in configuration, the template has been executed for the cost estimate. Just because the template was executed doesn't mean that any allocations have been made. The allocations depend on the condition of activation for each row. Each row that is activated contributes to the cost estimate.

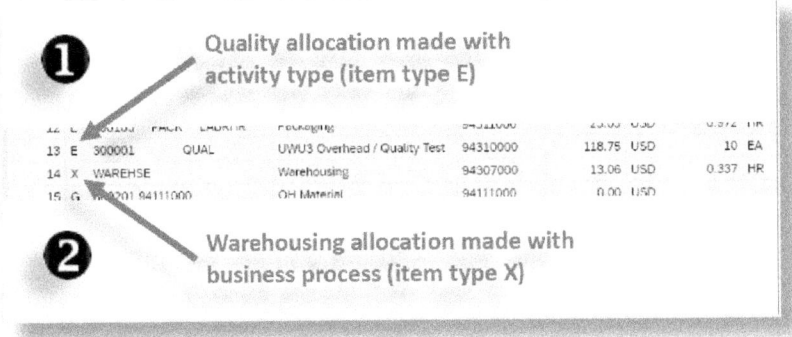

Figure 5.26: Itemization lines resulting from template allocation

Figure 5.26 shows the two additional items added to the cost estimate as a result of the template allocation. Item 13 represents the quality inspection and was made using activity type QUAL from cost center 300001. This is an activity type allocation, so the item type is E (internal activity). Item 14 is an allocation from business process WAREHSE and uses item type X (business process costs). Although three formula rows are defined in template UWU001, only the two that are active for the Chicago plant (UWU3) affected the cost estimate.

> ### Multiple costing items from one template row
>
> 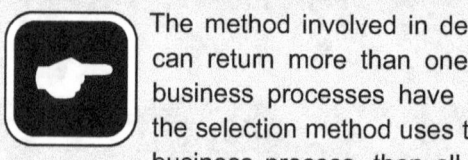 The method involved in determining the allocation object can return more than one result. For example, if three business processes have the same characteristics, and the selection method uses those characteristics to find the business process, then all three business processes are used in the allocation. To keep them separate, three different items of type X are included in the cost estimate itemization, assuming that template row is active.

6 Mixed-price costing

Certain materials can have alternative sources of procurement. These sources can include different methods of manufacturing, outsourcing to a subcontractor, and purchasing from a vendor. Several procurement alternatives can be active at any given time. To more accurately reflect the standard cost of these materials, all the different methods for making or acquiring them need to be accounted for in generating a cost estimate. Mixed-price costing provides a solution to achieve this.

6.1 Mixed-price cost estimate

Due to manufacturing capacity constraints, there can be two or more ways to procure a material. This can include using different production lines within the plant, engaging an outside manufacturer to make the material using supplied components, or purchasing the final material from a vendor. If demand is high enough to regularly require two or more alternatives for acquiring the material, then mixed-price costing can be used to take the ratio of different procurement methods into account in order to determine the standard cost of the material.

Universal Writing Utensils' Chicago plant (UWU3) regularly uses three methods to obtain blue ink (material H100). It has the capability of mixing the ink in-house, but it does not have the capacity to supply all the ink that it needs. The Los Angeles plant UWU2 also manufactures the blue ink and can ship excess ink to Chicago for use in manufacturing there. There is also a local subcontractor that produces the ink. Because these alternatives are all normally used, a decision was made to blend the individual costs together using a mixed-price cost estimate.

A mixed-price cost estimate looks a little different than a regular material cost estimate. The top level of the cost estimate combines the costs of the allowed procurement alternatives based on a pre-defined mixing ratio. Figure 6.1 shows the top level of the mixed-price cost estimate for the blue ink in plant UWU3.

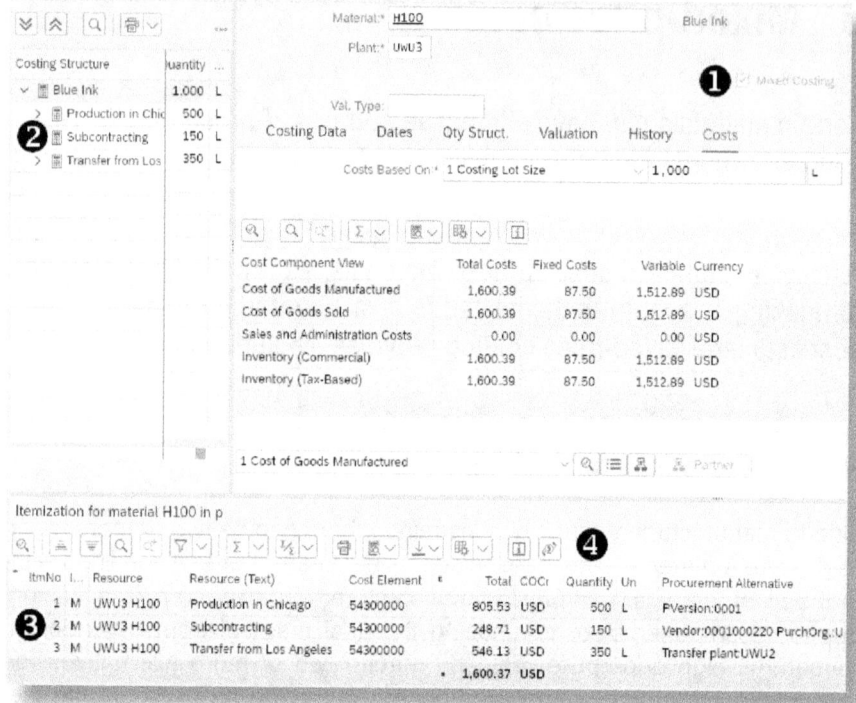

Figure 6.1: Top-level mixed-price cost estimate

Section ❶ of Figure 6.1 shows that the MIXED COSTING checkbox has been selected, indicating that this level of the cost estimate includes the costs of the procurement alternatives. Section ❷, in the COSTING STRUCTURE window, lists the procurement alternatives that were used in the cost estimate. The procurement alternatives include production in the Chicago plant, subcontracting from the Chicago plant, and stock transfer from the Los Angeles plant. Section ❸ shows the cost estimate itemization. At this costing level, there is an item for each of the procurement alternatives. The RESOURCE column displays the material being costed, and the RESOURCE (TEXT) column contains the description of the procurement alternative. The itemization quantities in the column under ❹ represent the pre-defined mixing ratio for each procurement alternative. In this case, the ratio is factored by the costing lot size, which is the selected view for the cost estimate values. Because the costing lot size is 1000 L, the mixing ratios are 50% PRODUCTION IN CHICAGO, 15% SUBCONTRACTING, and 35% stock TRANSFER FROM LOS ANGELES. The resulting cost is the weighted average of the calculated costs for each procurement alternative.

Mixed-price costing

A separate cost estimate is created for each of the procurement alternatives. These cost estimates exist independently of the material, and the cost estimate numbers used are assigned when the procurement alternatives are created. Drill down from the COSTING STRUCTURE to see each cost estimate.

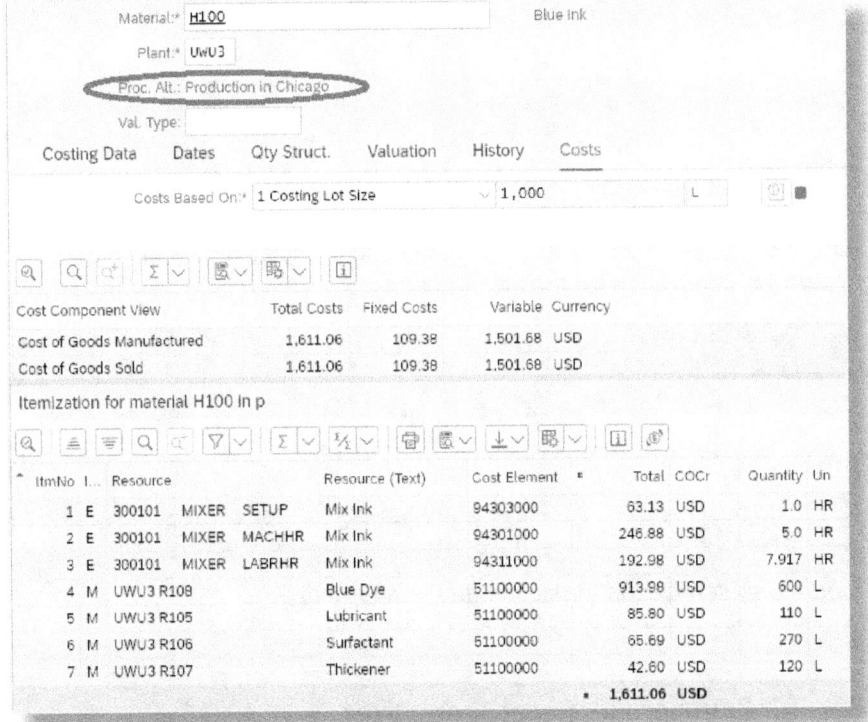

Figure 6.2: Procurement alternative 1 - production

Figure 6.2 represents the cost estimate of manufacturing procurement type. Note that the MIXED COSTING checkbox is no longer visible, and the procurement alternative (PROC. ALT.) is defined as PRODUCTION IN CHICAGO. The cost at this level is based on the material's costing lot size (1,000 L). This value is factored by the mixing ratio on the top-level mixed cost estimate. Each alternative has a similar cost estimate generated for it.

125

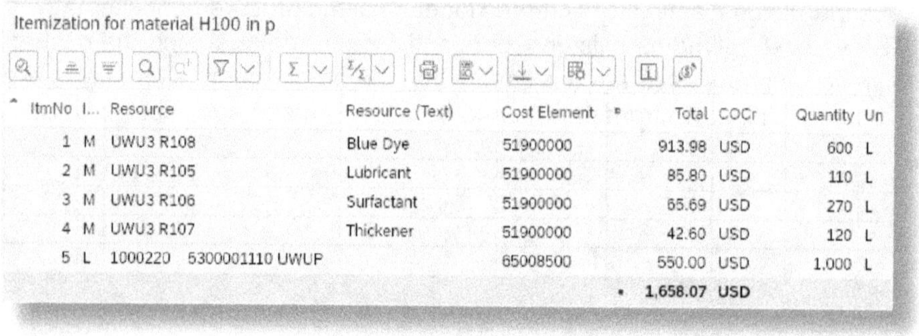

Mixed-price costing

Itemization for material H100 in p

ItmNo	I...	Resource		Resource (Text)	Cost Element	Total	COCr	Quantity	Un
1	M	UWU3 R108		Blue Dye	51900000	913.98	USD	600	L
2	M	UWU3 R105		Lubricant	51900000	85.80	USD	110	L
3	M	UWU3 R106		Surfactant	51900000	65.69	USD	270	L
4	M	UWU3 R107		Thickener	51900000	42.60	USD	120	L
5	L	1000220	5300001110 UWUP		65008500	550.00	USD	1.000	L
						1,658.07	**USD**		

Figure 6.3: Itemization for subcontracting alternative

Figure 6.3 shows the itemization for the subcontracting cost, and Figure 6.4 shows the itemization for the stock transfer cost.

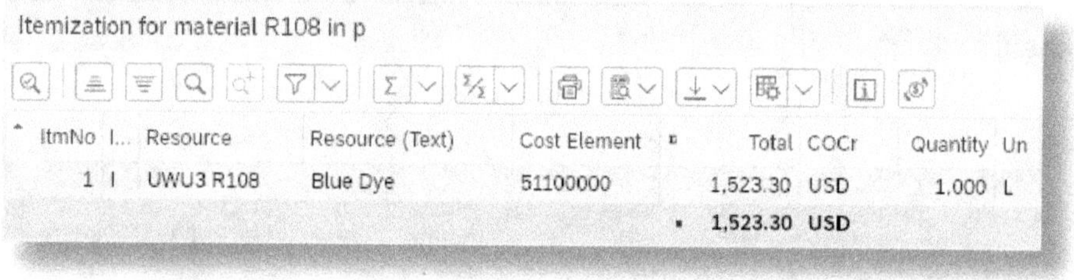

Itemization for material R108 in p

ItmNo	I...	Resource	Resource (Text)	Cost Element	Total	COCr	Quantity	Un
1	I	UWU3 R108	Blue Dye	51100000	1,523.30	USD	1.000	L
					1,523.30	**USD**		

Figure 6.4: Itemization for stock transfer alternative

6.2 Defining procurement alternatives

Mixed-price costing requires the possible procurement alternatives to be defined by plant and material. These procurement alternatives are assigned individual cost estimate numbers, which is why the procurement costing level can have its own cost estimates. Procurement alternatives should only be defined for those materials for which mixed-price costing is to be used.

GUI transaction CK91N is used to define the alternatives by material, plant, and valuation type. The Edit Procurement Alternatives Fiori app is also used for maintaining the alternative structures (see Figure 6.5).

Figure 6.5: Fiori tile for editing procurement alternatives

First, select the MATERIAL, PLANT, and if applicable, VALUATION TYPE (see Figure 6.6).

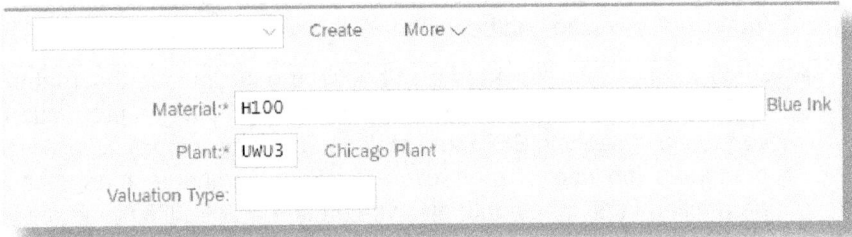

Figure 6.6: Procurement alternative material and plant

Next, click on Create with Fiori, or ☐ in the SAPGUI transaction, to create a new procurement alternative definition. A dropdown menu for selecting the category of the procurement alternative is displayed on the right side of the window (see Figure 6.7).

Figure 6.7: Process category dropdown menu

Depending on which category is selected, different information is required to support the alternative.

Five different types of procurement are supported:

- ▶ PURCHASE ORDER—This assigns costs from purchasing. To generate the costs using a specific PIR (purchasing information record), enter a valid purchasing organization and vendor. The relevant costing information is derived from the PIR assigned to the material, the vendor, and the purchasing organization. If vendor is entered, purchasing organization must be entered and vice versa. This is required to find the relevant PIR. If vendor and purchasing organization is left blank, then the system uses the search strategy defined in the valuation variant to determine the source of the cost. In addition, by using multiple purchase order alternatives, the costs from multiple vendors can be included in the cost estimate.

- ▶ PROCUREMENT (CHANGE INVOLVING STOCKS)—The opening inventory can be defined as its own procurement alternative, so that a high opening inventory value can be included in the cost estimate.

- ▶ PRODUCTION—This represents in-house production for the material. The quantity structure can either be defined using a production version or a specific BOM and task list (route or recipe). S/4HANA mandates the use of production versions in manufacturing, and production versions should always be used. For ECC6.0 and older systems, this is not required, but highly recommended. If there are multiple production alternatives, where production version is selected for one, production versions must be used for all alternatives.

- ▶ SUBCONTRACTING—The material is produced by a vendor using components supplied by the plant. Vendor, purchasing organization, and BOM usage and alternative must be defined.

- ▶ STOCK TRANSFER—The material is procured via stock transfer from another plant. The source plant must be defined.

When creating a procurement alternative, costing lot size should be checked, and a specific name assigned to CHANGEABLE NAME. Costing lot size defaults to that found in the material master, but it can be changed if so desired. Figure 6.8 shows the information required for an alternative to purchasing the material. Both the system-supplied generic name and the changeable name are viewable in the cost estimate.

Click on the CONFIRM button to accept the information entered. When all the alternatives have been defined, save the changes using the Save or ▣ button, depending on the user interface.

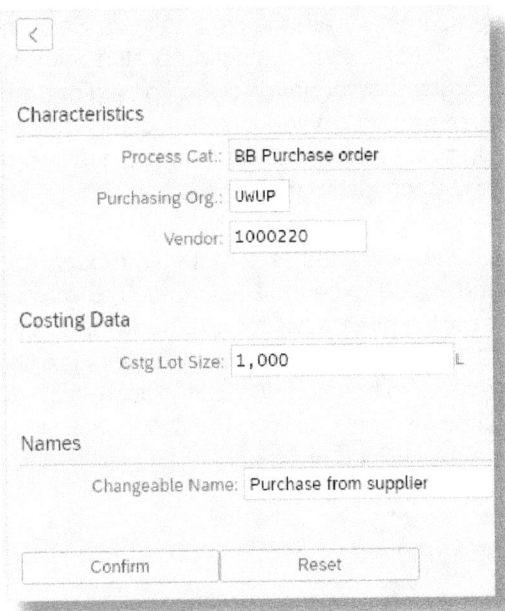

Figure 6.8: Defining a procurement alternative

Once confirmed, the alternative is added to the list of procurement alternatives for the material (see Figure 6.9).

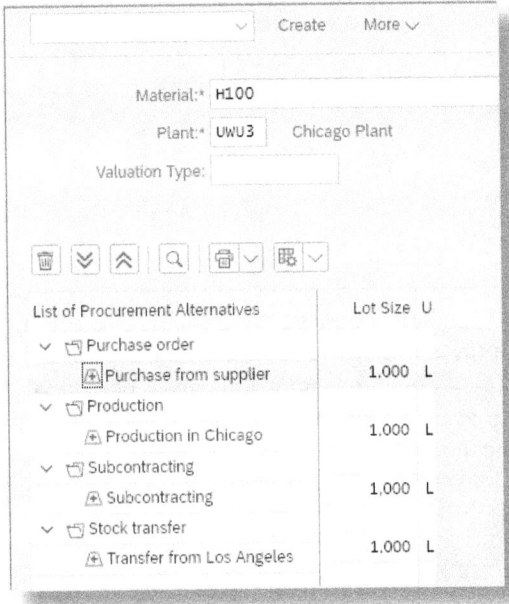

Figure 6.9: List of procurement alternatives for H100

In this example, there are four procurement alternatives defined. Each alternative uses a different category. There is no restriction on the number of alternatives that can exist in a given category. In a complex plant, for example, there may be two or more production versions that can be selected for manufacturing. Each production version can be used as a different procurement alternative in the mixed cost estimate.

Just because an alternative has been assigned to a material, it does not mean that it also shows up in the mixed-price cost estimate. The mixing ratio must be defined to use a specific alternative for it to show up in the cost estimate. GUI transaction CK94 or the Change Mixing Ratios Fiori tile maintains this data. There is also a link to this from the Edit Procurement Alternatives Fiori app using the dropdown menu GoTo • Change Mixing Ratios. This menu is accessible in the app by clicking on More ∨.

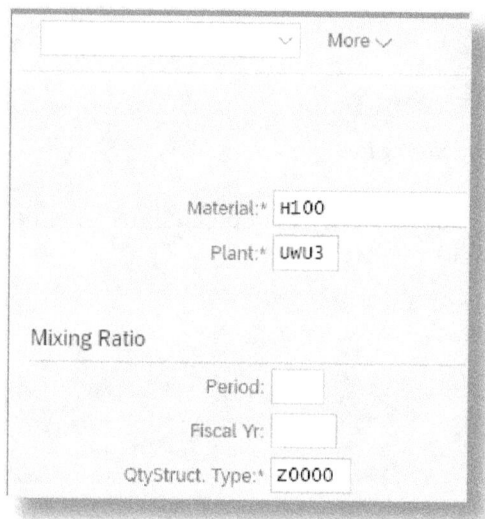

Figure 6.10: Change mixing ratios

Figure 6.10 shows the initial information required for creating the mixing ratio. MATERIAL, PLANT, and quantity structure type (QTYSTRUCT. TYPE) are required. Any costing version for a costing variant that does not have a quantity structure type assigned to it cannot process mixed-price cost estimates. The configuration for this is explained in Section 6.3. The additional selection of PERIOD and fiscal year (FISCAL YR) defines the initial date that this mixing ratio is valid.

Mixing Ratio of Procurement Alternatives								
	PCat	Val. Type	Changeable Name	Lot Size	VUM	App... QtyStrDate	MR	Mixing Ratio
	BB		Purchase from supplier	1,000	L		☐	
	BF		Production in Chicago	1,000	L		✓	50.000
	BL		Subcontracting	1,000	L		✓	15.000
	BU		Transfer from Los Angeles	1,000	L		✓	35.000

Figure 6.11: Define mixing ratios

When setting up the mixing ratios, each alternative can have a specific quantity structure date (Q$_{TY}$S$_{TR}$D$_{ATE}$) defined for it (see Figure 6.11). If the date is set, then that date is used as one of the criteria for selecting the structure to be used. For each procurement alternative, the mixing ratio is entered as either a percentage or as an equivalence number, depending on the configuration of the quantity structure type. If percentage is required by the quantity structure type, the total percentages must add up to 100 before saving. There is no restriction on using equivalence numbers, if so configured, but this can lead to some confusion as to how the mixed-price cost estimate was created. The ratio calculated from equivalence numbers is the number assigned to a specific procurement alternative divided by the sum of all the equivalence numbers. When a mixing ratio is entered, the MR (mixing ratio) indicator is automatically set, telling the system to include that procurement alternative in the mixed-price cost estimate. If an alternative has no mixing ratio number defined, it can be included in the cost estimate if that indicator is manually set. This allows the cost estimate for the alternative to be generated, even though it does not contribute to the overall cost estimate. This estimate can be viewed by drilling down into that alternative on the mixed-price level of the material cost estimate. In Figure 6.11, the PURCHASE FROM SUPPLIER alternative is not included in the cost estimate because there is no mixing ratio defined and the MR checkbox is not selected.

6.3 Mixed-price costing configuration

Certain configuration is required before a mixed-price cost estimate can be set up and processed. This includes defining a quantity structure type and assigning the quantity structure type to a costing version and costing type.

6.3.1 Quantity structure type

The quantity structure type determines how mixed costing is executed for a given material. It is assigned to the mixing ratio definition for the material and defines how the mixing ratio is to be used in costing. Configuration is processed via IMG menu path CONTROLLING • PRODUCT COST CONTROLLING • PRODUCT COST PLANNING • SELECTED FUNCTIONS IN MATERIAL COSTING • MIXED COSTING • DEFINE QUANTITY STRUCTURE TYPES. Select option DEFINE QUANTITY STRUCTURE TYPES FOR MIXED COSTING.

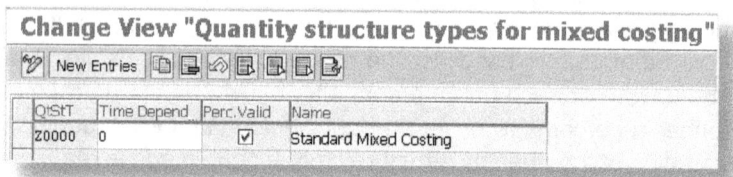

Figure 6.12: Mixed costing quantity structure configuration

Figure 6.12 shows the definition of a quantity structure type. A 5-character ID and name are assigned to the quantity structure type. TIME DEPENDENCY determines the time period for which the mixing ratio is valid. Allowed values are:

- ▶ 0—no time dependency. The ratio is valid without regard to the fiscal calendar.
- ▶ 1—based on fiscal year
- ▶ 2—based on period

The PERC. VALID checkbox determines whether to use percentages or equivalence numbers in defining the mixing ratios. If this is selected, then percentages are used, and the total for all alternatives must add up to 100%. If not selected, the system uses the entered numbers as a weighting factor which is divided by the sum of the factors to determine the contribution percentage of the procurement alternative.

6.3.2 Assigning to costing version

To activate mixed-price costing for a costing variant, the quantity structure type must be assigned to at least one costing version. This configuration is found using transaction OKYD or via IMG menu path CONTROLLING • PRODUCT COST CONTROLLING • PRODUCT COST PLANNING • SELECTED FUNCTIONS IN MATERIAL COSTING • MIXED COSTING • DEFINE COSTING VERSIONS.

Up to 99 costing versions are available for use for each costing variant. Assign the quantity structure type to each version that is applicable.

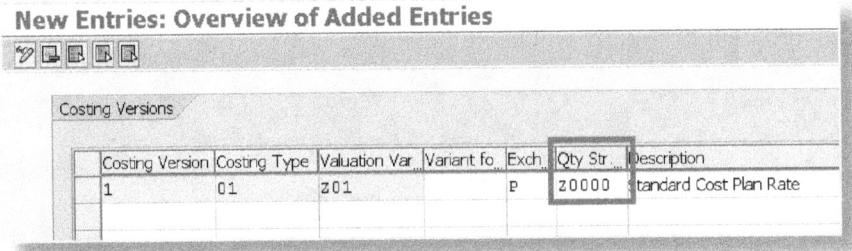

Figure 6.13: Maintain costing versions with OKYD

Figure 6.13 shows the definition of the costing versions. The quantity structure version is assigned by COSTING VERSION, COSTING TYPE, and VALUATION VARIANT. If multiple costing variants use the same costing type and valuation variant, this assignment applies to each costing variant. If costing type or valuation variant is left blank, then the version definition is valid for all costing variants using the defined costing type or valuation variant.

This configuration is also available in the costing variant configuration (OKKN) under the ASSIGNMENTS tab (see Figure 6.14). Clicking on ☐ , next to the COSTING VERSION button, changes the focus to transaction OKYD to update the costing version definitions.

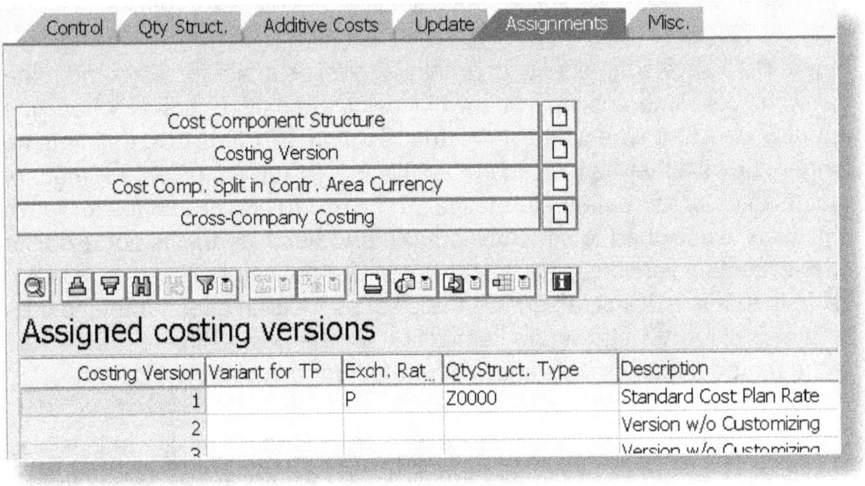

Figure 6.14: Valuation variant assignments tab

The example in Figure 6.14 shows that mixed costing is enabled for costing version 1 (QTYSTRUCT. TYPE set to Z0000), but it is not enabled for costing version 2. When running a cost estimate using costing version 2, a cost estimate is generated using the material master data alone, instead of the procurement alternative setup.

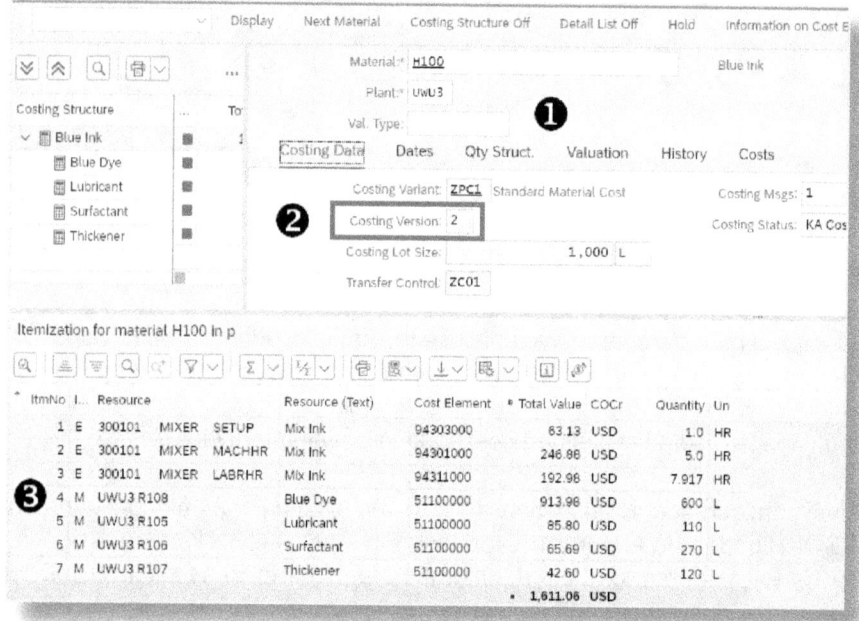

Figure 6.15: Costing version 2 cost estimate with no mixed price

Figure 6.15 shows the effects of running a cost estimate for the same material with the same costing variant but using a costing version where the quantity structure type was not defined. Section ❶ of the cost estimate no longer shows either an indication that this is a mixed-price cost estimate or that this is a procurement alternative. The existing procurement alternative definition is assigned to structure Z0000, and because this is not associated with costing version 2, the procurement alternatives are ignored. Section ❷ in the COSTING DATA tab shows the COSTING VERSION used for the cost estimate. Section ❸ shows the itemization for the cost estimate, as defined in the material master. This shows manufacturing in plant UWU3.

Creating a mixed-price cost estimate with an alternative mixing ratio is also possible. This is useful when determining the cost impact of selecting from among several mixing strategies and comparing them side by side. First, create an additional quantity structure type and assign it to a costing version.

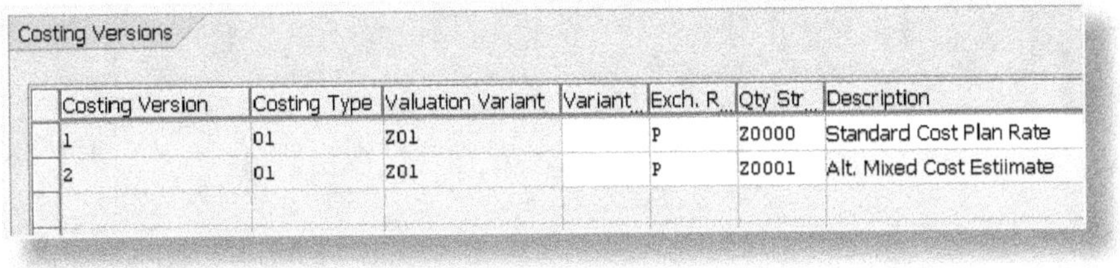

Costing Versions						
Costing Version	Costing Type	Valuation Variant	Variant	Exch. R	Qty Str	Description
1	01	Z01		P	Z0000	Standard Cost Plan Rate
2	01	Z01		P	Z0001	Alt. Mixed Cost Estimate

Figure 6.16: Costing version 2 with alternative quantity structure type

Figure 6.16 shows that COSTING VERSION 2 for COSTING TYPE 01 and VALUATION VARIANT Z01 has now been assigned quantity structure type Z0001. Z0001 was created to allow for an additional mixing ratio definition for the procurement alternatives for material H100. Next, define a mixing ratio for quantity structure type Z0001.

		Details for Alternative	Delete	Undo Changes		Mixing Ratios Only	More
Material:	H100					Blue Ink	
Plant:	UWU3	Chicago Plant					
Qty Structure Type:	Z0001	Alternative Mixed Costing					
Mixing Ratio of Procurement Alternatives							
PCat	Changeable Name		Lot Size	VUM	QtyStrDate	MR	Mixing Ratio
BB	Purchase from supplier		1,000	L		✓	40.000
BF	Production in Chicago		1,000	L			
BL	Subcontracting		1,000	L			
BU	Transfer from Los Angeles		1,000	L		✓	60.000

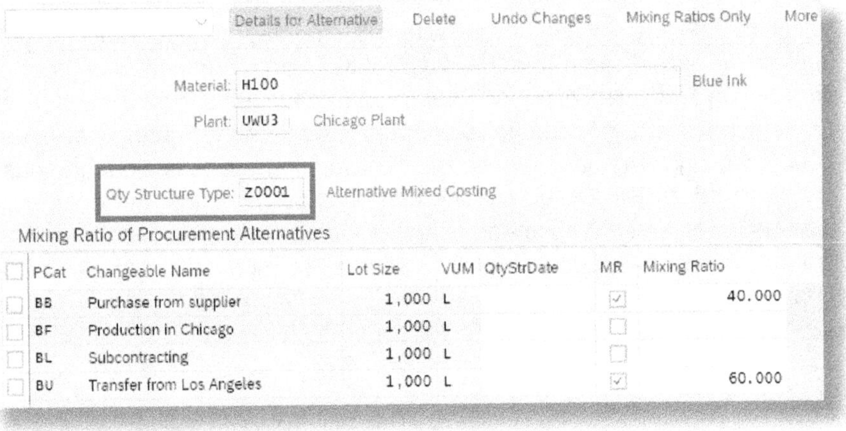

Figure 6.17: Mixing ratio for quantity structure type Z0001

The mixing ratio for Z0001 is defined in Figure 6.17. This shows that two of the procurement alternatives have been selected. Purchase from an external supplier is expected 40% of the time, and transfer from Los Angeles 60% of the time. Compare this with the definition for Z0000 in Figure 6.11. The procurement alternatives are always the same because they are defined independently of the quantity structure type. The resulting cost estimate is shown in Figure 6.18.

Mixed-price costing

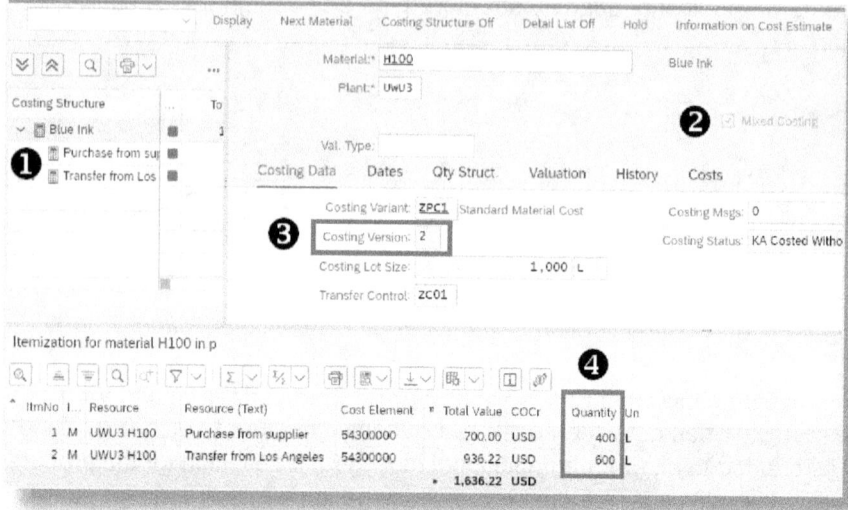

Figure 6.18: Cost estimate with mixing ratio Z0001

Sections ❶ and ❷ show that with the changed configuration for costing version 2 (indicated in section ❸), this is now a mixed-price cost estimate. The quantities assigned to each alternative are shown in section ❹. Costing version 1 uses the three alternatives defined for quantity structure Z0000. Costing version 2 shows only the two alternatives assigned to quantity structure Z0001. Mixed costing can be a powerful tool not only to determine costs based on planned usage of various procurement alternatives, but also to provide a good way to investigate the impact of using alternative strategies.

7 Additive cost estimates

Additive cost estimates are used to include costs in a material cost estimate that cannot be derived another way. Additive cost estimates are maintained similarly to the way unit cost estimates are generated, and the costs must be built up manually by entering them in the cost estimate. The costing variant determines whether additive costs can be included in a material cost estimate.

7.1 How additive cost estimates work

An additive cost estimate is created manually in a similar manner to a unit cost estimate. There is no separate quantity structure that can be assigned for additive costs, and the costs must be entered directly into the cost estimate. Each additive cost estimate must be assigned to a specific material. Items are added line by line, and a preliminary cost estimate is created when entry is complete. This preliminary cost estimate is then saved, and when a cost estimate is generated for the material, the line items of the additive cost estimate are included at the end of the itemization of the regular cost estimate. These costs also become part of the cost component split.

Tables for additive cost estimates

Additive cost estimates are stored in the same tables as cost estimates with quantity structure. The three main costing tables KEKO (Product Costing—Header Data), CKIS (Items Unit Costing/Itemization Product Costing), and KEPH (Product Costing: Cost Components for Cost of Goods Mfd) are used to store the data from both type of cost estimates. Although an additive cost estimate is developed the same way as a unit cost estimate, it is not treated as a unit cost estimate in the system. It is assigned to the same cost estimate number as the one used for cost estimates with quantity structure (stored for the material in table field MBEW-KALN1). There is an additional key in the product costing tables that is used to indicate that the cost estimate is an additive cost estimate (field KKZMA in the cost estimate tables). Assuming additive costs are allowed in the costing variant, the final cost estimate for the material includes both the "standard" costs based on the quantity structure plus all the costs assigned in the additive cost estimate.

> **Maintaining additive cost estimates is a manual process**
>
>  Additive cost estimates, such as unit cost estimates, require manual data entry, and may need to be changed or created on a regular basis. Additional custom coding is required to make this process more automatic.

7.2 Maintaining additive cost estimates

7.2.1 Generating the additive cost estimate

Additive cost estimates are created using GUI transaction CK74N or the Create Additive Costs Fiori tile (see Figure 7.1).

Figure 7.1: Fiori tile for creating additive cost estimates

The creation of additive cost estimates should be used when no additive cost estimate exists, or when a new one is needed, based on costing date or costing version. Once an additive cost estimate has been initially created, it can be changed using GUI transaction CK75N (Change Additive Costs Fiori tile). The corresponding display transaction is CK76N (Display Additive Costs Fiori tile).

The Universal Writing Utensils company transfers red ink (material H101) from its plant in Los Angeles to be used in manufacturing in its plant in Chicago. The company wants to account for shipping and handling costs for the movement of goods, along with the administrative costs associated with making the interplant shipment. The company has chosen to use additive cost estimates to do this. Normally, the cost at Chicago is derived directly from the Los Angeles cost, but this does not reflect any of the additional costs required to make the transfer. A standard shipment quantity for the ink is 10,000 L. This must be stored in drums (material V502), and each drum contains 500 L. The cost to ship a single load from Los Angeles to Chicago is 450.00 USD. There is an additional 125.00 USD of administrative costs that need to be accounted for in the shipment cost.

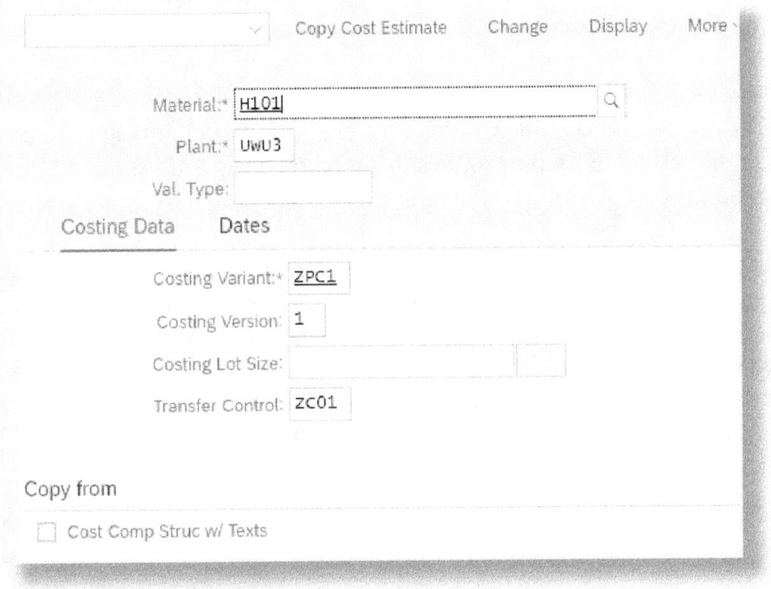

Figure 7.2: Create additive costs—enter costing data

Figure 7.2 shows the initial screen for creating an additive cost estimate. This looks very similar to CK11N and requires the same sort of information: COSTING VARIANT, COSTING VERSION, COSTING LOT SIZE, and TRANSFER CONTROL key. The COSTING VARIANT must match the one for the regular cost estimate in order for the material for the costs to be included in that cost estimate. If COSTING LOT SIZE is left blank, the system uses the costing lot size from the material master. In this case, since the shipment quantity is 10,000 and the costing lot size for the material is 1,000, there are two alternatives for entering the cost. If the default costing lot size is used, then all the additive costs entered in the itemization window must reflect the costs for that quantity. This means dividing all amounts by 10 (10,000 divided by 1,000) when creating the itemization. Another solution is to set the costing lot size for the additive cost estimate to 10,000. The stated costs can then be entered directly in the itemization. In our example, the company selected the option to manually enter the 10,000 liter costing lot size (see Figure 7.3). If the non-standard costing lot size is used, the system will display a warning message.

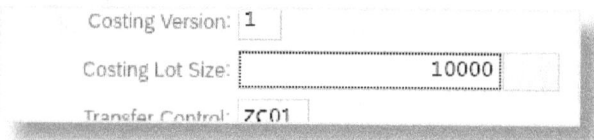

Figure 7.3: Cost lot size override

In the COPY FROM section of the window in Figure 7.2, there is a COST COMP STRUC W/TEXTS checkbox, which is used for prepopulating items in the additive cost estimate. In our example, this is left blank and all items have to be manually entered.

Like other cost estimates, additive cost estimates are also date dependent. The DATES tab shown in Figure 7.4 applies the same rules defined for normal cost estimates created with this specific costing variant. The difference in this case is that the QUANTITY STRUCTURE DATE is missing. Additive cost estimates have no quantity structure associated with them and there is no need to specify a structure date in the cost estimate.

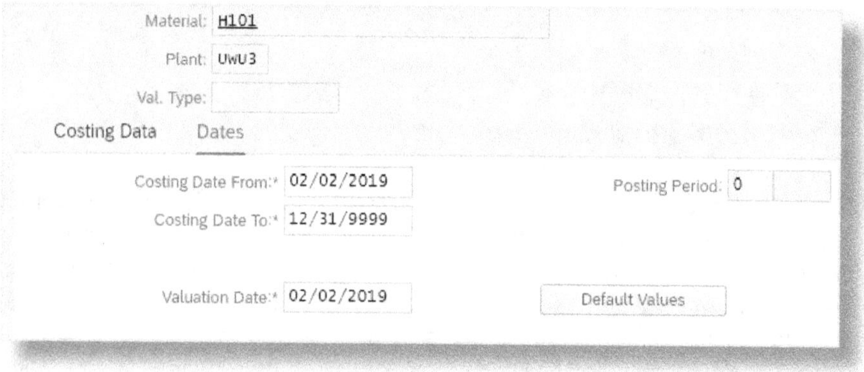

Figure 7.4: Additive cost estimate dates tab

First, the drum material is added. For a costing lot size of 10,000 L, there are 20 drums of 500 L each.

The itemization window (see Figure 7.5) is used to manually enter any item that is included in the cost estimate. Data entry and editing in this window follow the same rules as for unit cost estimates. An item type must first be entered, and then certain remaining fields can be used to further define what costs are associated with that line. For example, item category M refers to a material. A material and plant combination must be entered along with a quantity that would be associated with the costing lot size. That is all that needs to be entered for the material. The system finds the standard price for the material and then factors that against the QUANTITY. In this example, the standard is $1,500.00/100 PC and the quantity is 20. $1,500.00 divided by 100 multiplied by 20 equals 300.00, which is seen in the VALUE – TOTAL column. DESCRIPTION comes from the material master, and the COST ELEMENT is derived from the valuation class assigned to the material.

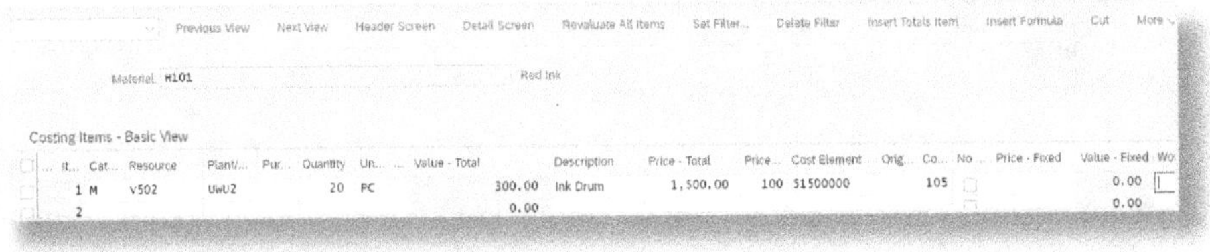

Figure 7.5: Itemization entry item with first item entered

The remaining two items in the additive cost estimate are not associated directly with any cost object. These items use item category V, which requires the quantity, description, price, price unit, and a cost element to be entered. Figure 7.6 shows the completed itemization. Note that QUANTITY is set to the costing lot size for the V items, and PRICE UNIT is also set to the costing lot size. The fourth item in the listing represents administrative costs using the V item type. Administrative costs are usually fixed. To enter a fixed cost for a V item, first enter the PRICE - TOTAL value and then enter the fixed portion of that in the PRICE - FIXED column. There is an additional text line that has been added at the beginning of the cost estimate, and a summation line has been added at the end to add together the non-material costs. Neither of these lines has any impact on the total cost of the additive cost estimate.

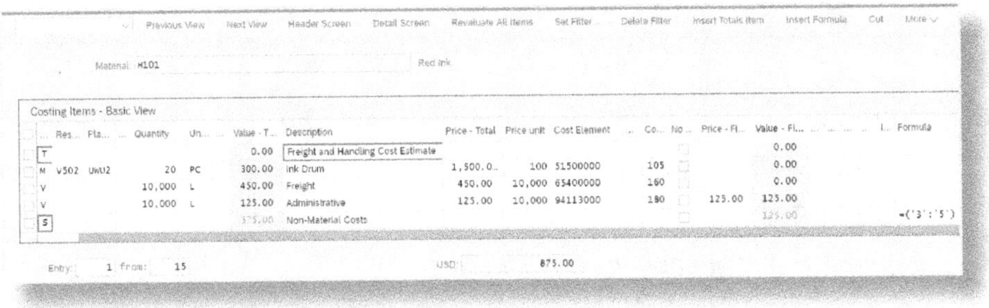

Figure 7.6: Completed itemization

The text item (T) and summarization item (S) are highlighted by the system to indicate that they are not part of the cost estimate, and are included for informational purposes only. The system gives a running total of the costs at the bottom of the window. In this example, the total is 875.00 USD per 10,000 L for the shipment.

> ### Costing lot size and quantities
>
>
>
> Be careful to match the quantities in an additive cost estimate with the costing lot size when first creating it.

The costing lot size is changeable from within the cost estimate list. Select CHANGE LOT SIZE... from the FUNCTIONS dropdown menu. This is accessible in the Fiori app by clicking on the More ⌄ button. Change the lot size to the desired value. When returning to the itemization list window, the quantities are adjusted to reflect the changed lot size. Certain quantities are independent of lot size. Setup time is an example of an item that does not change with lot size. The time is the same regardless of the amount of production. It is possible to enter item quantities that are independent of lot size. In Figure 7.7, item 4 is defined as independent of lot size. F is entered in the column LOT-SIZE INDEP., which means that regardless of the costing lot size quantity, the quantity entered does not change. The costs associated with this item do not necessarily have to be fixed, and a mixture of fixed and variable costs can be assigned. This setting only affects the quantity and not the per unit cost.

Costing Items - Basic View								
...	Item	...	Res...	Plan...	P...	Quantity	Uni...	Lot-Size ...	Value
	1	T							0
	2	M	V502	UwU2		20	PC		300
	3	V				10,000	L		450
	4	V				10,000	L	F	125
	5	S							575

Figure 7.7: Item independent of lot size

Figure 7.8 shows the result when the costing lot size is adjusted from 10,000 to 1,000. The quantities for items 2 and 3 have been changed to fit the new lot size of 1,000 and are ten times less than before. However, item 4 retains the original quantity of 10,000. The quantity has become fixed.

	Item	Res...	Plan...	P...	Quantity	Unit...	Lot-Siz...	Value
	1	T						0.
	2	M	V502	UwU2	2	PC		30.
	3	V			1,000	L		45.
	4	V			10,000	L	F	125.
	5	S						170

Costing Items - Basic View

Figure 7.8: Quantities after lot size change

The following item categories are available for additive cost estimates:

- **B**—base planning object. This requires base planning object ID, quantity, and cost element if not already assigned to the base planning object itself. Base planning objects are not intended for use in S/4HANA.

- **E**—internal activity. This requires cost center, activity type, quantity of activity, and unit of measure. This can also be derived from a work center and the work center's plant. The cost element comes from the definition of the activity type.

- **F**—external activity. This requires purchasing information record ID, plant, purchasing organization, quantity, and cost element.

- **L**—subcontracting. This requires purchasing information record ID, plant, purchasing organization, quantity, and cost element. The cost element is derived from the account assignment configuration for subcontracting (transaction event key FRL—external activity)

- **M**—material. This requires material number, plant, quantity, and unit of measure. Cost element is derived from the automatic account assignment configuration for transaction event key GBB (inventory posting offset), modifier VBR (consumption).

- **N**—external service. This requires service ID, plant, purchasing organization, quantity, and unit of measure. Cost element is derived from the valuation class assigned to the external service activity.

- **O**—arithmetical operation. This requires a formula and a cost element. Allowed operations are: add, subtract, multiply, and divide, for values of specific line items. Multiplication and division are also allowed for operations with constant values. However, the addition and subtraction operations are not allowed with constants.

- **P**—process (manual). This requires business process ID and quantity. Unit of measure is derived from the business process. The cost element is taken from the business process definition.
- **S**—total. Specify the item lines to total. Totals are not included in the cost. This is an information line only.
- **T**—text item. This requires a description and is not included in the cost.
- **V**—variable item. This requires quantity, price, price unit, and cost element. Text describing the cost should also be entered under description. Cost element can be derived from the cost component, depending on the configuration.

There are many different editing functions that can be used. To insert a line, select the line before where the new line should be inserted. Click on the [icon] button using the SAPGUI transaction or select INSERT ITEM from the More ∨ dropdown menu in the Fiori app. A new line is then inserted above the selected line. Enter the information.

To append a line to the end when changing a cost estimate, or, if there are no more new lines available when creating a cost estimate, click on the [icon] button using the SAPGUI transaction or select NEW ENTRIES from the More ∨ dropdown menu in the Fiori app.

In addition to the manual entry of line items, special editing functions allow for the explosion of a base planning object into its component line items (choose EXPLODE BASE PLANNING OBJECT... from the FUNCTIONS dropdown menu), the explosion of a material cost estimate into its component items (choose EXPLODE MATERIAL COST ESTIMATE... from the FUNCTIONS dropdown menu), and the copying of items from a material cost estimate (choose COPY COST ESTIMATE... from the FUNCTIONS dropdown menu). The FUNCTIONS menu is available in the Fiori app by clicking on the More ∨ button.

Saving an additive cost estimate is a two-step process. First, click on the Save ([icon]) button to perform a temporary save of the entries in the itemization window. The system then displays the resulting cost estimate.

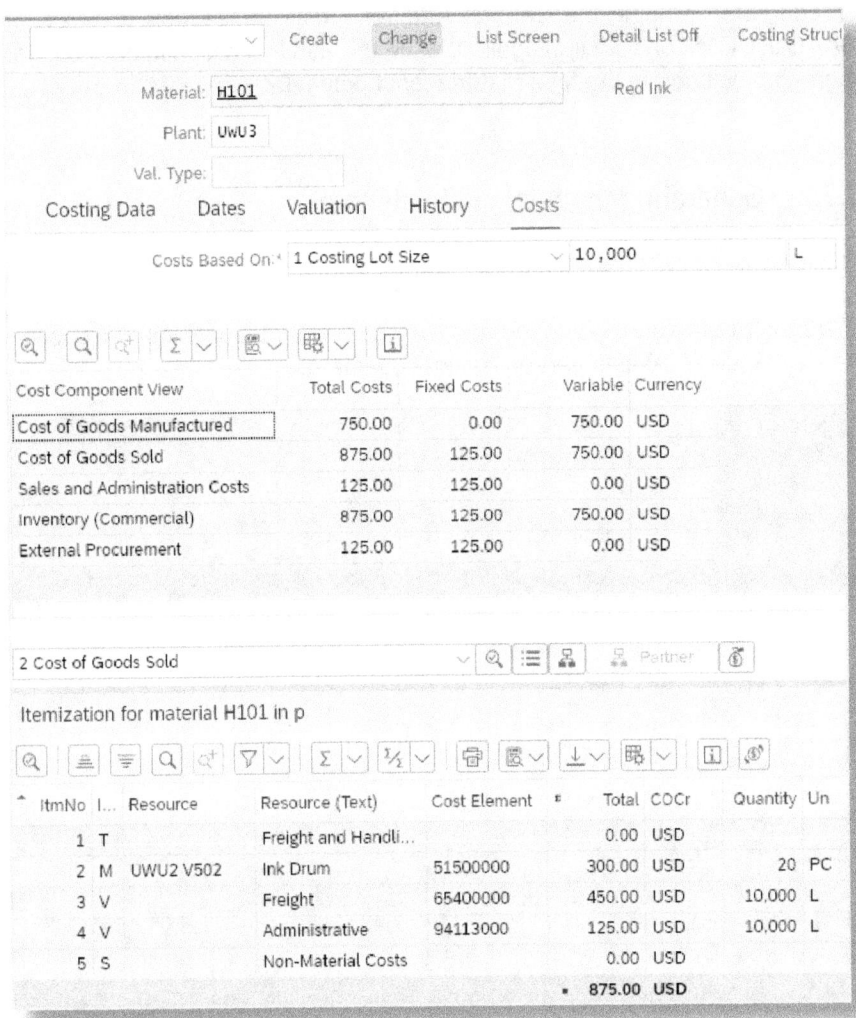

Figure 7.9: Resulting additive cost estimate

Figure 7.9 shows the final additive cost estimate. THE COST OF GOODS SOLD cost component view is selected to show all costs, including the administrative costs. Note that in the cost estimate itemization, the subtotal item has a value of 0. The subtotal is simply informational and is only displayed in the itemization entry window. Click on the List Screen (📝) button to go back to the data entry window. This button is also used to get to the itemization screen when running the Change Additive Costs transaction (CK75N for SAPGUI). Click on Save (🖫) again to save the additive cost estimate so that it can be included in the final material cost estimate.

7.2.2 Generating the total cost estimate

To see the cost estimate that includes the items from the additive cost estimate, run Create Cost Estimate (SAPGUI transaction CK11N) for the material. Prior to generating the additive cost estimate, only the first costing item in Figure 7.10 was part of the cost estimate.

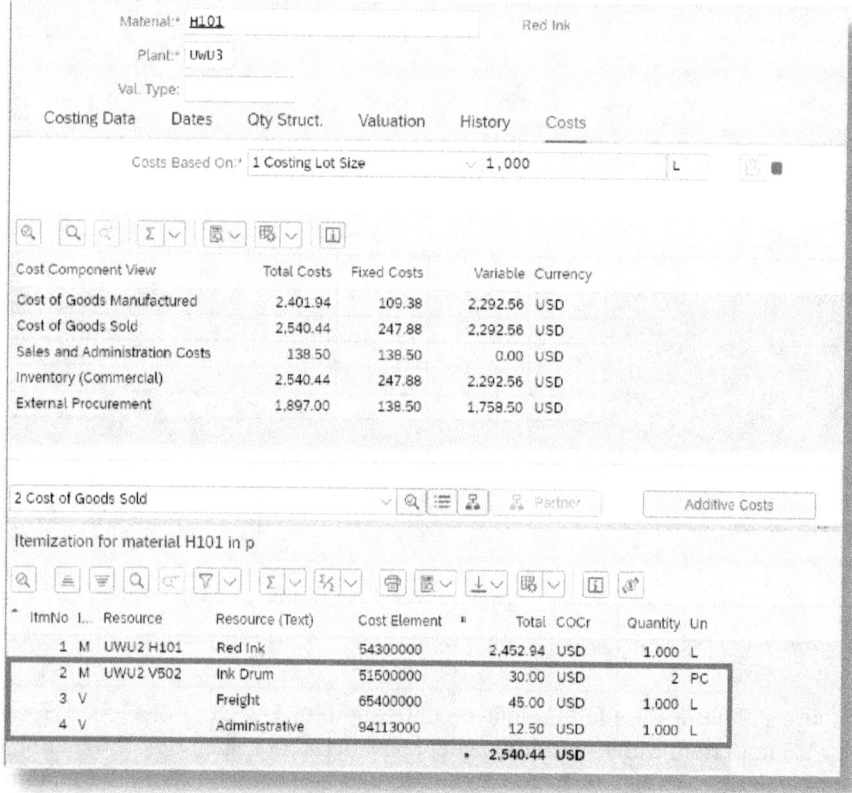

Figure 7.10: Cost estimate with additive costs

146

After creating the additive cost estimate, the recosted material includes the individual line items from the additive cost estimate (highlighted in the box in Figure 7.10). To see which costs are additive, click on the ADDITIVE COSTS button.

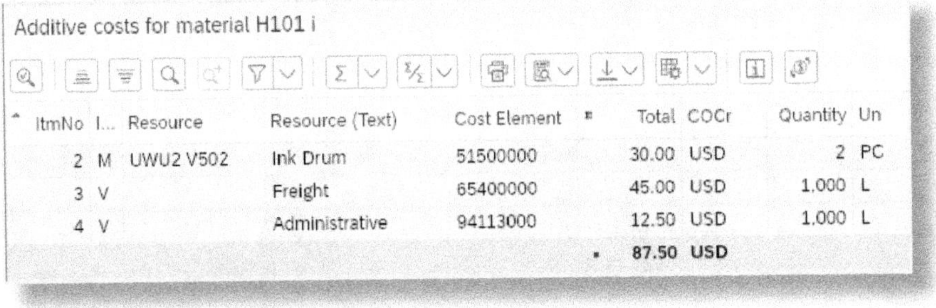

ItmNo	I...	Resource	Resource (Text)	Cost Element	Total COCr		Quantity	Un
2	M	UWU2 V502	Ink Drum	51500000	30.00	USD	2	PC
3	V		Freight	65400000	45.00	USD	1,000	L
4	V		Administrative	94113000	12.50	USD	1,000	L
					87.50	USD		

Figure 7.11: Cost itemization only showing additive costs

Figure 7.11 shows only those costs that are from the additive cost estimate. Note that any items of type S (total) and T (text) are not transferred to the combined cost estimate. Click on 🔍 (🔍) to return to the full itemization. Item 1 contains the cost of the interplant transfer. Items 2 through 4 are pulled from the additive cost estimate.

7.2.3 Deleting additive cost estimates

If additive cost estimates should no longer be part of the final cost estimate, the additive cost estimate needs to be removed. Additive cost estimates are deleted by running transaction CKR1. When first entering Reorganize Cost Estimates (SAPGUI transaction CKR1), click on the All Selections (📋) button to open all possible selections. This is required to make the selection for additive cost estimates visible.

147

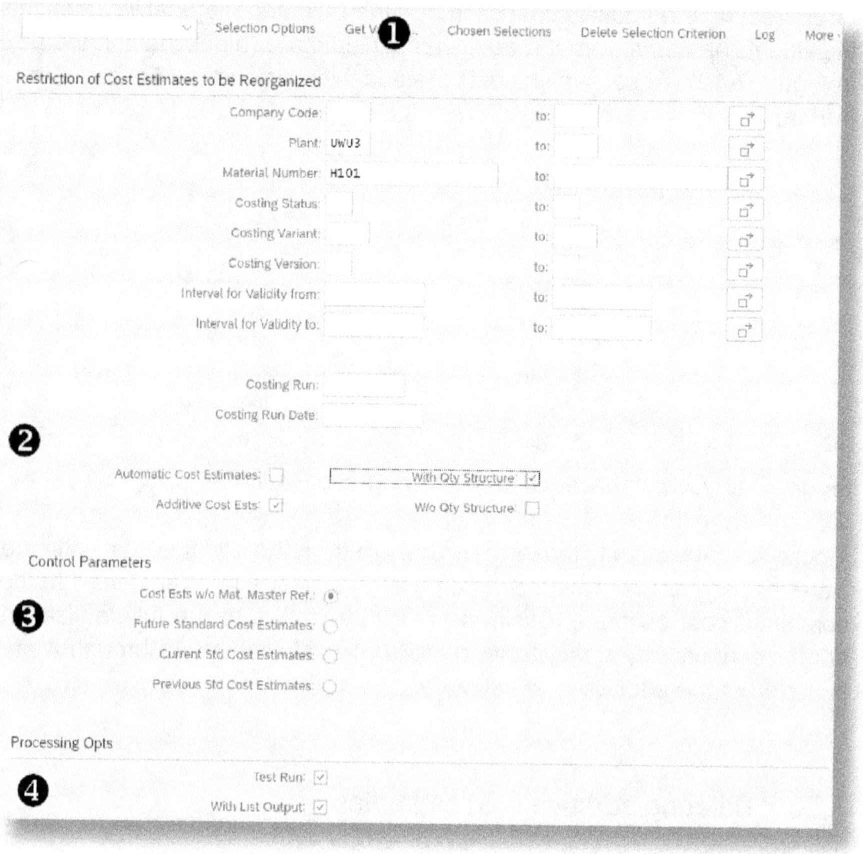

Additive cost estimates

Figure 7.12: Deleting the additive cost estimate

Figure 7.12 shows the Fiori version of the Reorganize Cost Estimates transaction. Looking at section ❶, the All Selections button has been clicked, thereby making all reorganization options available. In section ❷, the AUTOMATIC COST ESTIMATES and W/O QTY STRUCTURE checkboxes should be blank. Only ADDITIVE COST ESTS and WITH QTY STRUCTURE should be selected. Under CONTROL PARAMETERS (section ❸). COST ESTS W/O MAT. MASTER REF. should be selected. As a rule, the TEST RUN and WITH LIST OUTPUT parameters (in section ❹) should be selected when this is first executed to ensure that only the desired cost estimates are deleted.

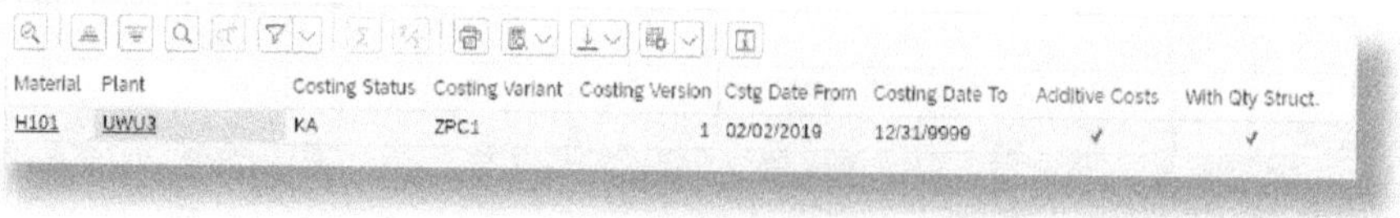

Material	Plant	Costing Status	Costing Variant	Costing Version	Cstg Date From	Costing Date To	Additive Costs	With Qty Struct.
H101	UWU3	KA	ZPC1	1	02/02/2019	12/31/9999	✓	✓

Figure 7.13: List of cost estimates to be deleted

Figure 7.13 shows the resulting report if WITH LIST OUTPUT is selected. Only after this initial test run, should TEST RUN be deselected to allow for the actual deletion to take place.

7.3 Additive cost estimate configuration

Additive costs are not included in cost estimates unless the costing variant has been configured to allow for them. There is also configuration to determine how additive costs are used in the cost estimate and whether certain types of additive costs are included in the cost estimate, even if additive costs are allowed.

7.3.1 Costing variant configuration

The use of additive costs is defined by costing variant. This is configured on the ADDITIVE COSTS tab of transaction OKKN. The IMG menu path is CONTROLLING • PRODUCT COST CONTROLLING • PRODUCT COST PLANNING • MATERIAL COST ESTIMATE WITH QUANTITY STRUCTURE • DEFINE COSTING VARIANTS. Select the costing variant and click on the ADDITIVE COSTS tab.

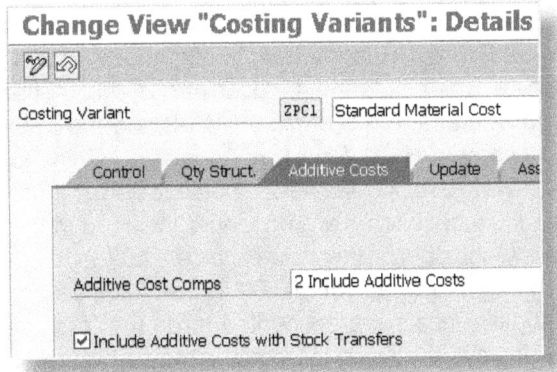

Figure 7.14: Costing variant additive costs

The configuration shown in Figure 7.14 shows two different options to maintain. The ADDITIVE COST COMPS selection defines whether additive costs are to be included and the behavior of additive costs when allocating overhead to the cost estimate. There are three options to choose from:

149

▶ 1 IGNORE ADDITIVE COSTS—Additive costs are ignored when creating the cost estimate. Any existing additive costs created when this option is not selected will be ignored and excluded from the final cost estimate.

▶ 2 INCLUDE ADDITIVE COSTS—Additive costs are assigned to the main cost estimate, but no overhead can be calculated using these costs as a basis.

▶ 3 INCLUDE ADDITIVE COSTS AND APPLY OVERHEAD—Additive costs are assigned and can also be used when calculating overhead using an overhead costing sheet.

The INCLUDE ADDITIVE COSTS WITH STOCK TRANSFERS checkbox is used to determine whether additive costs should apply to stock transfers or production in another plant. If selected, additive costs can be used to account for transport or other costs associated with shipping between two plants.

The costing example from Section 7.2 is for a material that is transferred from plant UWU2 (Los Angeles) to plant UWU3 (Chicago). The cost of the material UWU2 contains component R109 which has its own additive cost estimate. The first cost example looks at the impact of turning off the INCLUDE ADDITIVE COSTS WITH STOCK TRANSFERS function.

The cost estimate in Figure 7.10 was calculated with INCLUDE ADDITIVE COSTS and INCLUDE ADDITIVE COSTS WITH STOCK TRANSFERS both configured. The total COST OF GOODS SOLD view of the costs is 2,540.44 USD per 1,000 L. This contains the additive costs for material R109 at plant UWU2 and the additive costs for the transfer of material H101 from Los Angeles to Chicago. When INCLUDE ADDITIVE COSTS WITH STOCK TRANSFERS is deselected, Figure 7.15 shows that the three additive cost items are no longer included in the cost estimate and the COST OF GOODS SOLD view value is now 2,452.94 USD per 1,000 L. The additive costs associated with R109 in Los Angeles are still included. Because no additive costs are accounted for in the transfer, the cost estimate no longer displays the ADDITIVE COSTS button as before.

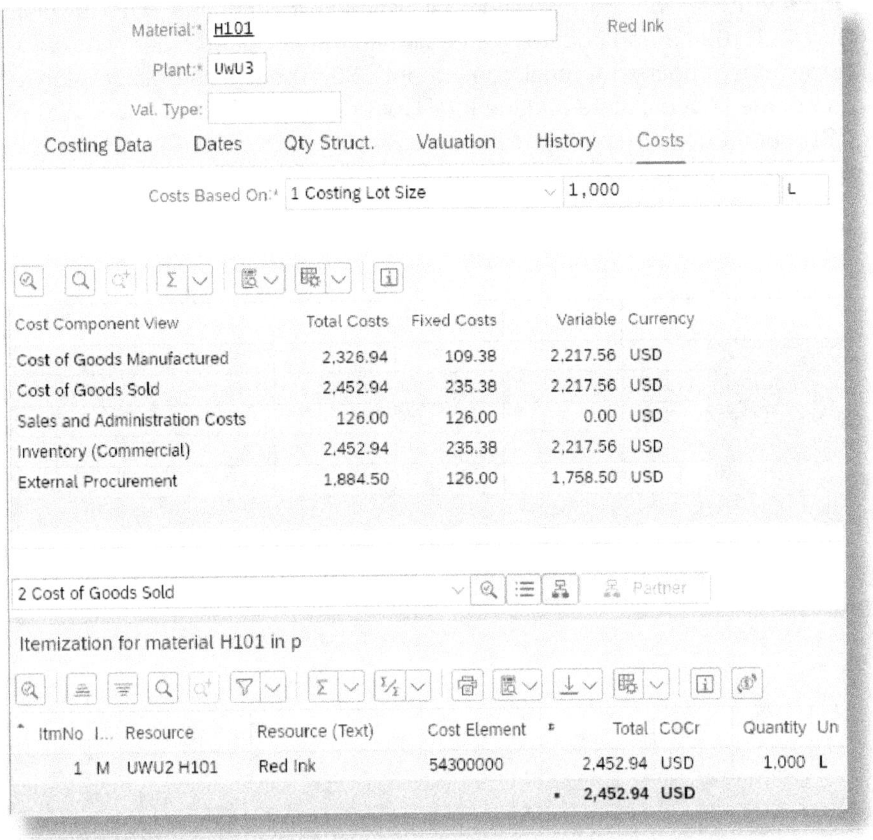

Additive cost estimates

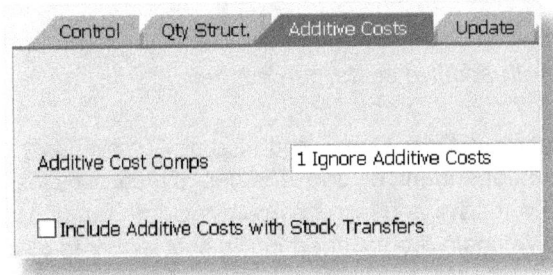

Material:*	H101				Red Ink		
Plant:*	UWU3						
Val. Type:							

Costing Data Dates Qty Struct. Valuation History Costs

Costs Based On:* 1 Costing Lot Size 1,000 L

Cost Component View	Total Costs	Fixed Costs	Variable	Currency
Cost of Goods Manufactured	2,326.94	109.38	2,217.56	USD
Cost of Goods Sold	2,452.94	235.38	2,217.56	USD
Sales and Administration Costs	126.00	126.00	0.00	USD
Inventory (Commercial)	2,452.94	235.38	2,217.56	USD
External Procurement	1,884.50	126.00	1,758.50	USD

2 Cost of Goods Sold

Itemization for material H101 in p

ItmNo I...	Resource	Resource (Text)	Cost Element	F	Total	COCr	Quantity	Un
1 M	UWU2 H101	Red Ink	54300000		2,452.94	USD	1,000	L
				•	2,452.94	USD		

Figure 7.15: Cost estimate using no additive costs with transfers

The next example has the additive cost configuration set to IGNORE ADDITIVE COSTS. This is shown in Figure 7.16.

Control	Qty Struct.	Additive Costs	Update
Additive Cost Comps		1 Ignore Additive Costs	
☐ Include Additive Costs with Stock Transfers			

Figure 7.16: Ignore additive costs configuration

151

Figure 7.17 shows the resulting cost estimate for material H101 at plant UWU3. R109 had an additive cost estimate that included SALES AND ADMINISTRATIVE COSTS defined in cost component 180. These costs are no longer part of the cost estimate and the total COST OF GOODS SOLD is now 2,326.94 USD per 1,000 L. The total for the SALES AND ADMINISTRATIVE COSTS view also is changed and has become 0.00 USD.

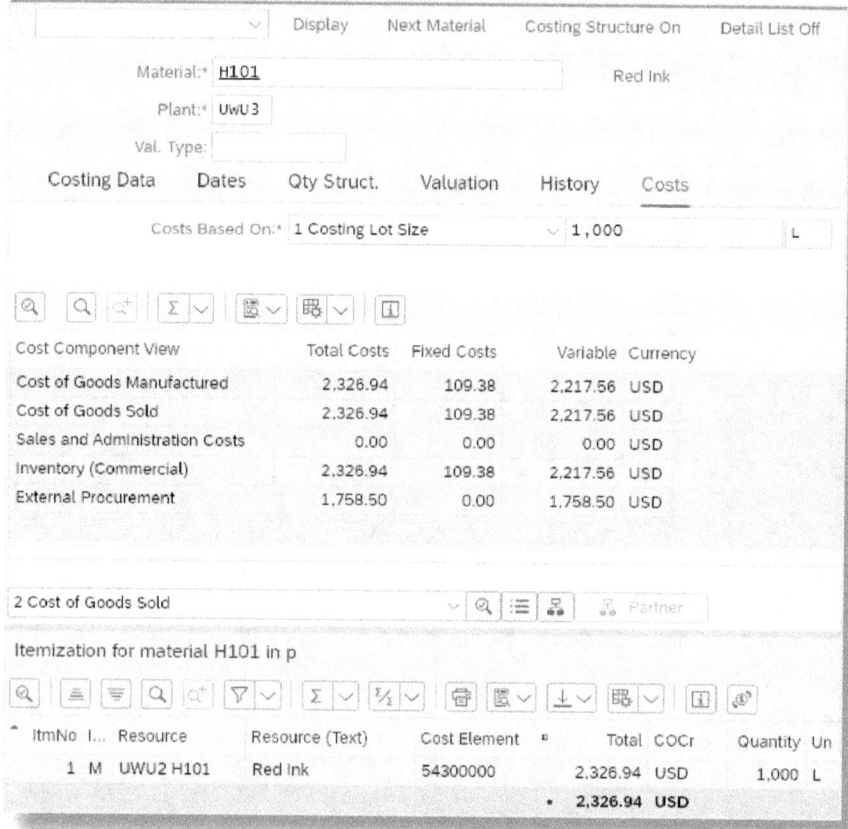

Figure 7.17: Cost estimate with additive costs ignored

The configuration settings ADDITIVE COST COMPS and INCLUDE ADDITIVE COSTS WITH STOCK TRANSFERS are independent of one another. If ADDITIVE COST COMPS is set to IGNORE ADDITIVE COSTS and INCLUDE ADDITIVE COSTS WITH COST TRANSFERS is selected, additive costs are included in the cost estimate of a transferred material.

7.3.2 Cost component structure with texts

A data entry template for entering additive costs can be set up using the COST COMP STRUC W/ TEXTS (cost component structure with texts) feature. When first creating an additive cost estimate, select this option in the COPY FROM section (see Figure 7.18).

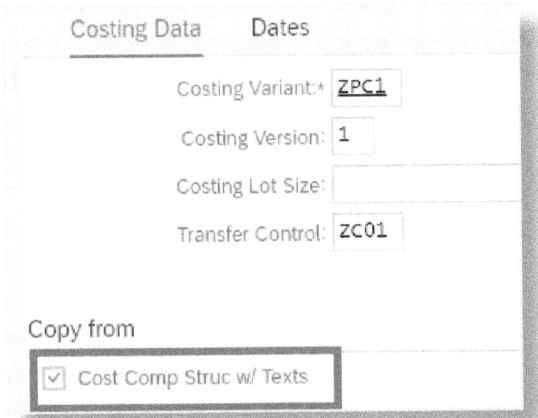

Figure 7.18: Cost component structure with texts selection

Using this feature prepopulates item lines in the additive cost estimate. This can only be used if the cost component split is configured to define the cost components to use. This configuration assigns a specific cost element or origin group to a cost component which is then used in the additive cost estimate.

Select the cost component configuration using transaction OKTZ or via IMG menu path CONTROLLING • PRODUCT COST CONTROLLING • PRODUCT COST PLANNING • BASIC SETTINGS FOR MATERIAL COSTING • DEFINE COST COMPONENT STRUCTURE. Select the cost component structure to be updated. Next, select the UPDATE OF ADDITIVE COSTS folder, as shown in Figure 7.19.

153

Additive cost estimates

Change View "Update of Additive Costs": Overview					
Dialog Structure	Cost Comp. Str.	Cost Com	Chart of Accts	Cost Element	Origin group
▽ ☐ Cost Component Struct	K1	160	YCOA	65400000	
▽ ☐ Cost Components w	K1	180	YCOA	94113000	
☐ Assignment: Cost					
☐ Update of Additiv					
☐ Transfer Structur					
☐ Cost Component Views					
☐ Assignment: Organiz. L					
☐ Cost Component Group					

Figure 7.19: Update of additive costs in cost component split

When creating new entries, enter the cost component structure, the cost component of that structure, the chart of accounts in which a cost element is defined, the cost element to assign to the additive cost, and an origin group, if desired. Repeat for any cost component to be used with specific text in the additive cost estimate.

When COST COMP STRUC w/ TEXTS is selected (see Figure 7.18), the system checks for any cost components that have not been defined and displays a warning message for each one when moving to the cost estimate editing window. A separate line item with item category V (variable) is created for each defined cost component, using the cost element specified in the configuration (see Figure 7.20).

Costing Items - Basic View										
Item	Resource	Plant/...	Pur...	Quantity	Un...	Value - Total	Description	Price - Total	Price	Cost Element	Orig.	Co...
1 V				1.000		0.00	Freight			65400000	160
2 V				1.000		0.00	Sales / Admin			94113000	180

Figure 7.20: Additive cost estimate—cost component with text

The description shows the name of the cost component, and the cost component and cost element are automatically defined. All that is needed is to specify the price. Additional items can be included in the cost estimate by using the available editing functions for inserting or adding items.

This configuration also supports an additional feature which can be used when COST COMP STRUC w/TEXTS is not selected for the additive cost estimate. To avoid having to determine a specific cost element for an additive cost estimate item, the cost component can be entered. The cost element is derived from the cost component configuration. Figure 7.21 shows how this is done. This should be used for items that do not have an automatic means for deriving the cost element, such as item types V or O. If there is no configured cost element or origin group for the cost component, the system displays an error.

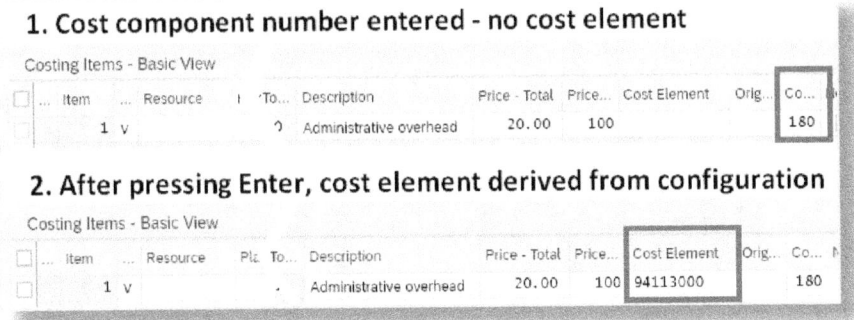

Figure 7.21: Deriving the cost element from the cost component

8 Co-products

Co-products are two or more products that are manufactured simultaneously using the same components and manufacturing operations. The splitting of the manufacturing costs among the various co-products is controlled by apportionment structures.

8.1 Joint production

Joint production is a means by which two or more products are manufactured simultaneously using the same production process. The results of the process consist of either co-products or by-products. *Co-products* are an intentional result of the manufacturing process, and the manufacturing cost is divided amongst the various co-products. *By-products* are typically residue left over from manufacturing that have small value and are kept in inventory either for reuse in other manufacturing processes or for external sales. A good example of a by-product is sawdust, which is a result of milling lumber.

8.1.1 By-products

By-products are represented in the BOM as a material with a negative quantity. Material H299 is a residual solvent left over from the ink manufacturing process at plant UWU2. The BOM for ink material H101 (red ink) defines H299 as a by-product of the manufacturing process (see Figure 8.1).

Item...	Item Category	Component	Component ...	Component Quantity	
0010	L(Stock item)	R109	Red Dye	63.000	L
0020	L(Stock item)	R105	Lubricant	12.000	L
0030	L(Stock item)	R106	Surfactant	22.000	L
0040	L(Stock item)	R107	Thickener	11.000	L
0050	L(Stock item)	H299	Solvent	-1.500	L

Figure 8.1: BOM with by-product

157

Co-products

A setting that is applicable to by-products and co-products is the Co-PRODUCT indicator in the GENERAL DATA section of the BASIC DATA tab of the component item (see Figure 8.2). This must be left blank for the component to behave as a by-product instead of a co-product. This mainly affects the manufacturing process, but also impacts the costing of co-products.

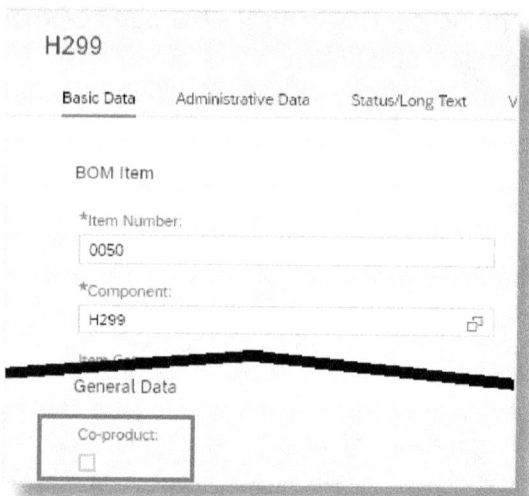

Figure 8.2: Co-product indicator for the BOM item

The resulting cost estimate is shown in Figure 8.3. Note that the item type is M for material, and the value and quantity are both negative values. This reduces the overall cost of the manufactured material.

ItmNo		Resource			Resource (Text)	Cost Element	=	Total COCr		Quantity	Un
1	E	200101	MIXER	SETUP	Mix Ink	94303000		87.94	USD	1.5	HR
2	E	200101	MIXER	MACHHR	Mix Ink	94301000		69.57	USD	1.546	HR
3	E	200101	MIXER	LABRHR	Mix Ink	94311000		57.79	USD	2.540	HR
4	M	UWU2 R109			Red Dye	51100000		1,518.30	USD	630	L
5	M	UWU2 R105			Lubricant	51100000		90.00	USD	120	L
6	M	UWU2 R106			Surfactant	51100000		55.00	USD	220	L
7	M	UWU2 R107			Thickener	51100000		38.50	USD	110	L
8	M	UWU2 H299			Solvent	55100000		3.45-	USD	15-	L
							•	1,913.65	USD		

Figure 8.3: Cost estimate with by-product

The material cost of the by-product material H299 is determined the same was as any other cost estimate. Its cost could be a result of a separate manufacturing process, or the cost could have been assigned. The by-product contributes to the cost component split of the main product based on how it is costed. For materials where the cost is directly assigned, only the cost component for the material's assigned cost element and/or origin group is used. If a full cost estimate is generated, then the entire cost component split is included in the main cost.

8.1.2 Co-products

Co-products can be either primary or secondary. A primary co-product is one for which a manufacturing order is created. The BOM for the co-product belongs to the primary co-product, and other co-products are assigned as components on the BOM with negative quantities, as is the case with by-products. The determination of how costs are split amongst the co-products is defined in the material master of the primary co-product.

No special material master settings are required for by-products. That is not the case with co-products. Due to the nature of production processing and the apportionment of costs, co-products must be explicitly declared. These settings are made in either the MRP 2 tab or the COSTING 1 tab of the material master. Material H231 (RED INK #2) is produced along with material H101 (red ink). Because of how the ink is processed, two different inks are produced with slightly different characteristics. Figure 8.4 shows the position of the co-product fields in the QUANTITY STRUCTURE DATA section of the COSTING 1 tab. The CO-PRODUCT checkbox indicates that this material is used as a co-product with one or more other materials. It does not determine that it is a primary co-product. The FXD PRICE checkbox indicates that the material has a fixed price that is not determined as part of a co-product apportionment structure. For costing purposes, a fixed price co-product is treated the same way as a by-product. This uses the *net realizable value* method for costing. This means that the value of the quantity of the co-product from the BOM is subtracted from the cost of the primary co-product without accounting for any method of dividing the costs. The CO-PRODUCT indicator needs to be set for the component in the BOM for fixed price co-products.

Co-products

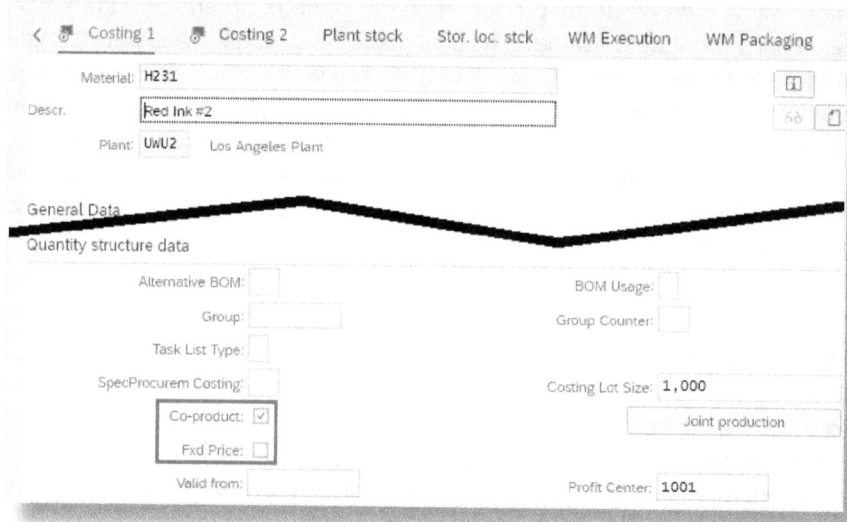

Figure 8.4: Co-product definition for material H231

The expected manufacturing quantity of the co-product is determined by assigning a negative value to it as a component of the primary co-product. Figure 8.5 shows material H231 added to the BOM of material H101 as a co-product. The value loaded is -30.00 L.

Item...	Item Category	Component	Component...	Component Quantity	
0010	L(Stock item)	R109	Red Dye	63.000	L
0020	L(Stock item)	R105	Lubricant	12.000	L
0030	L(Stock item)	R106	Surfactant	22.000	L
0040	L(Stock item)	R107	Thickener	11.000	L
0050	L(Stock item)	H299	Solvent	-1.500	L
0060	L(Stock item)	H231	Red Ink #2	-30.000	L

Figure 8.5: BOM showing material H231 as a co-product

The CO-PRODUCT checkbox must be selected for component H231 to indicate to the system that the special co-product logic should be used for this component (see Figure 8.6).

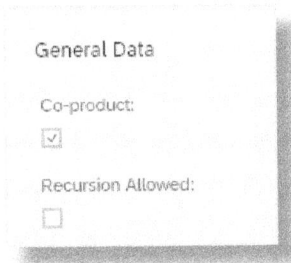

Figure 8.6: Co-product indicator for component H231

The original component quantities in the BOM were used to make 100 L of material H101. The combined quantity of H101 and H231 now appears to be 130 L for the same components; however, this is not correct. The BOM base quantity should be changed to 70 L. This, added to the 30 L for the co-product H231, gives a total product quantity of 100 L, which is correct for the components assigned to the BOM (see Figure 8.7).

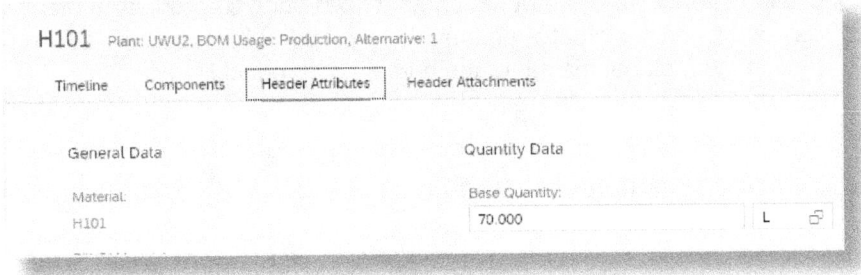

Figure 8.7: Adjusted BOM header base quantity

In addition to the BOM change, the routing or recipe base quantity should also be changed to reflect the lower quantity of the primary co-product. In this example, it is changed from 1,000 to 700, so that the cost split between the two co-products is factored correctly.

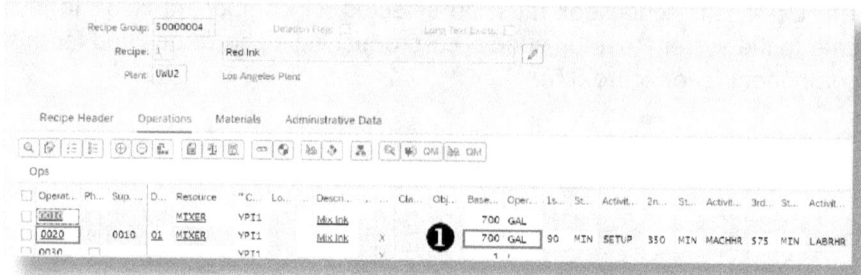

Figure 8.8: Recipe base quantity for primary co-product

Section ❶ in Figure 8.8 shows the adjustment. The above example was generated based on converting a quantity structure from making one product to making two co-products. The BOM quantities should be engineered with all co-products in mind. The base quantity of the BOM only refers to the primary co-product; however, the component quantities need to reflect not only the base quantity, but the quantities of all co-products as well. The same is true of the base quantities assigned to the recipes or routings. These base quantities refer only to the primary co-product, and the quantities associated with the other co-products must be accounted for.

Because material H231 is not set up as a fixed price co-product, a means of distributing the costs between the two co-products must be defined. This is done in the material master of the primary co-product H101.

8.2 Apportionment structures

8.2.1 Standard apportionment structures

The primary co-product must also be defined as a co-product, and if any of its subsidiary co-products are not fixed price, an apportionment structure must be set up to determine how the cost is to be split. Section ❶ of Figure 8.9 shows material H101 has been defined as a co-product. When the CO-PRODUCT checkbox is selected, the JOINT PRODUCTION button in section ❷ is enabled. Click on this button to define the apportionment structure.

Figure 8.9: Co-product definition for material H101

The BOM determines the relative quantities of the co-products. The apportionment structure defines how the costs are to be distributed between the products. Regardless of the co-product quantities defined in the BOM, the cost is divided amongst the co-products based only on the apportionment definitions. Take care to factor in the BOM quantities with the apportionment equivalence numbers to make sure that the costs are being divided correctly.

After clicking on the JOINT PRODUCTION button, the dialog box in Figure 8.10 appears. Enter a number and a description for the structure, then click on the EQUIVALENCE NUMBERS button at the bottom of the window.

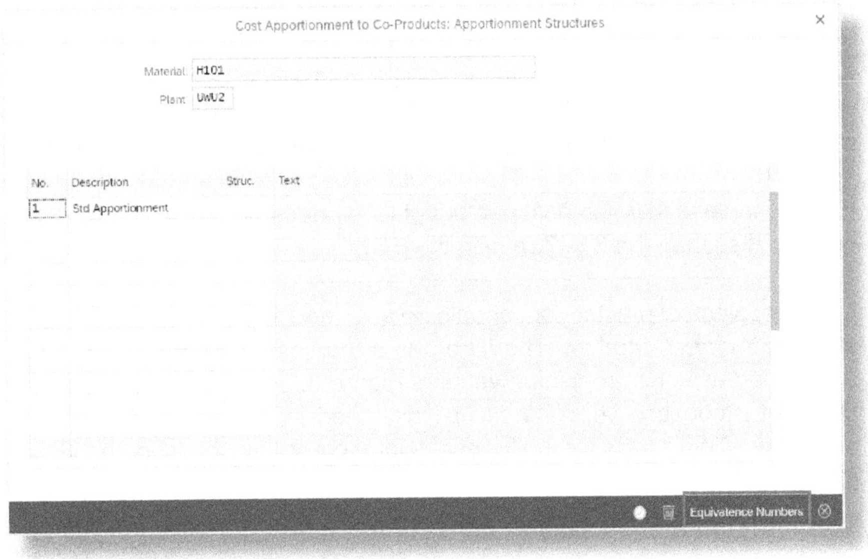

Figure 8.10: Apportionment structure dialog box

163

The EQUIVALENCE NUMBER dialog box (see Figure 8.11) is used to enter the list of co-products along with equivalence numbers to define the cost spread. The proportion of the costs assigned to each co-product is that material's equivalence number divided by the sum of the numbers for all co-products.

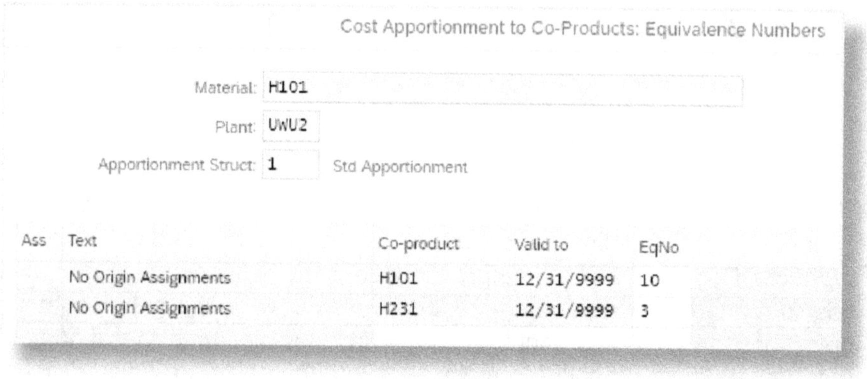

Cost Apportionment to Co-Products: Equivalence Numbers

Material: H101
Plant: UWU2
Apportionment Struct: 1   Std Apportionment

Ass	Text	Co-product	Valid to	EqNo
	No Origin Assignments	H101	12/31/9999	10
	No Origin Assignments	H231	12/31/9999	3

Figure 8.11: Equivalence numbers for the co-products

Enter the list of co-products starting with the primary co-product. Next, assign a weighting factor to each material, along with a number that represents the weighting of the cost distribution. To make the calculated cost of each co-product the same, the equivalence numbers must match the ratios of the subsidiary co-products to the base quantity of the primary co-product in the BOM. To do this, set the weighting for H101 in the EqNo (weighting) field to 7, and set the weighting for H231 to 3. This gives the same ratio as defined in the BOM (30.00 L of H231 for a base quantity of 70.00 L. However, the example in Figure 8.11 shows an equivalence number for H101 set to 10, and H231 set to 3. This should drive the cost per unit of material H231 to be less than the cost per unit of H101 because the ratio of H231 to H101 is less than the 3 to 7 ratio in the BOM.

One final piece of master data should be assigned to the production version of the primary co-product. The ID of the apportionment structure must be associated with the production version. Figure 8.12 shows the assignment. Different production versions can be assigned to different apportionment structures. This allows for a different yield of co-products based on the specific manufacturing process.

Figure 8.12: Apportionment structure in production version

The cost of the primary co-product using a costing lot size of 1,000 L is shown in Figure 8.13. The item type for the subsidiary co-product is A, not M as is the case for by-products and fixed price co-products. The cost of co-product H231 is also calculated based on the master data and shows up as a negative quantity and cost as is expected. The cost for H101 has increased slightly from what was seen in Figure 8.3 due to the weighting applied to the apportionment structure.

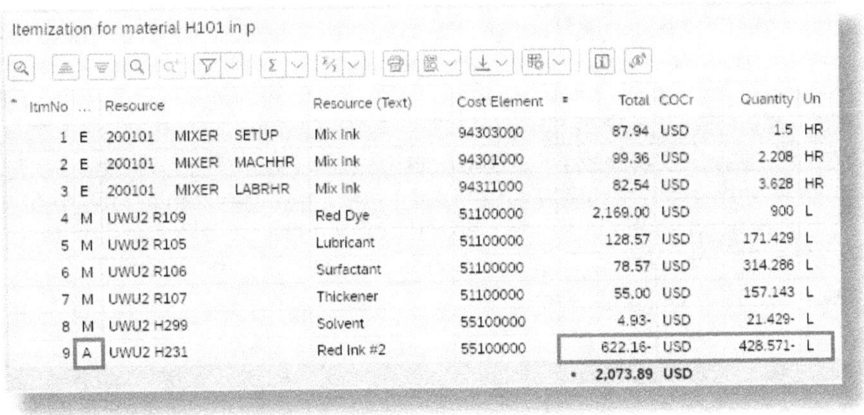

ItmNo	...	Resource			Resource (Text)	Cost Element	Total COCr		Quantity	Un
1	E	200101	MIXER	SETUP	Mix Ink	94303000	87.94	USD	1.5	HR
2	E	200101	MIXER	MACHHR	Mix Ink	94301000	99.36	USD	2.208	HR
3	E	200101	MIXER	LABRHR	Mix Ink	94311000	82.54	USD	3.628	HR
4	M	UWU2 R109			Red Dye	51100000	2,169.00	USD	900	L
5	M	UWU2 R105			Lubricant	51100000	128.57	USD	171.429	L
6	M	UWU2 R106			Surfactant	51100000	78.57	USD	314.286	L
7	M	UWU2 R107			Thickener	51100000	55.00	USD	157.143	L
8	M	UWU2 H299			Solvent	55100000	4.93-	USD	21.429-	L
9	A	UWU2 H231			Red Ink #2	55100000	622.16-	USD	428.571-	L
							2,073.89	USD		

Figure 8.13: Cost itemization for primary co-product

The QTY STRUCT tab of the cost estimate now contains a JOINT PRODUCTION section. This displays the primary co-product (PROCESS), production version (PROD. VERSION), and the APPORTIONMENT structure used for the cost estimate (see Figure 8.14). This is the primary co-product, so the process material is the same as the cost estimate material.

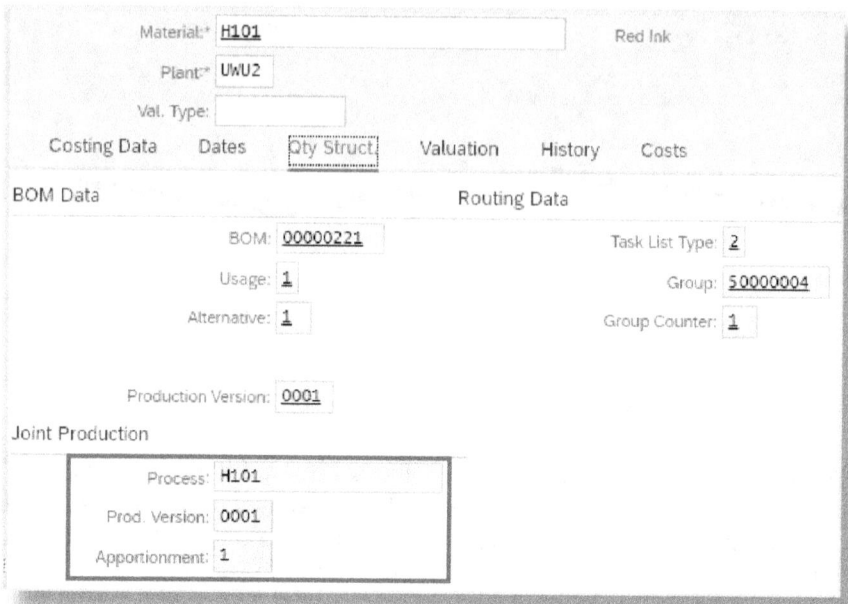

Figure 8.14: Joint production information in the cost estimate

A cost estimate can also be created separately for co-product H231 (see Figure 8.15). Section ❶ shows the costing lot size. This is the secondary co-product quantity calculated to be manufactured for each 1,000 L of the primary co-product that is made. 1,000 represents the costing loti size defined for the primary co-product. This is highlighted in Figure 8.13. The quantity was 30 L of H231 per 70 L of H101 (see Figure 8.5 and Figure 8.7). Adjusting the ratio of H231 to H101 for 1,000 L gives a quantity of 428.571 L. This is used as the costing lot size for this co-product's cost estimate. In section ❷, the primary co-product shows up as a co-product with negative quantity in the cost estimate.

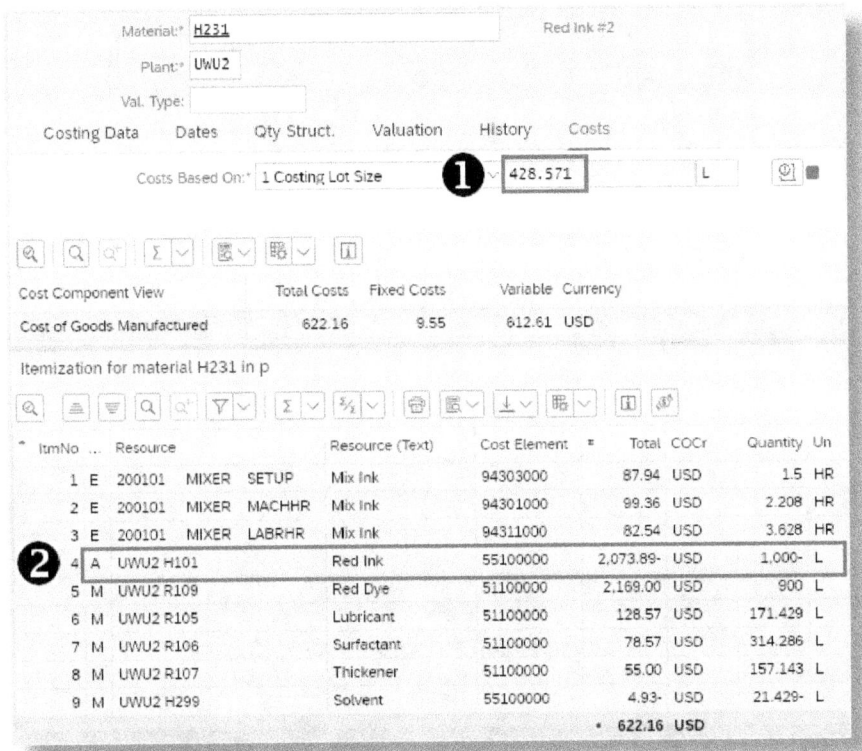

Figure 8.15: Cost estimate itemization of subsidiary co-product

The per unit cost for H231 is 622.16 USD divided by 428.571 L, which equals 1.45 USD per L. The per unit cost for H101 is 2,073.89 USD per 1,000 L, or 2.07 USD per L. Based on the assignment of the apportionment equivalence numbers, the costing result matched the expectations that the primary co-product would absorb more of the costs than the subsidiary co-product. The QTY STRUCT. tab for this cost estimate indicates the primary co-product, production version, and apportionment structure used to generate the cost estimate (see Figure 8.16). This provides the necessary information to determine how the cost estimate was generated for the non-primary co-product.

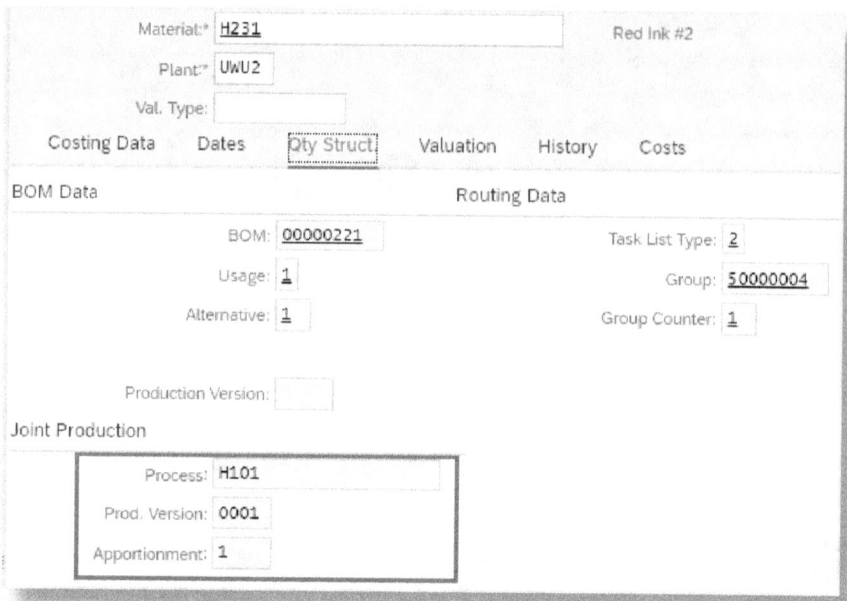

Figure 8.16: Quantity structure tab for co-product H231

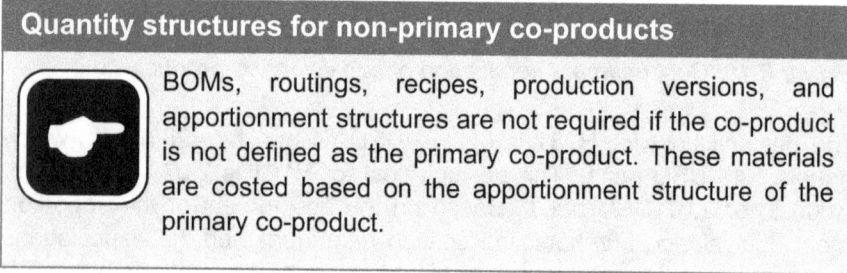

8.2.2 Source structures

The use of apportionment structures defined in Section 8.2.1 provides a method of splitting the total material costs. However, the costs to be divided can be broken down to cost element level, thereby providing a different way to allocate the costs amongst the various co-products. The previous example did not generate the desired cost split for Universal Writing Utensils. The company wants the component costs to be fully included in the cost of both co-products, but it wants the manufacturing costs to be split so that the primary co-product receives most of the cost. Because the major portion of the cost of the ink product is material cost, this should provide a much smaller difference in cost between the two co-products.

Using source structures within the apportionment structure allows the costs to be divided based on the individual cost elements that are in the cost itemization. Special cost element assignments are defined within the source structure. These assignments are then used when defining equivalence numbers for the co-products in the apportionment structure. Source structure configuration is found via IMG menu path CONTROLLING • PRODUCT COST CONTROLLING • PRODUCT COST PLANNING • SELECTING FUNCTIONS IN MATERIAL COSTING • COSTING IN JOINT PRODUCTION • DEFINE SOURCE STRUCTURE, or by using transaction OKEU (see Figure 8.17).

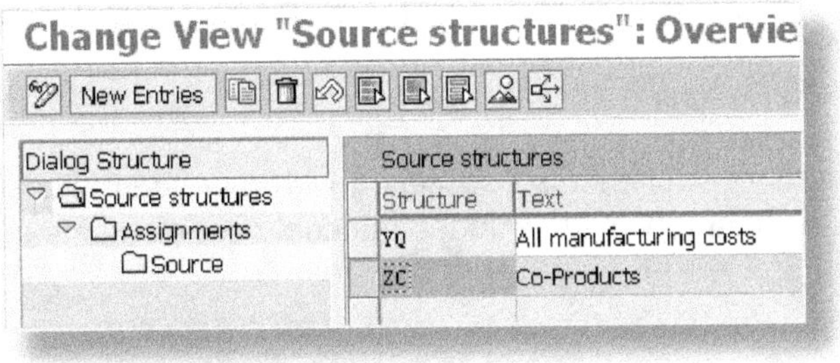

Figure 8.17: Source structure configuration

Each source structure has a set of assignments, and each assignment has either a range of cost elements or a cost element group defined for it. After selecting the source structure, double-click on the ASSIGNMENTS folder to define the different assignment categories.

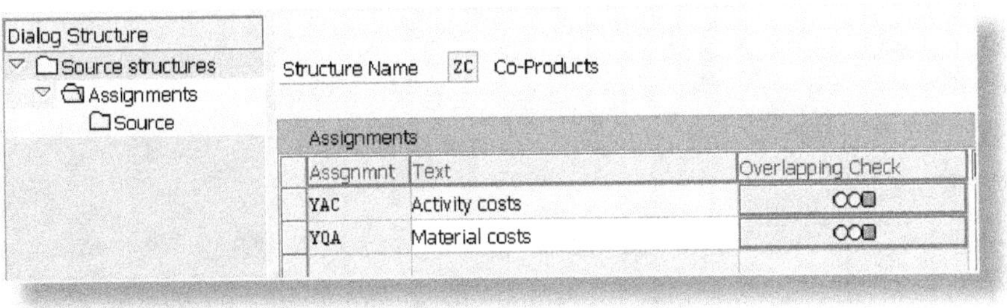

Figure 8.18: Assignment categories for structure ZC

Figure 8.18 shows two different assignments defined for source structure ZC (CO-PRODUCTS). Note the OVERLAPPING CHECK indicator. When this is green, there is no duplication of cost elements within any of the assignments. If the indicator is yellow, no cost elements have been defined yet. If the indicator is red, there are common cost elements in the assignments. A single cost element cannot be used in multiple assignments because its costs can only be apportioned to the co-products using one method. Select the assignment ID and double-click on the SOURCE folder to define the cost elements (see Figure 8.19). Enter either a range of cost elements or a cost element group.

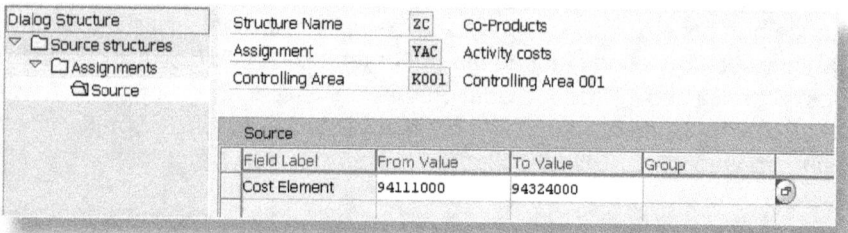

Figure 8.19: Cost elements assignments

ASSIGNMENT YAC contains cost elements associated with overhead allocation and activity type. Assignment YQA includes material cost elements in the range 50000000 to 55999999.

The source structures can now be assigned to an apportionment structure so that the cost distribution between the co-products can be more finely tuned. Figure 8.20 shows that a second apportionment structure has been assigned to material H101 in the material master. The previously-defined source structure ZC (CO-PRODUCTS) is assigned to it.

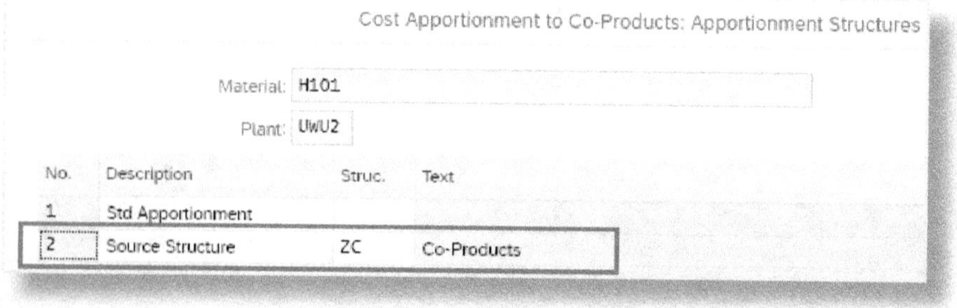

Figure 8.20: Source structure assigned to apportionment structure

After selecting this structure and clicking on the EQUIVALENCE NUMBERS button at the bottom of the window, the equivalence assignment window is displayed (see Figure 8.21).

Section ❶ shows that using the assignment from the source structure is now mandatory for defining the equivalence numbers. Section ❷ shows the numbers for each combination of assignment and co-product. Assignment YQA is used for the material costs, and because these costs need to be split evenly between the co-products, the ratio defined in the BOMs is used. The activity costs (YAC) are weighted more heavily with the primary co-product H101.

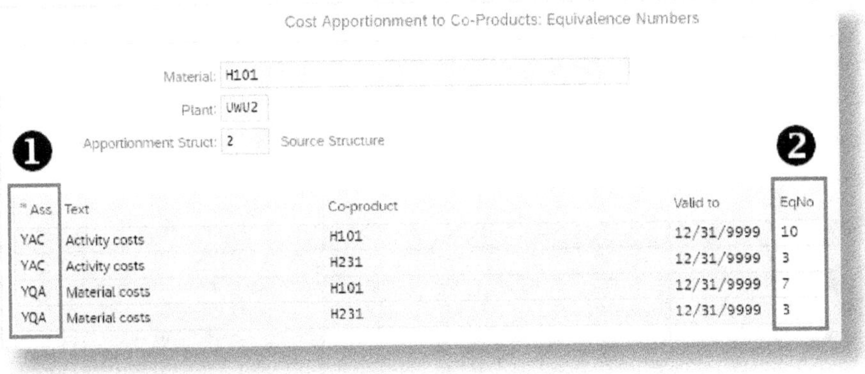
Cost Apportionment to Co-Products: Equivalence Numbers

Material: H101

Plant: UWU2

Apportionment Struct: 2 Source Structure

Ass	Text	Co-product	Valid to	EqNo
YAC	Activity costs	H101	12/31/9999	10
YAC	Activity costs	H231	12/31/9999	3
YQA	Material costs	H101	12/31/9999	7
YQA	Material costs	H231	12/31/9999	3

Figure 8.21: Equivalence definition using source structures

Because two apportionment structures have been defined for the primary co-product, assignment of each to a production version is mandatory so that the costing process can select the proper structure. To generate the following cost estimates, structure 2 is assigned to production version 0002, which is explicitly defined in the Costing 1 tab of material H101 for plant UWU2.

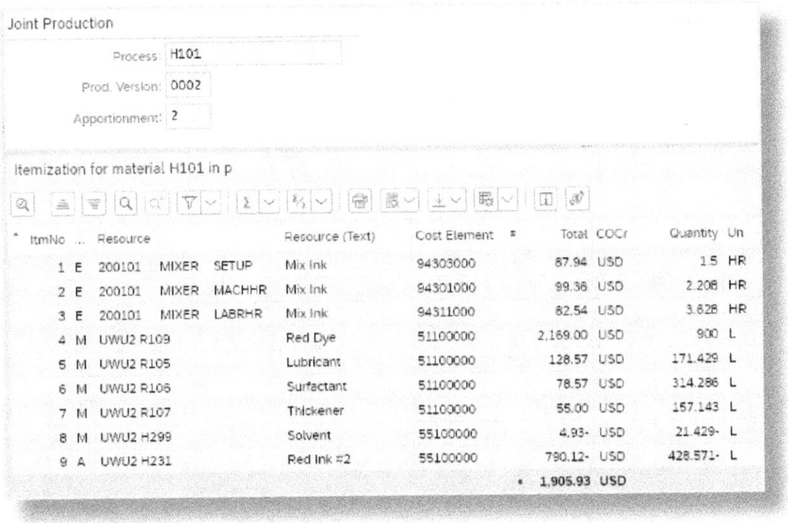
Joint Production

Process: H101

Prod. Version: 0002

Apportionment: 2

Itemization for material H101 in p

ItmNo	...	Resource	Resource (Text)	Cost Element	Total	COCr	Quantity	Un
1	E	200101 MIXER SETUP	Mix Ink	94303000	87.94	USD	1.5	HR
2	E	200101 MIXER MACHHR	Mix Ink	94301000	99.36	USD	2.208	HR
3	E	200101 MIXER LABRHR	Mix Ink	94311000	82.54	USD	3.628	HR
4	M	UWU2 R109	Red Dye	51100000	2,169.00	USD	900	L
5	M	UWU2 R105	Lubricant	51100000	128.57	USD	171.429	L
6	M	UWU2 R106	Surfactant	51100000	78.57	USD	314.286	L
7	M	UWU2 R107	Thickener	51100000	55.00	USD	157.143	L
8	M	UWU2 H299	Solvent	55100000	4.93-	USD	21.429-	L
9	A	UWU2 H231	Red Ink #2	55100000	790.12-	USD	428.571-	L
					• 1,905.93	USD		

Figure 8.22: Primary co-product itemization with source structure

Figure 8.22 shows the resulting cost estimate with a value of 1,905.93 USD per 1,000 L, or 1.91 USD per L. Figure 8.23 shows the cost estimate for material H231.

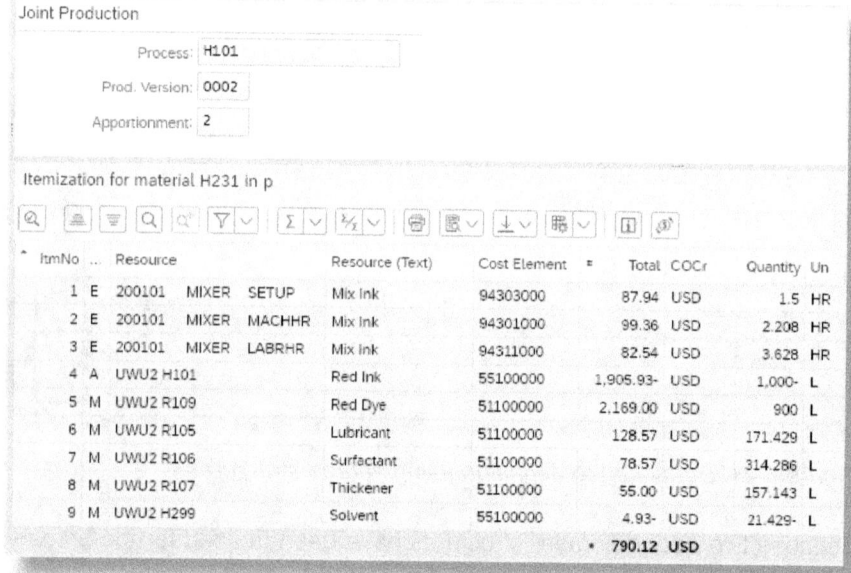

Figure 8.23: Subsidiary co-product itemization

The costing lot size is 428.571 based on the BOM definition, as it was in the example in Section 8.2.1. The resulting cost is then 790.12 USD per 428.571 L, or 1.84 USD per L. This results in a better distribution of the costs between the co-products.

9 Costing run

Companies normally have hundreds or thousands of materials that need cost estimates. It would be exceedingly difficult to cost all of these products individually. The costing run allows for multiple materials to be costed together, eliminating the need to work with materials one by one.

9.1 Costing run

Creating cost estimates individually can be extremely time-consuming. The costing run enables multiple materials to be costed together, thereby generating the cost estimates for all the selected materials. For costing variants that are used for material master update, marking and releasing steps can also be performed from the costing run. Mass costing using costing runs is available for all costing variants used for material cost estimates, but the costing run can only be used for cost estimates with quantity structure.

Costing runs have been traditionally managed with the SAPGUI transaction CK40N. However, as of S/4HANA version 1809, a new Fiori app has been developed, called Manage Costing Runs—Estimated Costs (see Figure 9.1).

Figure 9.1: Manage Costing Runs Fiori tile

The Fiori app provides an enhanced interface for accessing, creating, and running costing runs. New runs can be created either from scratch or by copying other runs. As of S/4HANA release 1809, runs can be set to repeat automatically at selected intervals, eliminating the need to create new runs manually each time. This has replaced two other Fiori apps, used for editing and deleting costing runs, which replicated the SAPGUI transactions

CK40N and CK44. These two transactions are still available in the system. The Fiori app has an enhanced search strategy using multiple parameters to show a list of only those runs that match the desired characteristics.

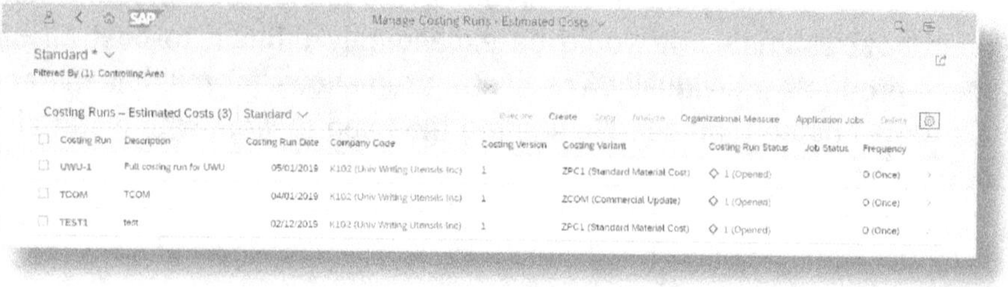

Figure 9.2: Selecting a costing run from the Fiori app

Figure 9.2 shows the window used to select a costing run to process. Click on the CREATE button to create a new costing run or choose one from the list.

A costing run is made up of three sections, as shown in Figure 9.3. The GENERAL DATA section defines the costing parameters used for all the cost estimates. The PROCESSING section contains the definition of the steps used to generate the cost estimates. The COSTING RESULTS section shows the list of materials selected and the results of selecting and costing at a high level.

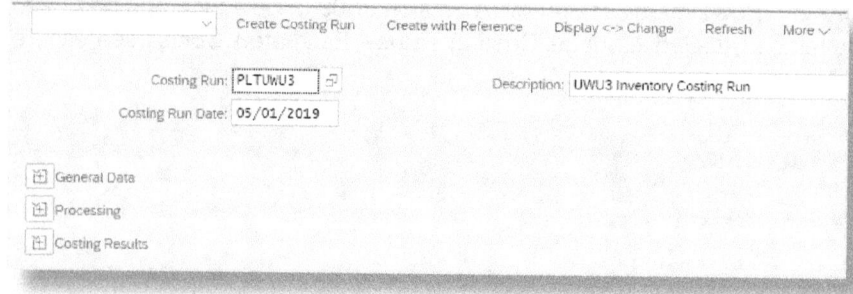

Figure 9.3: Costing run sections

9.1.1 General data section

The GENERA DATA section enables you to define the costing environment used when creating the cost estimates. There are four tabs of information.

Figure 9.4: Costing data for costing run

Figure 9.4 shows the COSTING DATA tab. This is similar to the costing data assigned for a single cost estimate, but some additional information is required. CONTROLLING AREA and COMPANY CODE must be defined. Costing lot size is not an available option, because it must be specified for all materials in the costing run. The same costing lot size is not necessarily applicable to all materials being costed. Although the company code must be selected, if cross-company code costing is enabled for the costing variant, then materials from multiple company codes can be costed within the same costing run. The SERVER GROUP setting is used to speed up processing. Materials are costed in levels, so there should be no interference when costing multiple materials simultaneously. When the SERVER GROUP is set up, the costing, marking, and release steps can be defined for parallel processing, allowing for two or more materials to be processed at the same time.

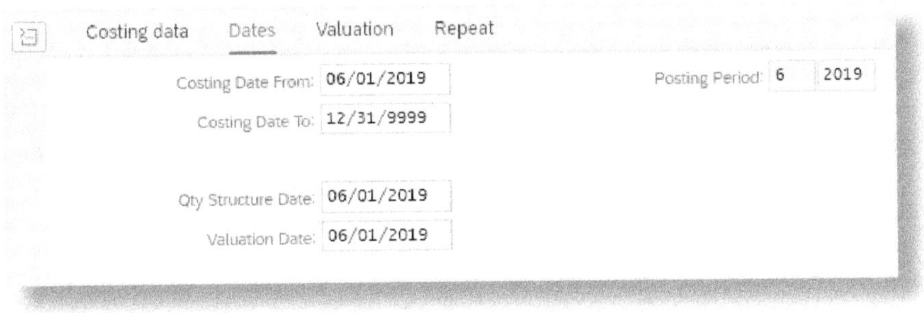

Figure 9.5: Dates selected for costing run

The DATES tab, shown in Figure 9.5, uses the default dates defined for the costing variant. If update is allowed by the costing variant, these dates can be changed.

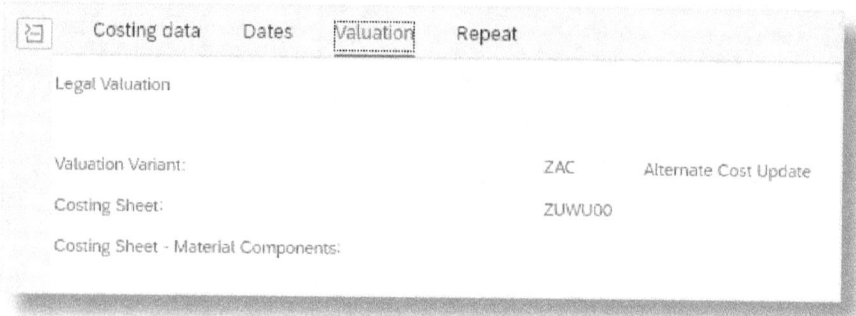

Figure 9.6: Valuation selections for costing run

The VALUATION tab, shown in Figure 9.6, is only informational. It shows the valuation data defined for the costing variant.

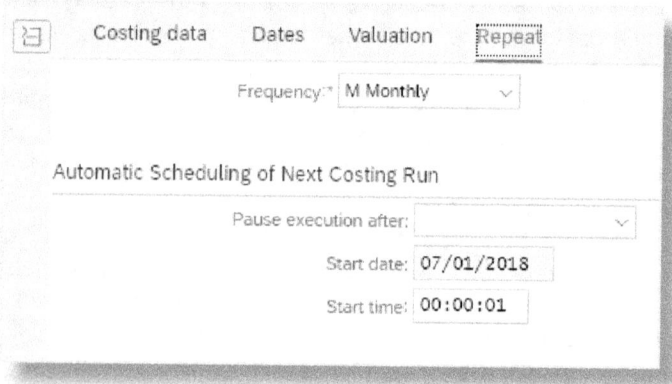

Figure 9.7: Costing run repeat setup

With S/4HANA release 1809, costing runs now offer a recurrence feature. This makes it possible to execute a costing run on a monthly, quarterly, or yearly basis without having to manually create the run each time. The REPEAT tab, shown in Figure 9.7, enables the parameters for a recurring costing run to be defined. If the costing run is only to run once, then the AUTOMATIC SCHEDULING OF NEXT COSTING RUN section is blank.

9.1.2 Processing section

Up to five flow steps can be defined for the costing run depending on the costing variant that is used. Prior to S/4HANA release 1809, a sixth step (Structure Explosion) was also used, but this has now been incorporated within the selection step. The steps are: SELECTION, COSTING, ANALYSIS, MARKING, and either RELEASE or PRICE UPDATE. Figure 9.8 shows only four steps and uses PRICE UPDATE instead of RELEASE which indicates that this is a costing run for an inventory costing variant that updates the auxiliary price fields in the material master. Costing variants that do not have the ability to update the material master only have the use of the first three steps because marking and price updates are not available for them.

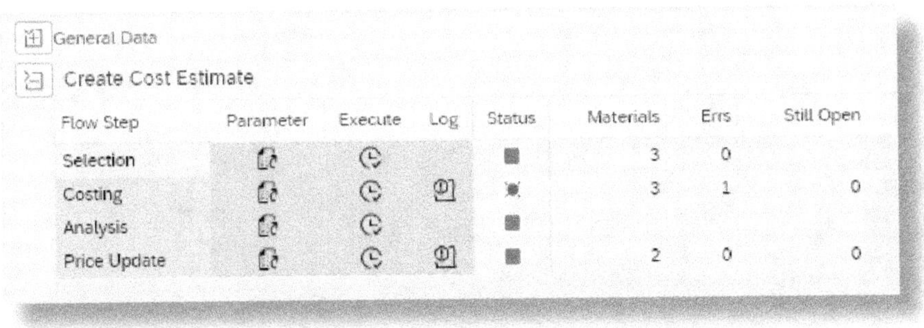

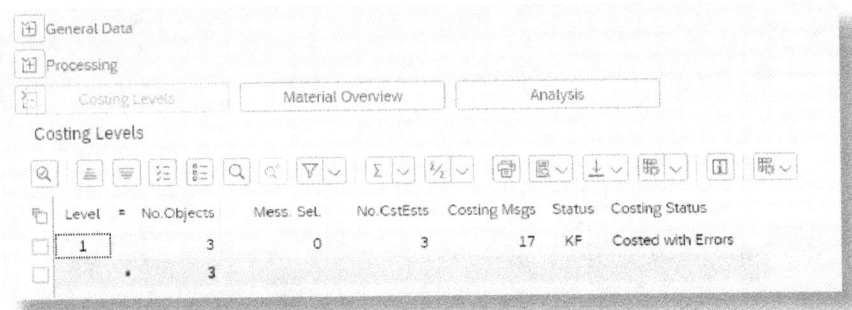

Figure 9.8: Processing section for costing run

9.1.3 Costing results section

There are three possible views in the COSTING RESULTS section. This section does not become active until after the selection step is processed.

Figure 9.9: Costing levels processed for costing run

The default display (see Figure 9.9) shows the costing levels from the selection process. This gives an overview of the costing process for each costing level. The costing run in the example only has one level. The costing level defines a group of materials that should be costed prior to the next higher level and is indicative of a material's place in the fully exploded BOM structure. This is updated after each costing run step, except the ANALYSIS step, and shows the number of materials for each level, the number of logged messages for that level, and the highest status for any material in the level. If any material's status indicates an error, the error status is displayed for the level. Click on the COSTING LEVELS button to return to this if one of the other reports has been selected.

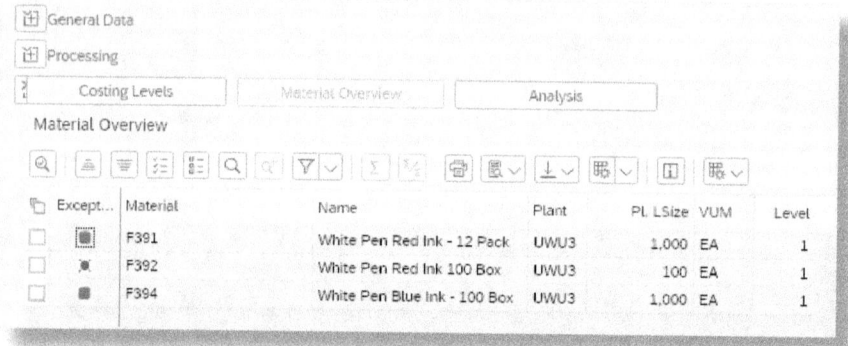

Figure 9.10: Materials processed in costing run

Click on the MATERIAL OVERVIEW button to see the list of materials selected, regardless of level (see Figure 9.10). Every material that was selected, along with its status, is included in the report. If the costing step has been executed, double click on a material to set the cost estimate details for that material.

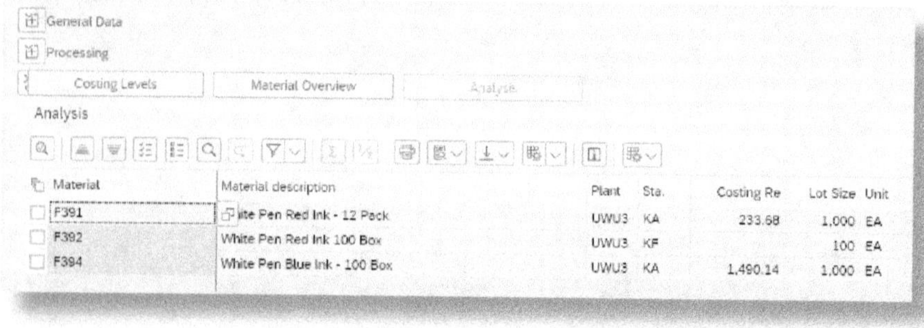

Figure 9.11: Analysis report for costing run

The analysis report is only available after the analysis step has run. Click on the ANALYSIS button to see the report (see Figure 9.11). The detail cost estimate can also be displayed by double clicking on a material.

9.2 Creating a costing run

The costing run creation process differs slightly, depending on whether transaction CK40N or the Fiori app is used. Click on the ▢ button to create a new costing run. Parameters are entered using the tabs described in Section 9.1.1. Using the Manage Costing Runs—Estimated Costs Fiori app, click on the CREATE button.

Figure 9.12 shows the Fiori window displayed when creating a new costing run. For ease of input, this combines the information from several tabs in the costing run GENERAL DATA section. In section ❶, under BASIC DATA, a name and date are assigned to the costing run. Section ❷ is used to load the costing parameters for the COSTING DATA tab. In Section ❸, the costing dates for the DATES tab are assigned. The radio buttons and fields in section ❹ determine whether the costing run will be processed on a recurring basis, and how often. This is accessible from the REPEATS tab. Section ❺ displays the VALUATION data associated with the costing variant selected. This is available on an existing costing run in the VALUATION tab.

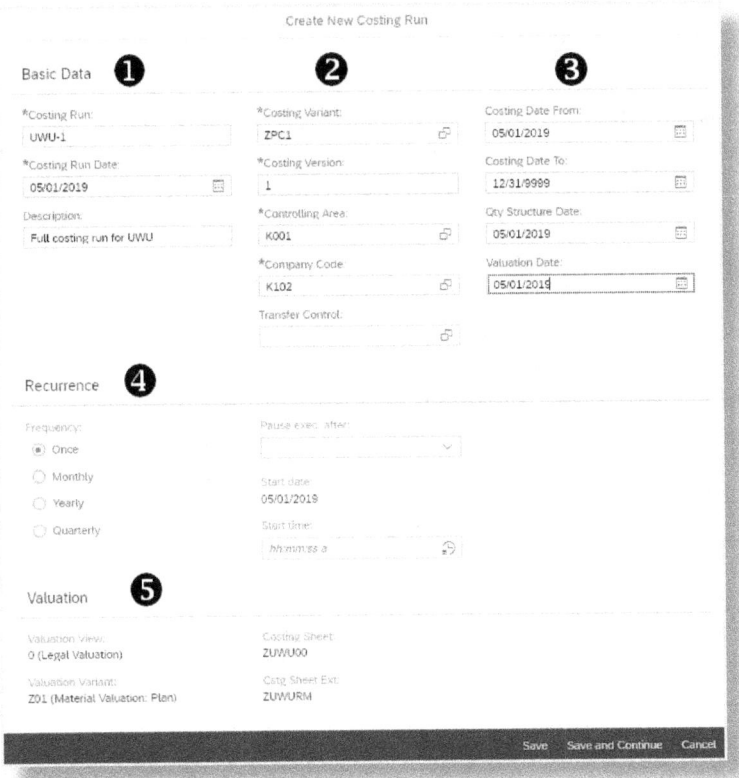

Figure 9.12: Creating a costing run in Fiori

As of S/4HANA release 1809, costing runs offer a recurrence feature. Recurrence allows a costing run to be executed on a monthly, quarterly, or yearly basis without having to manually create the run each time. When the costing run is created, you can define a recurrence frequency and the step after which execution of the next run should stop. The next run is then scheduled automatically after completion of the current run, and the start date is set based on the recurrence frequency. Upon completion of the specified step, processing pauses to allow you to check the results before continuing. To use this feature effectively, the date control configuration should be defined to use the costing date, quantity structure date, and valuation date matching the frequency assigned to the costing run. Because the new costing run is scheduled at the time the current costing run is executed, the costing date should be set to represent a future date. If monthly recurrence is selected, set the COSTING DATE FROM selection in the data control configuration to N—START OF NEXT MONTH or F—START OF NEXT POSTING PERIOD. Likewise, if the recurrence is defined as yearly, set it to J—START OF NEXT FISCAL YEAR. There is no date option for quarters, so the dates for a quarterly run need to be adjusted manually once it has been automatically created. For details on configuring the date control settings, see book one of this set "SAP® S/4HANA Product Cost Planning Configuration and Master Data".

After the initial creation of the costing run, costing run parameters can still be changed. Changes can occur until the time that the first step is executed.

9.3 Selection

The purpose of the selection step is to define the list of materials to be costed and to set up the order in which they are costed. The list of materials can be defined directly within the selection step, or the selection step can use the materials from another costing run or from a specially defined selection list. First, the list of parameters specifying the selection criteria must be defined. Prior to this definition, the PROCESSING SECTION looks like that shown in Figure 9.13.

To update the selection parameters, click on the 📝 button (▶ in CK40N) on the SELECTION line. Figure 9.14 shows the top portion of the selection parameter window.

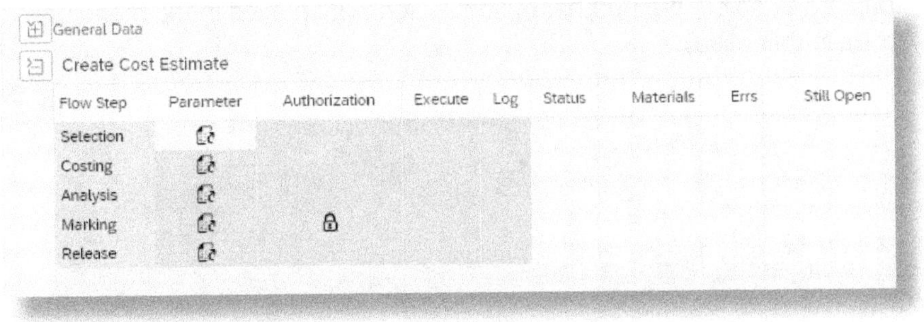

Figure 9.13: Empty processing section

9.3.1 Material selections

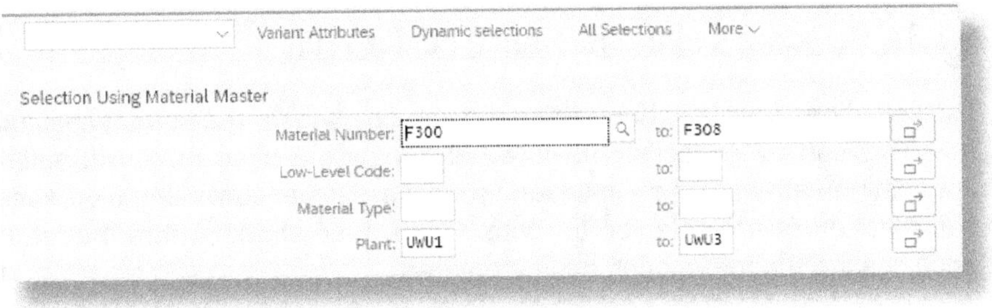

Figure 9.14: Selections using material master

Ranges of materials, low-level codes, material types, and plants can be entered. LOW-LEVEL CODE is a planning field that indicates the lowest bill of material level in which the material appears. In this case, the specific range of materials F300 through F308, for plants UWU1, UWU2, and UWU3, are selected.

9.3.2 Dynamic selections

Dynamic selections allow for a further refinement in selecting the materials than with the standard options. Click on DYNAMIC SELECTIONS (in CK40N). A list is displayed, showing additional fields in the material master, which can be used in the selection process. Figure 9.15 shows two additional fields: DF AT CLIENT LEVEL (global deletion flag) and DF AT PLANT LEVEL (deletion flag for the plant). Only if neither of the deletion checkboxes is selected for a material, will it be included in the costing run. When dynamic selections are enabled, the number of fields used is displayed in the menu bar (2 ACTIVE in this case).

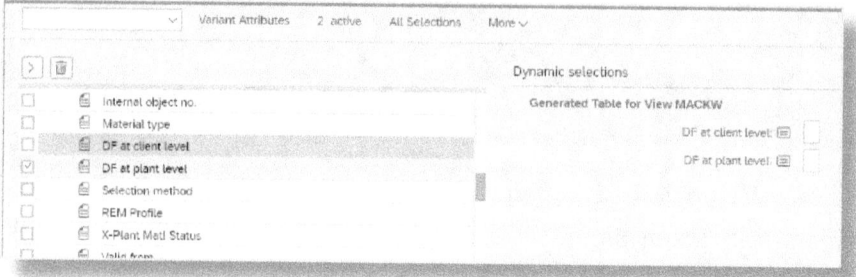

Figure 9.15: Dynamic selections

9.3.3 Selections using reference costing run

The selections from another costing run can be used for the current costing run. This can be especially useful when creating costing runs with different costing variants for comparison purposes. This ensures that the exact same materials are selected for both. Figure 9.16 shows where the reference costing run information can be entered.

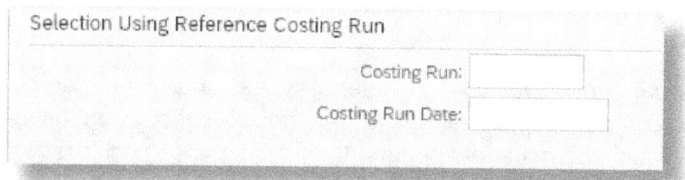

Figure 9.16: Selections using reference costing run

9.3.4 Selections with a selection list

Selection lists can be created for use as the source of materials to be processed in the costing run. For example, the Display Materials To Be Costed Fiori app (SAPGUI transaction CKAPP01) can create a list of materials that, as yet, have not been costed, and which can be used in costing runs. Enter the SELECTION LIST, as shown in Figure 9.17.

Figure 9.17: Selections using selection list

9.3.5 Additional selection criteria

Valuation class can be used as an additional selection option to specify the materials to be costed. Figure 9.18 shows where valuation class can be entered, if desired.

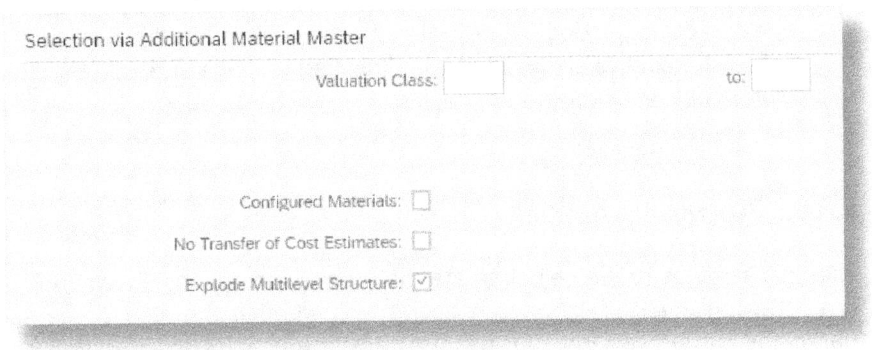

Figure 9.18: Additional selection criteria

There are also three checkboxes that can be selected, that affect the behavior of the costing run:

- CONFIGURED MATERIALS—when this is selected, only configured materials (see Chapter 4) are included in the selection. If this is not selected, then only non-configured materials are included. If an implementation has a mix of configured and non-configured materials, two separate costing runs are required to make sure that all materials are costed.

- NO TRANSFER OF COST ESTIMATES—in system versions prior to S/4HANA release 1809, this was also known as ALWAYS RECOST MATERIAL. If this is not selected, the system uses the transfer control setting of the costing variant to determine if a material is to be included in the selection. Any material with an existing cost estimate that would not be recosted based on the transfer control setting is not included in the selection list. For example, materials with a currently released standard cost estimate for the year would not be selected for a standard cost costing variant. If this checkbox is selected, then the setting for transfer control is overridden and the material is recosted. This setting does not impact any materials that are included in the structure explosion based on the exploded bill of materials for a material in the selection list. If the material is not in the primary selection, then transfer control settings always apply.

▶ EXPLODE MULTILEVEL STRUCTURE—As of S/4HANA release 1809, quantity structure explosion is now part of the selection step rather than a separate, optional step in the process flow. Based on the material in the primary selection, if this parameter is set, all materials in the exploded bill of materials are included in the cost run if transfer control allows for it. Use this flag to make sure all possible materials are processed.

9.3.6 Processing options

The final settings for the selection are the processing options shown in Figure 9.19. BACKGROUND PROCESSING determines whether the step is run as part of the current session, or run in the background. If BACKGROUND PROCESSING is chosen, a batch job is created that can either be run immediately or scheduled to run at some time in the future. PRINT LOG determines whether the log generated by the step is sent to the print spooler or just made available for viewing from the costing run. A log is created if messages are generated as part of the process.

Figure 9.19: Processing options

9.3.7 Executing the selection step

After all the parameters have been entered and saved, the step is now ready to execute (see Figure 9.20). It does not have to be executed at this time, and the other costing run steps can be configured prior to executing this step.

Figure 9.20: Selection ready to execute

Clicking on the button in the EXECUTE column processes the step. Figure 9.21 shows the successful completion of the operation. The status reflects the most severe message status for any of the materials processed. Green indicates that the highest message for any of the materials is informational only, or that no messages were generated. Yellow indicates that at least one of the materials had a warning message, and red indicates that at least one material had an error message. If the button is displayed in the LOG column, a log file is available for viewing.

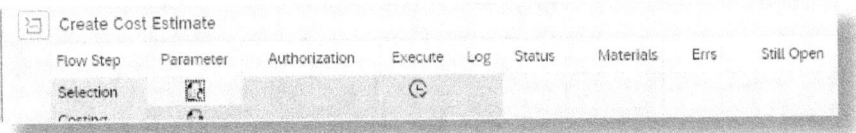

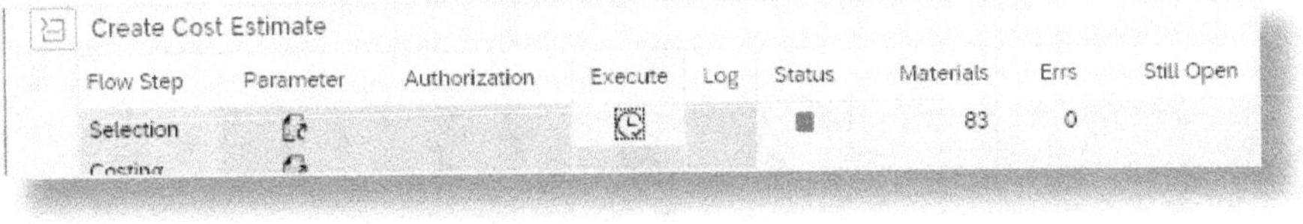

Figure 9.21: Selection execution complete

A primary function of the selection step is to determine the order in which the materials should be costed. This is done using costing levels. The lowest level materials are those that have no lower level components in the selection list. These reside in level 1. The next level up has materials that use the level 1 materials as components. The next level includes at least some of its components from level 2 and can also include level 1 materials. This continues until the highest level material is reached. Figure 9.22 shows that five levels have been determined for this costing run. When the costing step is executed, level 1 is processed first, then level 2, and so on, until level 5 is complete. This ensures that materials are only costed once.

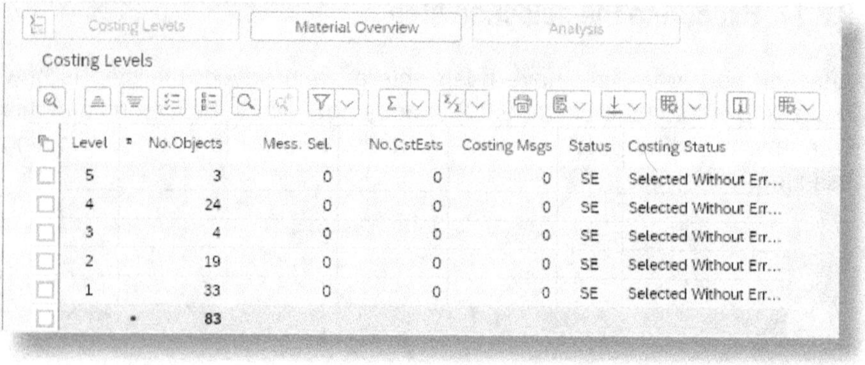

Level	No.Objects	Mess. Sel.	No.CstEsts	Costing Msgs	Status	Costing Status
5	3	0	0	0	SE	Selected Without Err...
4	24	0	0	0	SE	Selected Without Err...
3	4	0	0	0	SE	Selected Without Err...
2	19	0	0	0	SE	Selected Without Err...
1	33	0	0	0	SE	Selected Without Err...
·	83					

Figure 9.22: Costing levels after selection

9.4 Costing

9.4.1 Defining costing step parameters

The costing run creates cost estimates level by level, based on the selections in the previous step. Figure 9.23 shows the parameters used to control the material costing process.

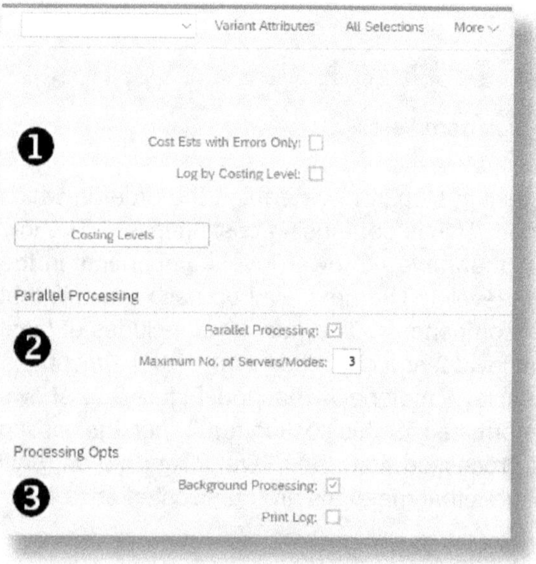

Figure 9.23: Costing step parameters

Section ❶ contains processing options. The COST ESTS WITH ERRORS ONLY checkbox can be selected when repeating a costing run in order to only cost those materials that had costing errors (status KF) from the previous time this particular costing step was executed. Be careful when choosing this option because there are times when material cost estimates with a status KA contain components that costed with errors, making the upper level cost invalid. LOG BY COSTING LEVEL is selected in order to create multiple logs based on level. This is usually set when a large number of errors is expected from the costing run. The costing step can also be run for specific costing levels. This is only available if NO TRANSFER OF COST ESTIMATES is not chosen in the selection step. Click on the COSTING LEVELS button and the selection window in Figure 9.24 is then displayed. Deselect the levels that shouldn't be costed.

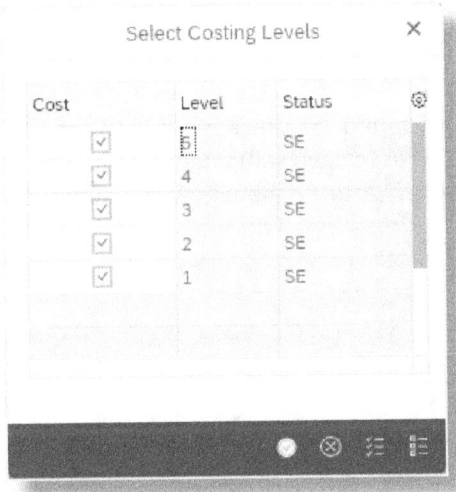

Figure 9.24: Costing level selection window

Section ❷, PARALLEL PROCESSING in Figure 9.23, contains the settings for running simultaneous cost estimates. Select PARALLEL PROCESSING and then enter the number of processes. To avoid system issues, check with the system administrator to determine the maximum number that should be selected.

Section ❸ contains the settings for how the step should be run. Select BACKGROUND PROCESSING when there is a large number of materials to be costed. Select PRINT LOG only if it is necessary to have a printed copy. The log is available for viewing within the costing run. Save the settings when complete.

9.4.2 Executing the costing step

After the settings are saved, the ⏵ button is displayed in the EXECUTE column next to the COSTING step. Click on that button to start the costing function. If background processing has been selected, enter the runtime information. If a background job has been requested, clicking on the REFRESH button (SAPGUI 🗘) shows the current status of the step. Figure 9.25 shows the costing step partially complete, with 27 materials still to be costed.

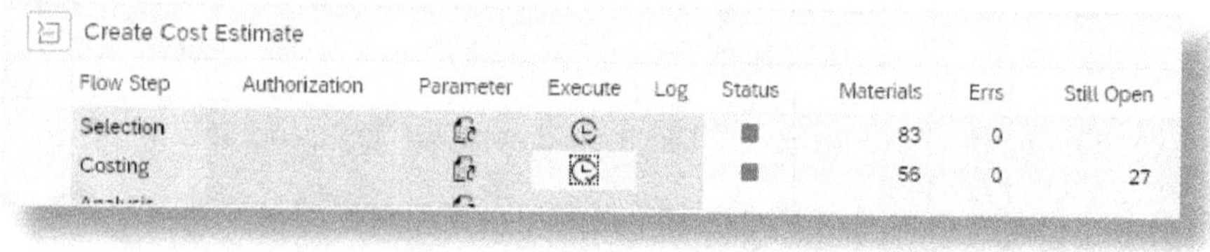

Figure 9.25: Step progress information

When the step is complete, the COSTING LEVELS display shows the resulting status and number of messages generated. Figure 9.26 shows that the status for all cost estimates was set to KA (costed without errors). However, messages were generated when some of the materials were costed on levels 1, 2, and 3.

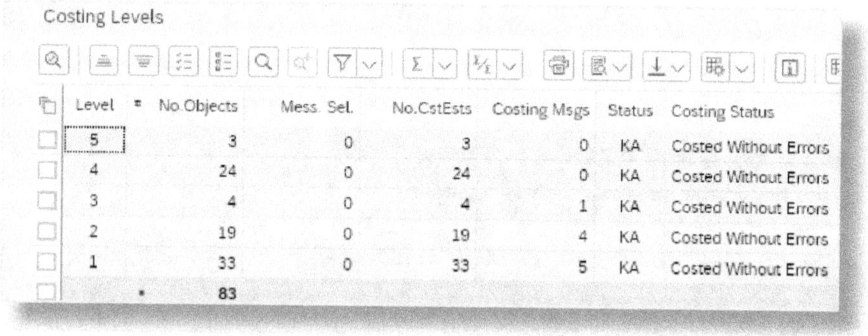

Figure 9.26: Level status after costing

Click on the 📄 button next to any step to display the messages for that step. Figure 9.27 shows the log. Although all the messages are informational only, these messages show problems with several of the cost estimates that are likely to cause the resulting costs to be incorrect. A good practice is to check on the costing messages before going on to the next step, even if there are no warnings or errors logged.

COSTING RUN

Information	10					
Warnings						
Error						
Total	10					

Except...	Msg. Ty...	Material	Plant	AppAr	MsgNo	Message Text
■	I	R101	UWU2	CK	776	No valid source of supply found for material R101 plant UWU2
■	I	R102	UWU2	CK	776	No valid source of supply found for material R102 plant UWU2
■	I	R103	UWU2	CK	776	No valid source of supply found for material R103 plant UWU2
■	I	R104	UWU2	CK	776	No valid source of supply found for material R104 plant UWU2
■	I	R100	UWU2	CK	776	No valid source of supply found for material R100 plant UWU2
■	I	H103	UWU2	CK	361	Value of costing item 00004 in itemization is 0
■	I	H104	UWU2	CK	361	Value of costing item 00004 in itemization is 0
■	I	H105	UWU2	CK	361	Value of costing item 00004 in itemization is 0
■	I	H106	UWU2	CK	361	Value of costing item 00005 in itemization is 0
■	I	H107	UWU2	CK	361	Value of costing item 00005 in itemization is 0

Figure 9.27: Log generated from costing step

9.5 Analysis

The ANALYSIS step is not necessary for the completion of the costing run, but it is useful and provides a good overview of the costs of all the selected materials. After clicking on the ⊞ button, a list of report variants is displayed. Each variant defines a specific set of options that can be used when creating the report. Figure 9.28 shows the variant SAP&COCKPIT selected.

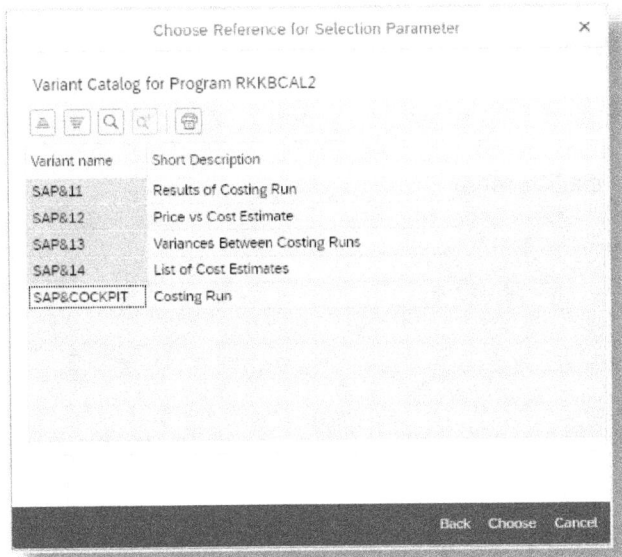

Figure 9.28: Analysis report variant selection

189

The selections in Figure 9.29 are displayed. Report selections can be made from here. Click on the ALL SELECTIONS button (for CK40N) to open up additional report selection criteria, including the selection of a specific report layout.

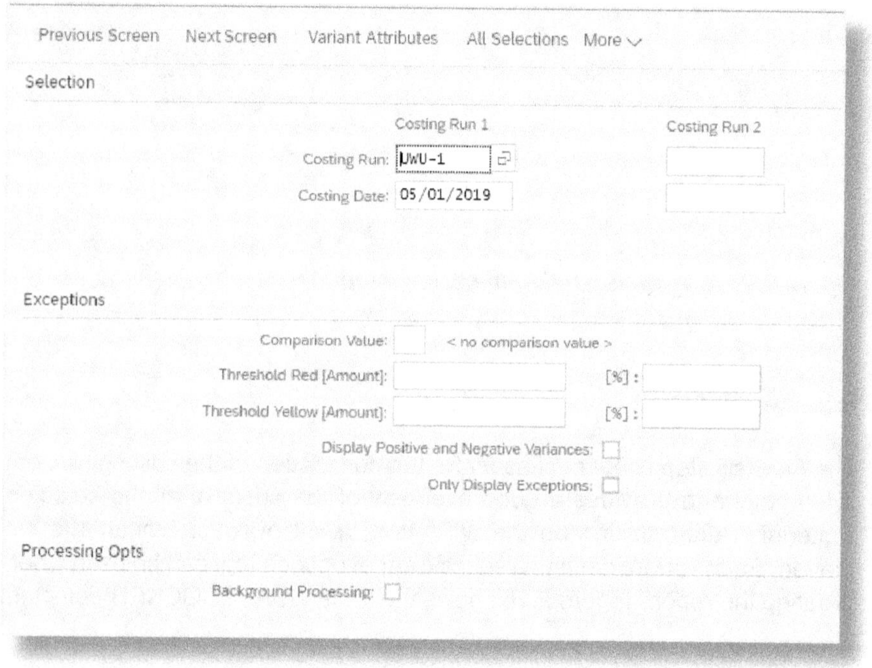

Figure 9.29: Selections for the report

Execute the report. Figure 9.30 shows the report resulting from the selections. This is also made available for the ANALYSIS button of the COSTING RESULTS section of the costing run.

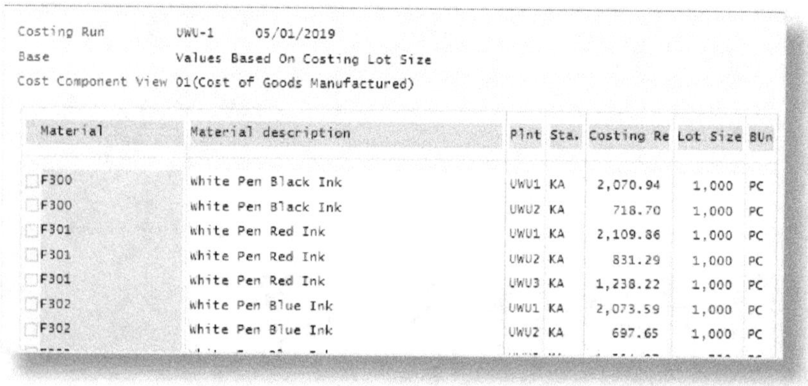

```
Costing Run        UWU-1     05/01/2019
Base               Values Based On Costing Lot Size
Cost Component View 01(Cost of Goods Manufactured)
```

Material	Material description	Plnt	Sta.	Costing Re	Lot Size	BUn
F300	white Pen Black Ink	UWU1	KA	2,070.94	1,000	PC
F300	white Pen Black Ink	UWU2	KA	718.70	1,000	PC
F301	white Pen Red Ink	UWU1	KA	2,109.86	1,000	PC
F301	white Pen Red Ink	UWU2	KA	831.29	1,000	PC
F301	white Pen Red Ink	UWU3	KA	1,238.22	1,000	PC
F302	white Pen Blue Ink	UWU1	KA	2,073.59	1,000	PC
F302	white Pen Blue Ink	UWU2	KA	697.65	1,000	PC

Figure 9.30: Analysis report

9.6 Marking

The marking step is only assigned to a costing run if the costing type assigned to the costing variant has PRICE UPDATE set to STANDARD PRICE.

9.6.1 Enabling marking

Marking must be enabled for the period of the costing run. If it is not enabled for the selected costing run, the lock icon is displayed in the AUTHORIZATION column (see Figure 9.31).

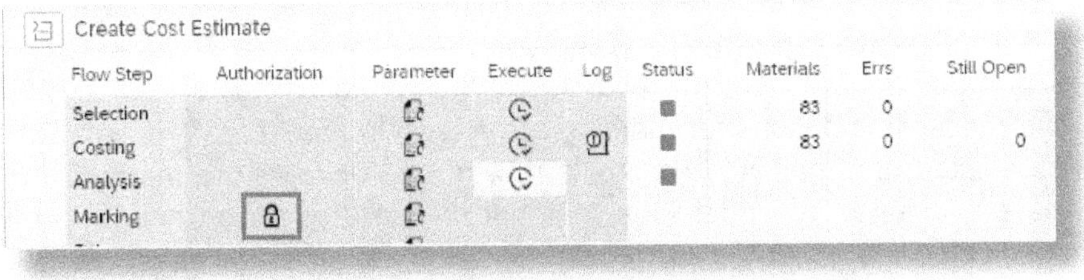

Figure 9.31: Lock icon for marking step

Click on the lock icon to enable marking for the period associated with the costing run. Select the company code and then make sure the COSTING VARIANT and COSTING VERSION of the costing run are entered (see Figure 9.32). If cross-company code costing is enabled in the costing variant, make sure that all company codes used in the costing run are processed. When complete, the 🔓 icon replaces the closed lock icon.

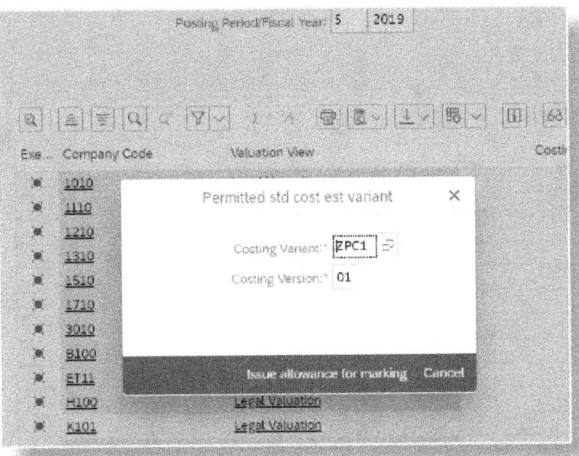

Figure 9.32: Unlocking marking for the period

> **Issuing the marking allowance**
>
>
> The Manage Costing Run – Estimated Costs Fiori app enables marking for multiple company codes and periods, without creating a costing run with a MARKING step. Click on the ORGANIZATIONAL MEASURE button at the top of the costing run selection window. A list of company codes and periods is displayed. Select the company code/period combinations to update and then enter the costing variant and costing version to enable marking.

9.6.2 Defining marking parameters

The processing options for marking are shown in Figure 9.33. If TEST RUN is selected, the marking process is run, but no updates are made to the material master. To update the material master, this option needs to be deselected. WITH LIST OUTPUT provides a list of the materials along with the new values to be loaded. If the operation is run in the background, this is a spooled report. Otherwise, it is displayed as part of the step completion processing. If PARALLEL PROCESSING is selected, the SERVER GROUP/NUMBER OF SES. information is displayed. Enter the parallel processor and the number of sessions. The usual default is 5. The BACKGROUND PROCESSING option determines if the operation is run in the current session or as a background job. Select this option if there are a large number of materials to mark.

Figure 9.33: Marking parameters

9.6.3 Executing the marking step

Click on the ⓒ button to execute the marking step. The log file displays the number of materials that were successfully marked and shows any errors that occurred. Figure 9.34 is an example of the marking report that is generated if WITH LIST OUTPUT is selected. If group and company code currencies are different, the value of both is displayed in the report.

Material	Plnt	Val. Type	Sta.	Executed	Crcy type	Crcy	Plan. Pr.	Std price	MvAvgPrice	per	Pr.	with QS	CENo	Currency and Valn.	Valuation view
F305	UWL2		VO	3	10	USD	69.77	0.01	0.00	100	S	E	100009926	Company code currency	Legal Valuation
F305	UWL2		VO	3	30	EUR	55.82	0.01	0.00	100	S	E	100009926	Group currency	Legal Valuation
F305	UWL3		VO	3	10	USD	108.52	0.01	0.00	100	S	E	100010931	Company code currency	Legal Valuation
F305	UWL3		VO	3	30	EUR	86.82	0.01	0.00	100	S	E	100010931	Group currency	Legal Valuation
F302	UWL2		VO	3	10	USD	69.77	0.01	0.00	100	S	E	100009920	Company code currency	Legal Valuation
F302	UWL2		VO	3	30	EUR	55.82	0.01	0.00	100	S	E	100009920	Group currency	Legal Valuation
F302	UWL3		VO	3	10	USD	189.98	0.01	0.00	100	S	E	100010602	Company code currency	Legal Valuation

Figure 9.34: Marking report

9.7 Cost updates

Two different types of material cost updates can be processed in the costing run. If the step is labeled RELEASE, the standard cost is updated from the marked cost. This is only available when the costing type of the costing variant has PRICE UPDATE set to STANDARD PRICE. Three other price updates are supported for a costing type: TAX-BASED PRICE, COMMERCIAL PRICE, and PRICES OTHER THAN STANDARD PRICE. If the costing type is defined for any of these price updates, then the final step is labeled PRICE UPDATE. For a full explanation of the different types of price updates, see book one of this set "SAP® S/4HANA Product Cost Planning Configuration and Master Data".

9.7.1 Defining release parameters

The parameters associated with executing the RELEASE step are the same as those for the MARKING step. Figure 9.35 shows the settings with PARALLEL PROCESSING not selected. BACKGROUND PROCESSING is recommended in order to release standard costs for a future date. This allows the cost estimates to be released automatically just after midnight on the first day of the period without having to manually process the RELEASE step at the proper time. Costs can only be released during the period associated with the costing date. To release costs in the current period, either foreground or background processing can be used.

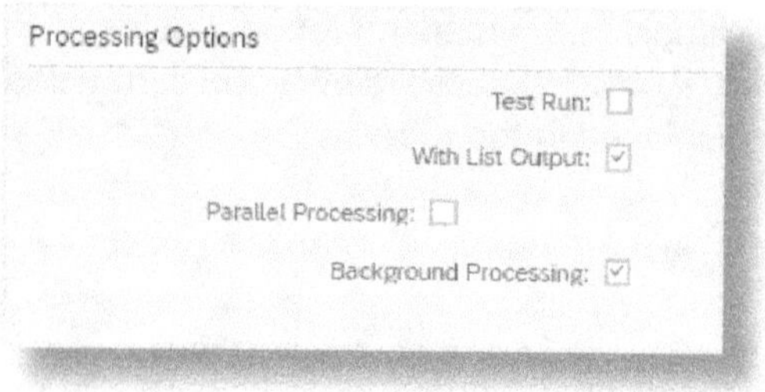

Figure 9.35: Release step parameters

9.7.2 Defining price update parameters

Figure 9.36 shows the parameters for the price update of a costing run using costing variant ZOTH. The costing type assigned to ZOTH has PRICE UPDATE defined as PRICES OTHER THAN STANDARD PRICE. Any of the nine updatable cost fields can be processed. For this cost run, COMMERCIAL PRICE 3 has been selected.

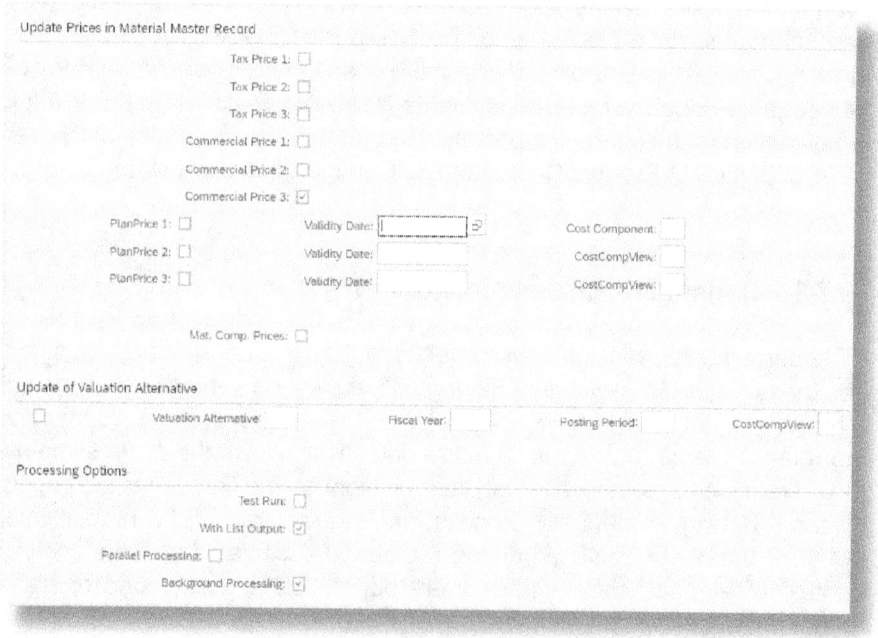

Figure 9.36: Price update parameters

If the costing type defines the PRICE UPDATE field to be TAX-BASED PRICE, then only the three tax prices can be selected. If the field is set to COMMERCIAL

PRICE, then only the three commercial prices can be selected. Because no time parameter is involved with these types of price updates, the jobs can be run either in the foreground or the background.

9.7.3 Executing the cost update step

Click on the ⟳ to process the cost update. A log is generated at completion of processing. If WITH LIST OUTPUT is selected, a report appropriate to the costing type of the costing variant is created. Figure 9.37 shows a portion of the list generated for the costing run using costing variant ZOTH. COMMERCIAL PRICE 3 is updated for the materials in the list.

Executed	Material	Plnt	Val. Type	Crcy	Price Unit	PrUnit	Tax prc.1	Tax pr. 2	Tax pr. 3	Comm.pr.1	Comm.pr.2	Com1 pr. 3	PlndPric
3	F391	UWU3		USD	0	100	0.00	0.00	0.00	0.00	0.00	254.89	0.00
3	F394	UWU3		USD	0	100	0.00	0.00	0.00	0.00	0.00	1,641.06	0.00

Figure 9.37: Price update report for other prices

Updates of standard prices can also generate inventory revaluations if the materials updated have stock quantities at the time of the update. Inventory revaluation documents are created for all materials. The document numbers are included in the step log.

9.8 Deleting costing runs

Costing run information can be deleted by using transaction CK44, or in the Manage Costing Runs – Estimated Costs Fiori app. When using the app, select the costing runs to be deleted (section ❶ of Figure 9.38). Next, click on the DELETE button (section ❷).

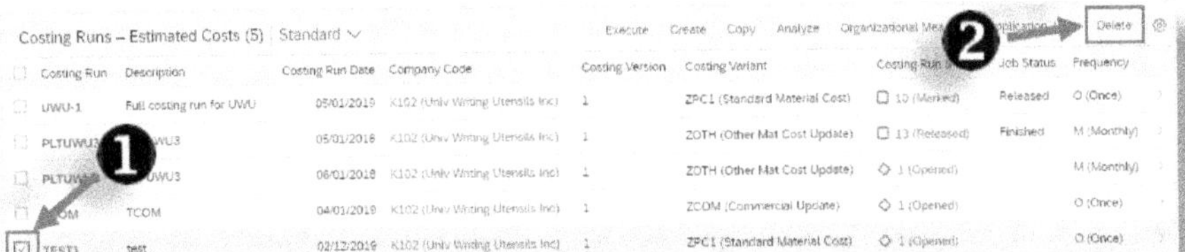

Figure 9.38: Selecting the costing runs to delete

A dialog box is displayed to confirm that the deletion process should be performed (see Figure 9.39). Click on the DELETE button to process the deletion.

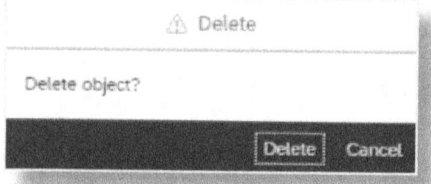

Figure 9.39: Delete dialog box

When a costing run is deleted, the selection list is deleted. Cost estimates, marking data, and release data are not deleted.

10 Alternative costing variants

Costing variants are used for much more than developing standard costs. Both books in this series have centered on developing standard costs. However, there are many other types of cost estimates that can be used to analyze the costs of materials. Some of these can be used for updating alternative fields in the material master, and others can be used for making alternative cost estimates for comparison purposes. This chapter provides a very high-level discussion of what these alternative costing variants can be used for.

10.1 Reference variants

The reference variant was introduced in book one "SAP® S/4HANA Product Cost Planning Configuration and Master Data". This is not a variant that can be used by itself for material costing. It is a means by which an existing cost estimate can be used as a building block for a new cost estimate. The resulting cost estimate can then be used for comparison purposes or for alternative valuation views of the materials. The benefit of using a reference variant is that there is no need to read the quantity structures used by the original cost estimate. There are two advantages to this. First, the costs are calculated faster because there is no need to search for a valid quantity structure. Second, because quantity structures can change over time, the costs generated using the reference variant are guaranteed to reflect the original quantity structure settings of the reference cost estimate.

To maintaining the reference variant, use transaction OKYC or follow IMG menu path CONTROLLING • PRODUCT COST CONTROLLING • PRODUCT COST PLANNING • MATERIAL COST ESTIMATE WITH QUANTITY STRUCTURE • COSTING VARIANT: COMPONENTS • DEFINE REFERENCE VARIANT. REFERENCE VARIANT 1 is defined to use current raw material prices, keeping all other costs from cost estimates using costing variant ZPC1 constant. The reference variant is then assigned to a new costing variant which uses the PLANNED PRICE 2 field in the material master to define an expected future raw material price. There are three tabs in the reference variant definition: COST ESTIMATE REF., RE-

VALUATION, and MISC. Figure 10.1 shows the COST ESTIMATE REF. tab, which defines the TRANSFER CONTROL. This is used to determine which costs are to be transferred from the existing cost estimate.

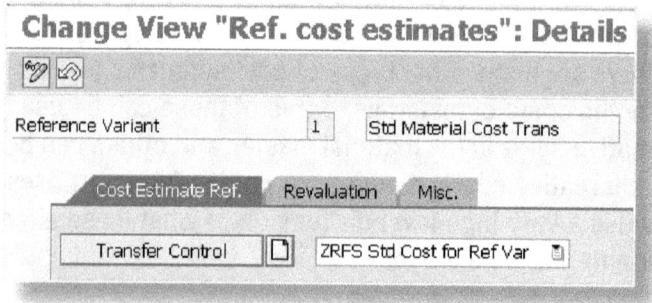

Figure 10.1: Cost estimate reference tab

A special transfer control is assigned here. This transfer control is set up to use an existing cost estimate of a specific costing variant as the source of costs. Figure 10.2 shows the use of the OTHER COST ESTIMATES strategy, along with a specific COSTING VARIANT (ZPC1) and COSTING VERSION. The PERIODS field is set to 999 to indicate that the most recent cost estimate is to be used. Transfer control configuration is processed using transaction OKKM or via IMG menu path CONTROLLING • PRODUCT COST CONTROLLING • PRODUCT COST PLANNING • MATERIAL COST ESTIMATE WITH QUANTITY STRUCTURE • COSTING VARIANT: COMPONENTS • DEFINE TRANSFER CONTROL. ONLY THE SINGLE-PLANT TAB IS APPLICABLE.

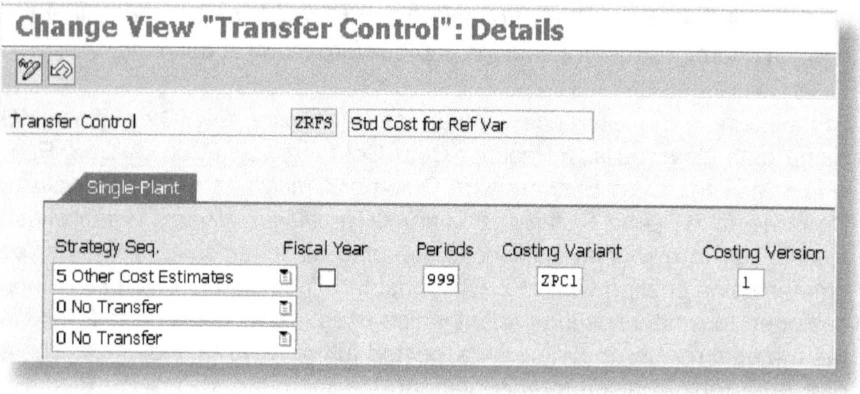

Figure 10.2: Reference variant transfer control definition

The REVALUATION tab of the reference variant configuration defines which costs are to be recalculated in the new cost estimate (see Figure 10.3). In this example, only MATERIAL COMPONENTS is selected for new costs calculation.

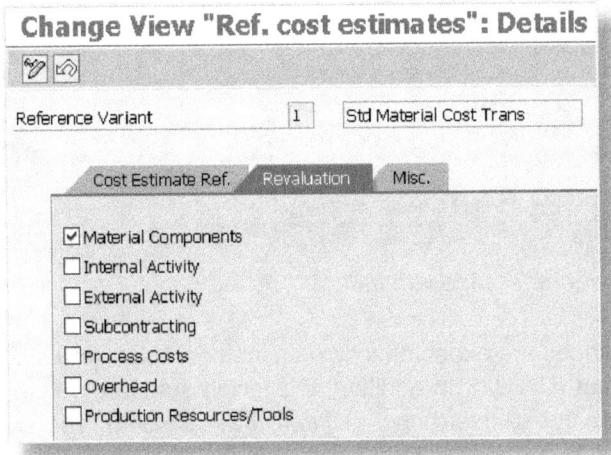

Figure 10.3: Defining components to revalue

The MISC. tab determines whether additive costs are to be transferred (see Figure 10.4).

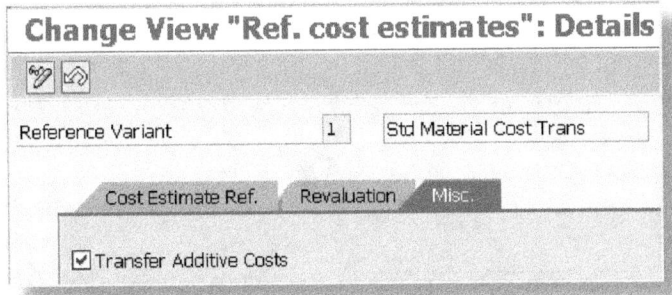

Figure 10.4: Defining behavior of additive costs

The reference variant can now be assigned to a costing variant. Figure 10.5 shows REFERENCE VARIANT 1 assigned to COSTING VARIANT ZRMC. This costing variant uses the PLANNED PRICE 2 field to store expected future raw material costs.

199

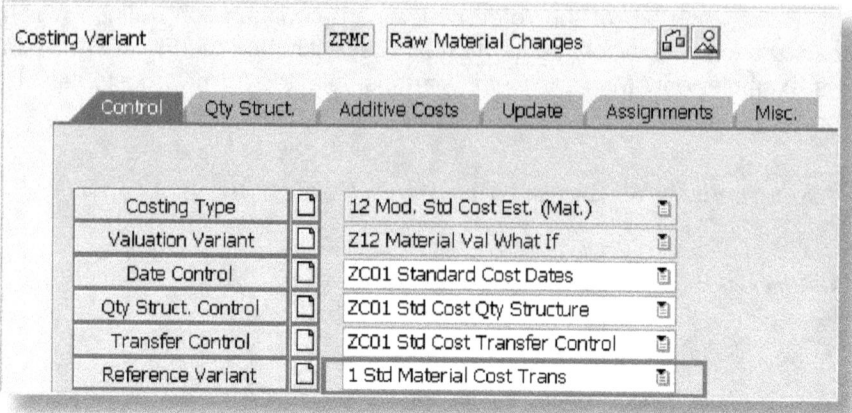

Figure 10.5: Assigning the reference variant

Raw material price changes are expected to impact material H101 (red ink) at the Los Angeles plant (UWU2). In addition, the recipe standard values have changed because the standard cost estimate was released. The expected raw material price increases have been entered into the PLANNED PRICE 2 fields of the raw materials. A cost estimate for this material is created using costing variant ZRMC (see Figure 10.5).

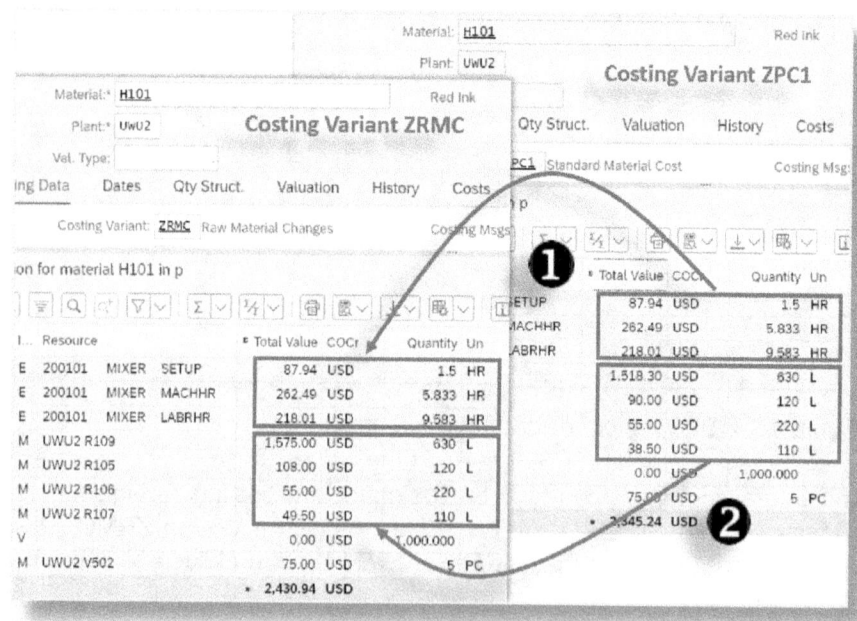

Figure 10.6: Cost estimate with reference variant

Figure 10.6 shows a comparison of the cost estimate using COSTING VARIANT ZRMC and the reference cost estimate using COSTING VARIANT ZPC1. Section ❶ shows that the activity costs and quantities remain the same even though the recipe standard values have changed. Section ❷ shows the updated raw material costs in the ZRMC cost estimate versus what was in the reference cost estimate.

10.2 Inventory costing

10.2.1 Tax-based and commercial inventory

SAP allows for the update of special inventory cost estimates using the lowest-value method of price determination. The system looks at goods movements and pricing history for raw materials in order to help determine a value that more accurately reflects the true worth of those purchased items. Using the values calculated for the purchased materials, inventory cost estimates can be made for manufactured materials to include these raw material values in order to get a truer picture of the costs for the intermediate materials and finished products. Special costing variants are created to generate these cost estimates, and the results can be updated in special fields on the ACCOUNTING 2 tab of the material master. Two sets of three values are updatable. There are three tax-based and three commercial inventory prices that use the lowest-value method when updating the costs. In Figure 10.7, section ❶ shows the tax-based price fields and section ❷ shows the commercial price fields.

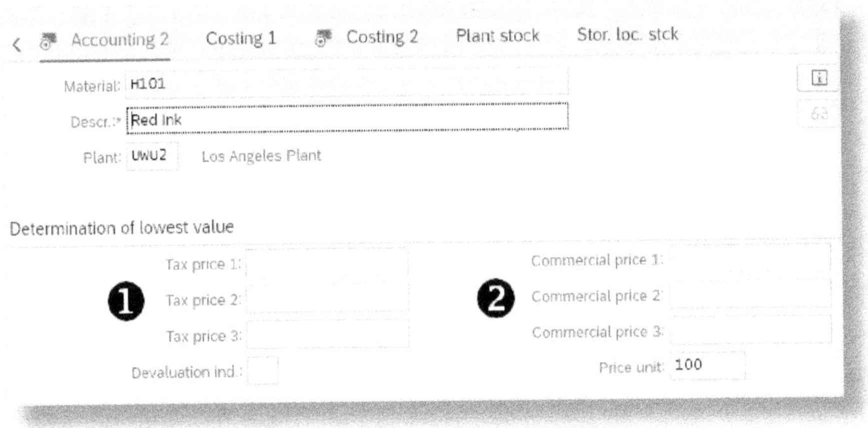

Figure 10.7: Lowest value inventory update fields

The costing type used by a costing variant for inventory costing must use one of two different price update strategies. The tax-based inventory updates must use TAX-BASED PRICE, as shown in Figure 10.8.

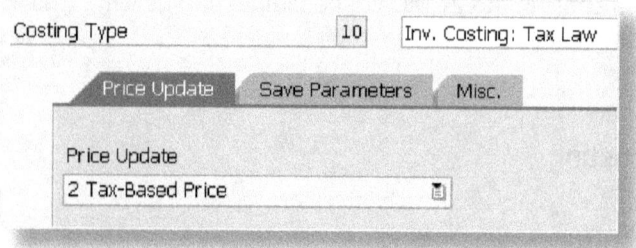

Figure 10.8: Tax-based price update configuration

Commercial inventory fields are updated when the costing type price update is set to COMMERCIAL PRICE (see Figure 10.9).

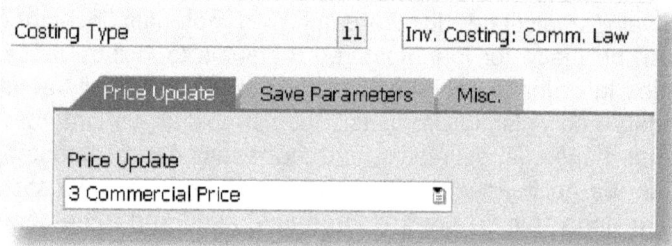

Figure 10.9: Commercial price update configuration

Costing variants with one of these two costing types can only update prices in manufactured materials. Raw material inventory price fields are updated using a transaction such as MRN0, which looks at material receipts in order to determine the lowest value to update the inventory price fields in the ACCOUNTING 2 tab of the material master. The prices assigned to these fields for the raw material should then be used as the source of raw material prices when using a costing variant defined for inventory costing purposes. This setup is made in the valuation variant in the MATERIAL VAL. tab. Figure 10.10 shows an example of a valuation variant set up to use one of the tax-based price fields as a source of raw material costs.

The definition of the cost components in the cost component split configuration determines if a contributing cost is eligible for either of these types of inventory cost. Only the costs associated with cost components that are defined for COMMERCIAL INVENTORY are used in the calculation of a commercial inventory price (see section ❶ in Figure 10.11). This corresponds to cost component view INVENTORY (COMMERCIAL). Only those costs defined for TAX INVENTORY are used for calculating a tax-based inventory cost (see section ❷). This corresponds to cost component view INVENTORY (TAX-BASED).

Priority	Strategy Sequence		Incl. Additive Costs
1	A Valuation Price 1 Based On Tax Law		✓
2	4 Planned Price 1		✓
3	L Price from Purchasing Info Record		✓
4	7 Valuation Price According to Price Control in ...		✓
5			☐

Figure 10.10: Valuation variant using tax-based raw material values

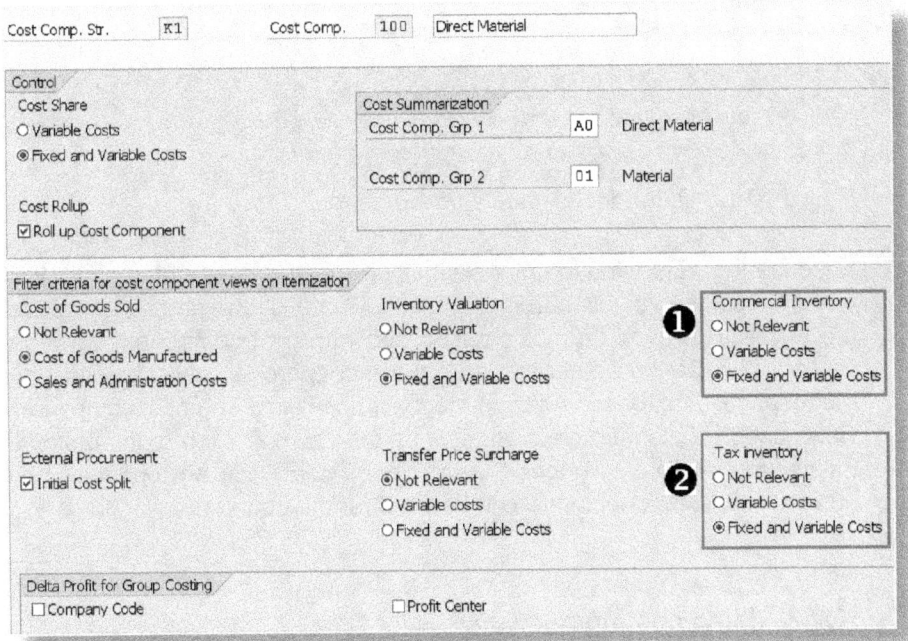

Figure 10.11: Cost component configuration

When prices are updated in the material master, the system uses the determination of lowest value strategy to find the proper value. This value is compared to the value calculated in the cost estimate, and the lower of the two values is updated in the material master. An example of this is found in book one "SAP® S/4HANA Product Cost Planning—Configuration and Master Data".

10.2.2 Updating other prices

There is another method that can be used to update the inventory price fields without using the determination of lowest value method. If the costing type price update is set to PRICES OTHER THAN STANDARD PRICE (see Figure 10.12), the six inventory price fields on the ACCOUNTING 2 tab of the material master can be selected for update, as well as the three planned price fields on the COSTING 2 tab.

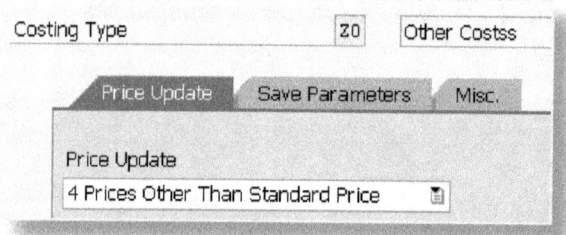

Figure 10.12: Other prices update configuration

Because the determination of lowest value method does not apply to this costing type, the valuation from the cost estimate is always used to update the prices. However, the costs associated with cost component views INVENTORY (TAX-BASED) and INVENTORY (COMMERCIAL) are still used for updating the respective tax-based and commercial price fields. The cost component views used for planned price updates on the COSTING 2 tab of the material master are manually assigned at the time those fields are updated. Any defined cost component view can be used for the update.

10.2.3 Using costing relevancy

Costing relevancy other than 100% (X) or 0% (blank) can be used for inventory cost estimates for BOM components and routing/recipe operations. The factors used for 100% and 0% come pre-defined with the system and cannot be changed. Other factors are created using transaction OKK9 or via IMG menu path CONTROLLING • PRODUCT COST CONTROLLING • PRODUCT COST

PLANNING • PRICE UPDATE • PARAMETERS FOR INVENTORY COST ESTIMATE • DEFINE RELEVANCY TO COSTING. Factor IDs are one character long and are assigned a name (see Figure 10.13).

Costing Relevancy	Name
	Not Relevant to Costing
A	75% Relevant to Costing
B	50% Relevancy to Costing
C	25% Relevancy to Costing
X	100% Relevant to Costing

Figure 10.13: Costing relevance codes

Once the factors are defined, they can be assigned to a valuation variant using transaction OKK7, or via IMG menu path CONTROLLING • PRODUCT COST CONTROLLING • PRODUCT COST PLANNING • PRICE UPDATE • PARAMETERS FOR INVENTORY COST ESTIMATE • DEFINE PRICE FACTORS (see Figure 10.14). The valuation variant can be wildcarded using the string +++. If the wildcard is used, the relevancy factor is valid for all valuation variants except those that are explicitly defined. The system first looks in the configuration for a specific valuation variant. If that matches the costing variant assignment, then that factor is used. If there is no match, the system then looks for the wildcard variant definition, if any. To create a new factor for a valuation variant, select the costing relevancy ID and then define the percentages used for relevancy for both fixed and variable costs. A price factor can be defined with different percentages for fixed and variable costs. The value entered is a multiplier, and 75% should be expressed as 0.750.

Valuation Variant	Costing Relevancy	Fxd Prc. Factor	Var. Price Factor
001	B	0.500	0.500
004	A	0.750	0.750
ZAC	A	0.750	0.750
ZAC	B	0.500	0.500
ZAC	C	0.250	0.250

Figure 10.14: Assignment of costing relevancy factors

These new relevancy factors can now be assigned to the BOM. In Figure 10.15, RELEVANCY TO COSTING is in the column to the right of FIXED QUANTITY. Normally, this is found in the item details under the STATUS/LONG TEXT tab after drilling into the BOM item.

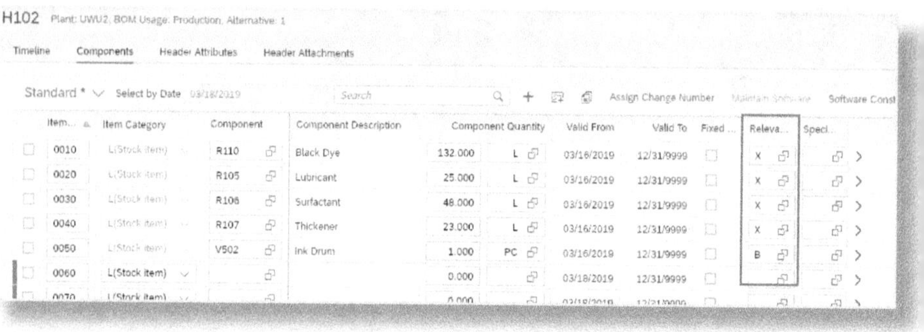

Figure 10.15: BOM components

The relevancy for costing indicator specifies how much of the value of the costing item is to be included in the cost. Two of the IDs are fixed by SAP. Leaving the field blank indicates that no cost is determined for that component. X indicates that the item is 100% cost relevant, meaning that the full cost is included in the cost estimate. Pricing factors other than blank and X are configured for each valuation variant in which they are to be used. The factor values are assigned at that time. As long as a factor is defined, it can be used in a BOM or routing operation. If a non-blank factor does not pertain to the specific valuation variant used in the cost estimate, it is treated as an X. For any cost estimate that is intended to be used to update the standard cost (costing type 01), a costing item can only be either 100% relevant or 0% relevant. Any non-blank factor is always treated as an X. Item 0050, for material V502 (see Figure 10.15), has its relevancy to costing factor set to B. This corresponds to 50% of the item cost (see Figure 10.14). The factor 0.500 is assigned to B for valuation variants 001 and ZAC.

The standard value of V502 is 15.00 USD per PC. The valuation variant ZAC is assigned to costing variant ZOTH. A cost estimate using this costing variant gives a value of 31.25 USD for a quantity of 4.167 PC (see Figure 10.16). The full value is 4.167 multiplied by 15.00 USD, equaling 62.51 USD. In this example, the 0.5 factor was applied to the cost, yielding a value of 31.25 USD.

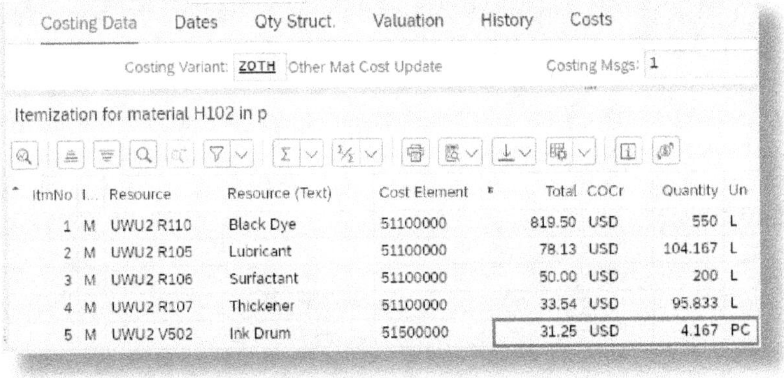

Costing Data | Dates | Qty Struct. | Valuation | History | Costs

Costing Variant: ZOTH Other Mat Cost Update | Costing Msgs: 1

Itemization for material H102 in p

ItmNo	I...	Resource	Resource (Text)	Cost Element	Total	COCr	Quantity	Un
1	M	UWU2 R110	Black Dye	51100000	819.50	USD	550	L
2	M	UWU2 R105	Lubricant	51100000	78.13	USD	104.167	L
3	M	UWU2 R106	Surfactant	51100000	50.00	USD	200	L
4	M	UWU2 R107	Thickener	51100000	33.54	USD	95.833	L
5	M	UWU2 V502	Ink Drum	51500000	31.25	USD	4.167	PC

Figure 10.16: Costing relevancy for costing variant ZOTH

If the same cost estimate is created using costing variant ZPC1, which is intended for updating standard costs, the result is different, even though the same factor value is assigned to the valuation variant. Figure 10.17 shows that the full value is assigned to material V502 in the cost estimate, even though the same costing relevancy factor was used.

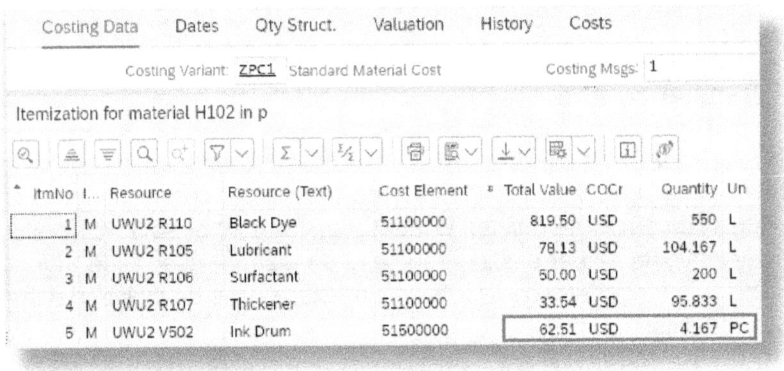

Costing Data | Dates | Qty Struct. | Valuation | History | Costs

Costing Variant: ZPC1 Standard Material Cost | Costing Msgs: 1

Itemization for material H102 in p

ItmNo	I...	Resource	Resource (Text)	Cost Element	Total Value	COCr	Quantity	Un
1	M	UWU2 R110	Black Dye	51100000	819.50	USD	550	L
2	M	UWU2 R105	Lubricant	51100000	78.13	USD	104.167	L
3	M	UWU2 R106	Surfactant	51100000	50.00	USD	200	L
4	M	UWU2 R107	Thickener	51100000	33.54	USD	95.833	L
5	M	UWU2 V502	Ink Drum	51500000	62.51	USD	4.167	PC

Figure 10.17: Costing relevancy for costing variant ZPC1

10.3 What-if costing

Costing variants do not need to be set up in order to update fields in the material master. Cost estimates can be created for various purposes including making cost comparisons. An example of this is the cost estimate in Section 10.1. Costing variant ZRMC was set up to assess the impact of prospective raw material prices on the product costs.

Typically, costing variants for what-if analysis purposes would not be allowed to update the material master. The costing type should reflect this by using NO UPDATE in the PRICE UPDATE field in the costing type configuration (see Figure 10.18).

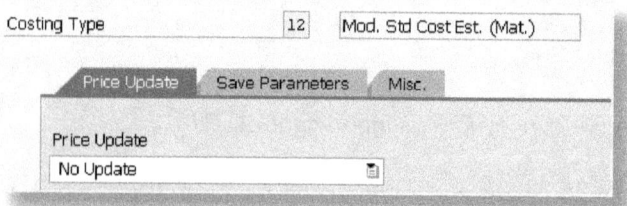

Figure 10.18: Costing type setting for no material master update

Other costing variant and valuation variant settings are useful for what-if costing purposes.

10.3.1 Transfer control

To make sure that all materials are costed in the scenario, the transfer control can either be forced to allow for no transfer of cost estimates, or the costing variant can be defined without transfer control so that there is no transfer of costs. Other costing sources can also be used (see Figure 10.19). This can force certain lower level costs to always be included if the cost estimate exists.

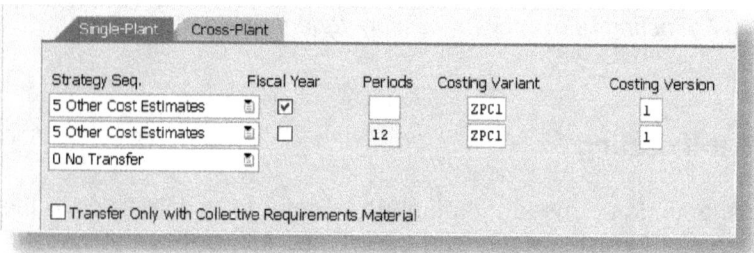

Figure 10.19: Special transfer control for what-if costing

10.3.2 Material valuation

The MATERIAL VAL. tab of the valuation variant configuration can be changed to specify an alternative source for purchased material costs (see Figure 10.20). In this case, PLANNED PRICE 2 is used as the primary source. However, other sources can be used, such as latest purchase order prices or one of the inventory cost fields from the ACCOUNTING 2 tab of the material master. This provides great flexibility in determining the raw material costs to be used when compared to the standard cost estimate.

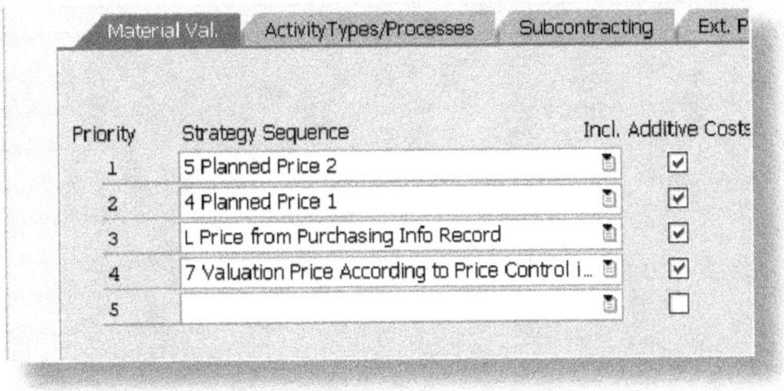

Figure 10.20: Valuation variant for raw material what-if costs

10.3.3 Activity types

Alternative activity type pricing or CO costing versions can be used to bring different values for manufacturing costs into the cost estimate. This could involve using forecast rates based on specific cost center plans assigned to different versions (see Figure 10.21).

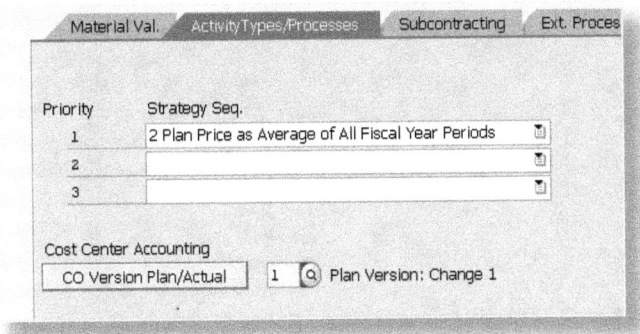

Figure 10.21: Activity type valuation using alternative plan version

209

10.3.4 Overhead

Different overhead allocation rates can be defined using different overhead costing sheets. Each sheet can have its own definition of cost bases and overhead rate assignment to provide alternative views of the cost (see Figure 10.22).

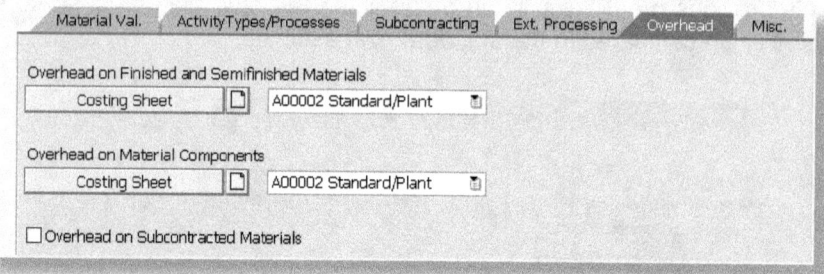

Figure 10.22: Overhead with alternative costing sheets defined

10.3.5 Costing version

Each costing version within the same costing variant can have its own exchange rate type, quantity structure type for mixed costing, and transfer price variant for profit center valuation costing. Figure 10.23 shows a setup using two different quantity structure types for mixed costing.

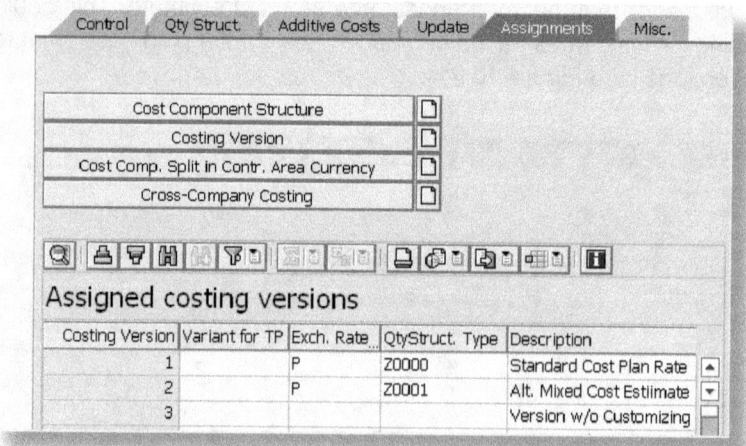

Figure 10.23: Costing version configuration in the costing variant

10.3.6 Reference variant

Reference variants can be used to ensure that certain costs remain the same as in the reference cost estimate, and that others are recalculated based on the criteria defined in the valuation variant. The example in Section 10.1 shows how this can be done.

10.4 Group costing

Group costing is a tool used for analysis of cost flow across legal entities within a corporation. Using the Material Ledger functionality, the movement of materials can be tracked in multiple currencies using parallel valuation. Group costing is a method of defining material costs to help understand what goes into these cost flows. Product cost planning supports three different valuation approaches: legal valuation, group valuation and profit center valuation. Material movements can be viewed using these three approaches. The standard view is *legal valuation*. The legal valuation view is mandatory and reflects statutory requirements for inventory valuation among the various legal entities that make up the corporation. When goods are shipped between company codes, the receiving company needs to be treated like an external customer, and some sort of profit must be recognized with these transactions. Corporations set up transfer prices to be assigned to the materials to reflect this profit.

Within the organization, however, the intercompany profit obscures the determination of the total corporation profit and is eliminated during consolidation activities at period end. The *group valuation* view is used to track goods movements without the internal markups required for legal valuation. Values flow using the source company's procurement and manufacturing costs without applying the transfer price uplift.

A third approach is *profit center valuation*. This applies to the movement of goods between profit centers, even within the same company code. Using this approach, individual profit centers are treated as independent companies with internal transfer prices. This allows for a better understanding of business unit performance, even though from a legal view, these business unit profits are automatically eliminated. This view works opposite to group valuation in that transfer pricing is accounted for in the cost estimate instead of being eliminated from it.

The following example uses the GROUP VALUATION view to demonstrate how product costs are determined. A costing type can only have one valuation approach assigned to it, so a different costing type and costing variant must be created for each valuation view. Figure 10.24 shows the VALUATION VIEW setting on the PRICE UPDATE tab of the costing type configuration. This particular costing type is set for GROUP VALUATION.

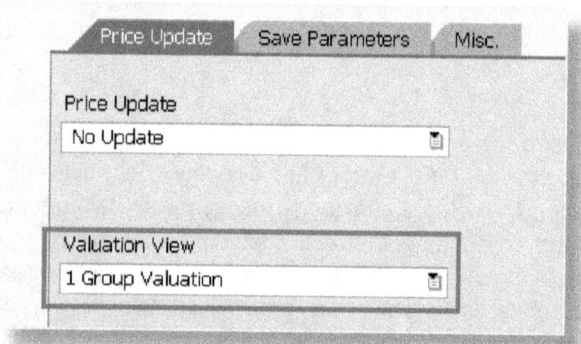

Figure 10.24: Costing type with group valuation

One cost component (170) is set up to account for the intercompany profit. Section ❶ in Figure 10.25 shows COMPANY CODE selected under DELTA PROFIT FOR GROUP COSTING. Only one of the options may be chosen for this setting. COMPANY CODE corresponds to group valuation, and PROFIT CENTER corresponds to profit center valuation. If COMPANY CODE is selected, this cost component cannot be used for inventory valuation purposes. Section ❷ shows that this has been disabled for this cost component. In addition, no cost elements can be assigned to this cost component. The system automatically determines the markup, and it can be assigned to its own TRANSFER PRICE SURCHARGE cost component view for better visibility in the cost estimate.

Universal Writing Utensils ships black ink (material H102) from the Chicago plant (UWU3) to the Gent plant in Belgium (UWU1) for use in manufacturing pens with black ink. The legal valuation standard cost contains a markup to account for transfer price. This is displayed in Figure 10.26. The itemization shows the standard cost estimate using costing variant ZPC1 in the COST OF GOODS MANUFACTURED cost component view. A 500.00 EUR markup per 1,000 L has been used. The valuation view is set to LEGAL VALUATION in the costing type used for this costing variant.

ALTERNATIVE COSTING VARIANTS

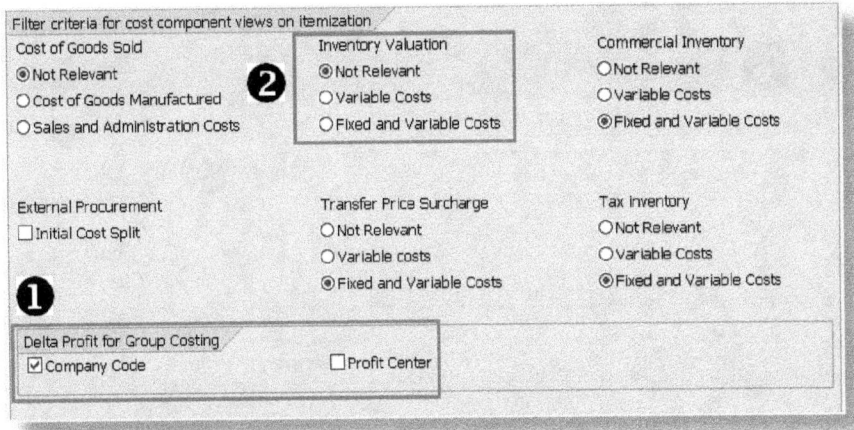

Figure 10.25: Cost component configuration for group costing

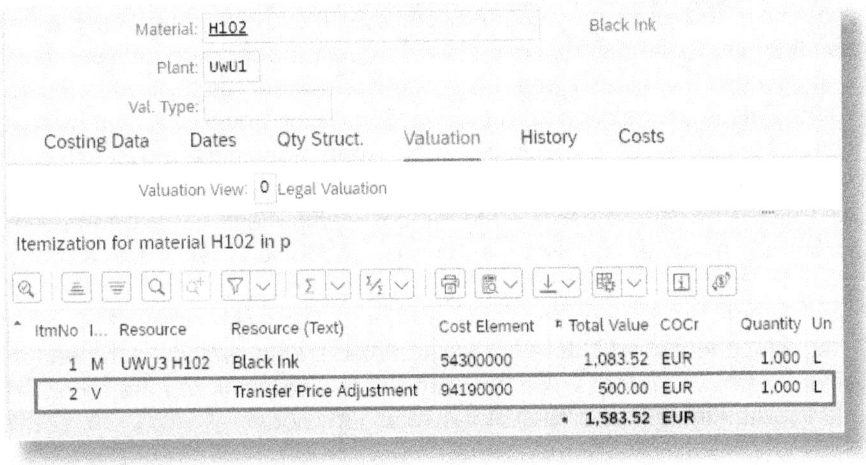

Figure 10.26: Standard cost estimate including transfer price

This material is now costed again using the group costing variant ZUGP. Figure 10.27 shows the cost estimate using the COST OF GOODS MANUFACTURED cost component view. It does not include the transfer uplift costs as in the standard cost estimate. Section ❶ highlights that the valuation view for this cost estimate uses GROUP VALUATION instead of legal valuation. Section ❷ shows the cost estimate without the transfer uplift that was seen in the previous cost estimate.

213

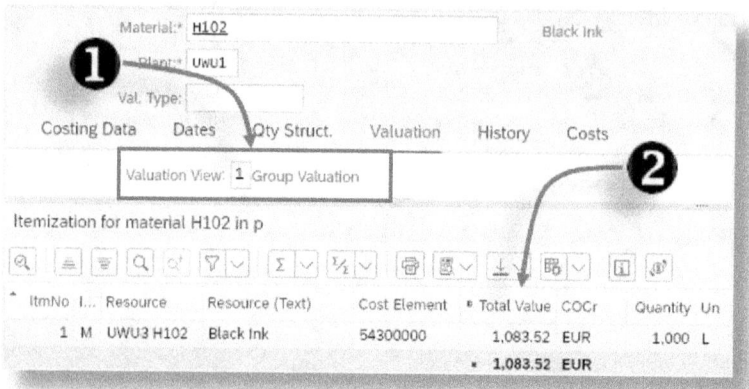

Figure 10.27: Group cost estimate with no transfer price -COGM

However, this cost does not disappear from the cost estimate. When creating a cost estimate for group valuation, the system looks at the standard cost at the receiving plant and compares it to the standard cost at the sending plant. The difference is the delta profit for shipping between company codes. This is assigned to the cost component, as defined in Figure 10.25. This is also assigned to the TAX SURCHARGE and TAX INVENTORY cost component views, so it should be visible when switching the cost estimate view to either one. This does not show up in the itemization because no cost elements can be assigned to the cost component. Items on the itemization list must have a cost element assigned. However, there is a special cost component set up for this, so it shows up in the cost component view. Figure 10.28 shows the value assigned to cost component 170 in the cost component split. This value is calculated by the system based on the differences in standard value between the source plant and the receiving plants when the plants are in different company codes.

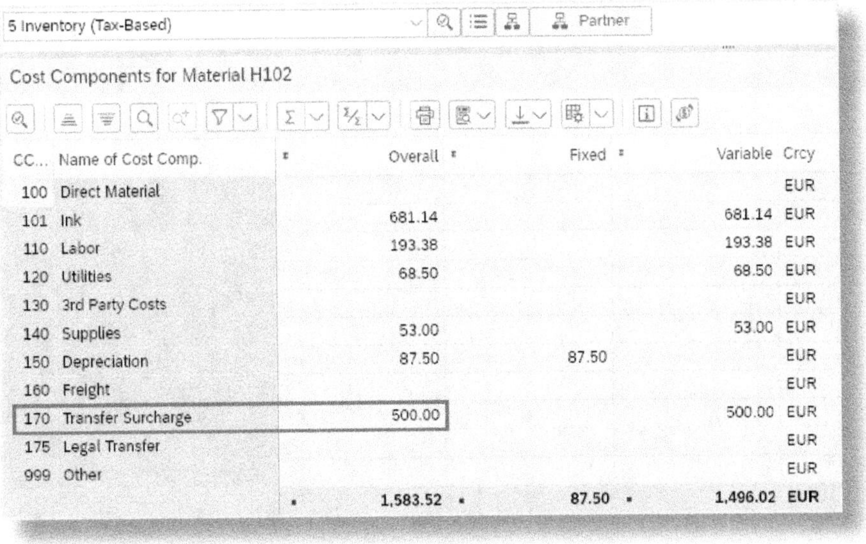

Cost Components for Material H102

5 Inventory (Tax-Based)

CC...	Name of Cost Comp.	Overall	Fixed	Variable	Crcy
100	Direct Material				EUR
101	Ink	681.14		681.14	EUR
110	Labor	193.38		193.38	EUR
120	Utilities	68.50		68.50	EUR
130	3rd Party Costs				EUR
140	Supplies	53.00		53.00	EUR
150	Depreciation	87.50	87.50		EUR
160	Freight				EUR
170	Transfer Surcharge	500.00		500.00	EUR
175	Legal Transfer				EUR
999	Other				EUR
		1,583.52	87.50	1,496.02	EUR

Figure 10.28: Cost component view with transfer surcharge

11 Cost estimate reorganization

Cost estimates are created for a variety of reasons, even if they are not used for updating the material master. Occasionally, some of these cost estimates, as well as some of the cost estimates that are used for material updates, need to be removed from the system.

11.1 Deleting cost estimates

There are several reasons that cost estimates need to be removed from the system, such as:

- Cost estimates for what-if analysis are no longer needed and are causing clutter in the system.
- A standard cost estimate was marked for future release but after review, it is found to be erroneous and needs to be deleted.
- A cost estimate that was released this period needs to be rerun.
- Cost estimates with status KF (Costed With Errors) are no longer required.

These are only a handful of reasons why cost estimates should be deleted. There are two methods to enable cost estimates to be removed from the system. One method is to use archiving (transaction CKR3) so that essential cost estimate information that is not immediately needed in the system is kept offline for later referral. Archiving of cost estimates should be coordinated with other archiving objects.

The other alternative is to delete the cost estimate without archiving. This is done using the Reorganize Cost Estimates Fiori app or SAPGUI transaction CKR1. This transaction recognizes two different classes of cost estimates that can be deleted: cost estimates without reference in the material master, and those that are referenced directly by the material master. The second class always refers to standard cost estimates. These can be marked (future) cost estimates, the standard cost estimates currently in use, or the cost estimates that were previously used as the standard.

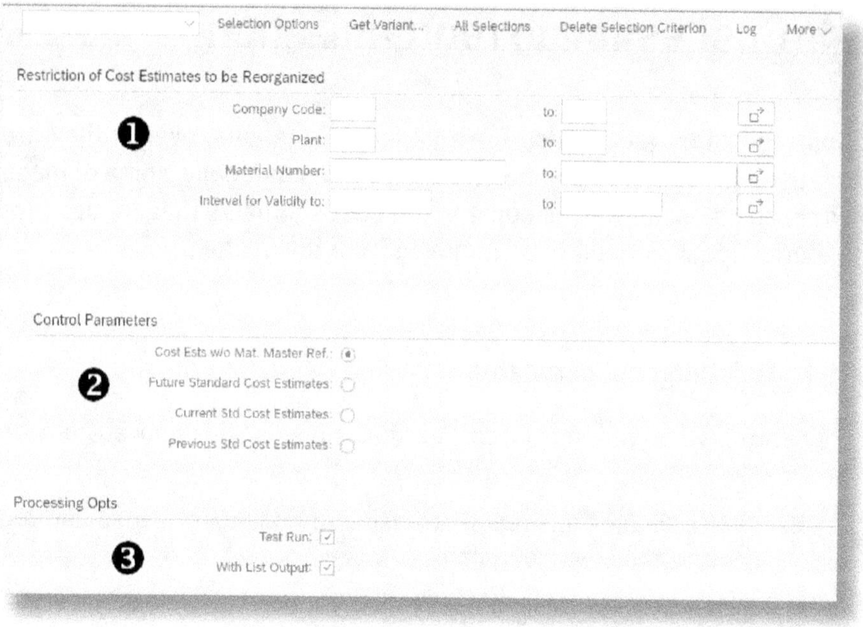

Figure 11.1: Initial window for deleting cost estimates

Figure 11.1 shows the initial window that is displayed when running the transaction. There are three sections. Section ❶ is used to define specific cost estimate parameters, such as material and validity dates, to identify the cost estimates to select.

Section ❷ specifies the class of cost estimate to be considered. The relevant option is selected by clicking on the corresponding radio button; only one of the four options can be selected at a time. COST ESTS W/O MAT. MASTER REF. includes any cost estimate that is not directly referenced in the COSTING 2 tab of the material master. This includes any cost estimate that does not have VO (marked) or FR (released) status, or any cost estimate that has status FR but is older than the previous standard cost estimate. Any inventory cost estimates are also dealt with using this setting, even if they have been used to update the material master. This is because the material master does not have a direct reference to those cost estimates. FUTURE STANDARD COST ESTIMATES refers to any cost estimate that has VO status (marked). CURRENT STD COST ESTIMATES refers to the cost estimates that currently represent the standard cost for the materials, and has status FR. There can be unexpected consequences if these are deleted without immediately creating new cost estimates to take their place. PREVIOUS STD COST ESTIMATES refers to those cost estimates that represent the standard that was set immediately prior the current standard. Older released cost estimates are not included because they are no longer directly associated with the material in the COSTING 2 tab.

In section ❸, select the options to be used when processing the deletion. Leave TEST RUN unchecked to perform the actual deletion. Select WITH LIST OUTPUT to see a list of the cost estimates that were deleted.

> ### Delete cost estimate processing options
>
>
> Always select the TEST RUN checkbox when first running the deletion. This prevents unnecessary grief if the options selected include cost estimates that shouldn't be deleted. Another safeguard is to always select WITH LIST OUTPUT to ensure that a full list of the cost estimates to be deleted is displayed.

When deleting the cost estimates that are associated with the material master, using the default window selections is usually sufficient to delete the proper cost estimate. However, when deleting cost estimates without reference to the material master, more information is required to be sure that the proper cost estimates are chosen. Click on the All Selections button, or click on 🗇 if running transaction CKR1, to display the additional selection parameters (see Figure 11.2).

Restriction of Cost Estimates to be Reorganized		
Company Code:	to:	
Plant: UWU2	to:	
Material Number:	to:	
Costing Status:	to:	
Costing Variant:	to:	
Costing Version:	to:	
Interval for Validity from:	to:	
Interval for Validity to:	to:	
Costing Run:		
Costing Run Date:		
Automatic Cost Estimates: ✓	With Qty Structure: ✓	
Additive Cost Ests: ✓	W/o Qty Structure: ✓	

Figure 11.2: Full cost estimate selection parameters

The cost estimates are then deleted from the system and are no longer accessible. If FUTURE STANDARD COST ESTIMATES was selected in the initial window, the future planned price and period are reset in the COSTING 2 tab of the material master for each cost estimate that was deleted. If PREVIOUS STD COST ESTIMATES was selected, then the same is true for the previous planned price and period.

Special processing is used when the CURRENT STD COST ESTIMATES option is selected. A warning message CK669 – DELETING CURRENT STANDARD COST ESTIMATE CAN CAUSE INCONSISTENCIES is displayed when the Execute button is pressed. The system does not proceed until the message is acknowledged. The deletion of current standard cost estimates should be avoided if at all possible because it can cause problems with the material ledger and with the calculation of work-in-process and can create variances for manufactured materials. If the deletion takes place, the current planned standard price is deleted along with the period the cost estimate was released. The accounting standard price is not changed, but there is no cost estimate to back it up. This can be an issue in countries where there is a requirement to link a standard to a document identifying how the standard was created.

Using the expanded parameters allows the selection of specific costing variants and costing versions. This is especially helpful if multiple costing variants are being used for various purposes. Cost estimates selected can also be restricted to a specific costing run. The bottom four selections can further restrict the cost estimates to be deleted. Either AUTOMATIC COST ESTIMATES or ADDITIVE COST ESTIMATES, or both, must be selected. Automatic cost estimates refer to any cost estimate with quantity structure or without quantity structure associated with a material. Additive cost estimates are special cost estimates that are used to assign costs to a cost estimate with quantity structure that cannot be determined using the standard quantity structures available. Deletion can be further restricted by selecting either WITH QTY STRUCTURE or W/O QTY STRUCTURE. By default, all four options are selected.

When the selections have been made, click on Execute (⊕) to begin the deletion process. If WITH LIST OUTPUT is selected, a report lists all cost estimates that have been deleted (see Figure 11.3).

COST ESTIMATE REORGANIZATION

Co...	Material	Plant	C...	Cos...	Cstg Date Fr...	Posti...	Year
ZCOM	H101	UWU2	KA	1	03/11/2019	3	2019
	R105	UWU2	KA	1	03/11/2019		
	R106	UWU2	KA	1	03/11/2019		
	R107	UWU2	KA	1	03/11/2019		
	R109	UWU2	KA	1	03/11/2019		
	R109	UWU2	KA	1	03/10/2019		
ZOTH	H101	UWU2	KA	1	03/11/2019		
	H101	UWU2	KA	1	03/10/2019		
	R105	UWU2	KA	1	03/11/2019		
	R106	UWU2	KA	1	03/11/2019		
	R107	UWU2	KA	1	03/11/2019		
	R109	UWU2	KA	1	03/11/2019		
ZPC1	R109	UWU2	KA	1	01/19/2019	1	

Figure 11.3: Output listing for deleted cost estimates

11.2 Archiving cost estimates

Cost estimates can also be archived using archiving object CO_COPC. Archiving deletes the selected cost estimates from the system, but stores the information in an archive file for later retrieval. When archiving with transaction SARA, the archiving object must be entered. The special archiving transaction CKR3 automatically selects the CO_COPC archiving object. There are two steps to the archiving process for cost estimates. Figure 11.4 shows the initial window for setting up the archiving section. The WRITE and DELETE buttons process the archiving session. The READ button can be used to access archived cost estimates.

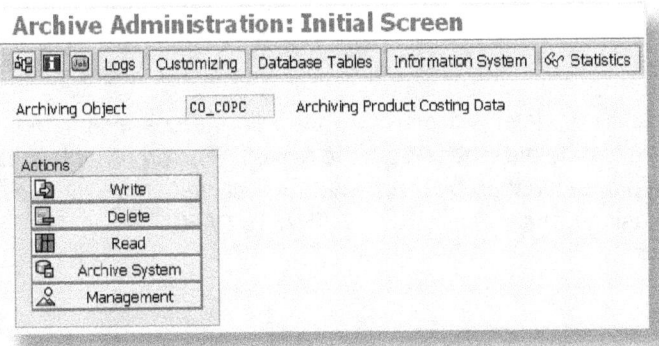

Figure 11.4: Archiving cost estimates initial window

The first step is WRITE. In this step, cost estimates are selected and written to an archive file. The selection parameters are defined first (see Figure 11.5). They are similar to the parameters for deleting without archiving. A run variant is created to execute the WRITE step in the background.

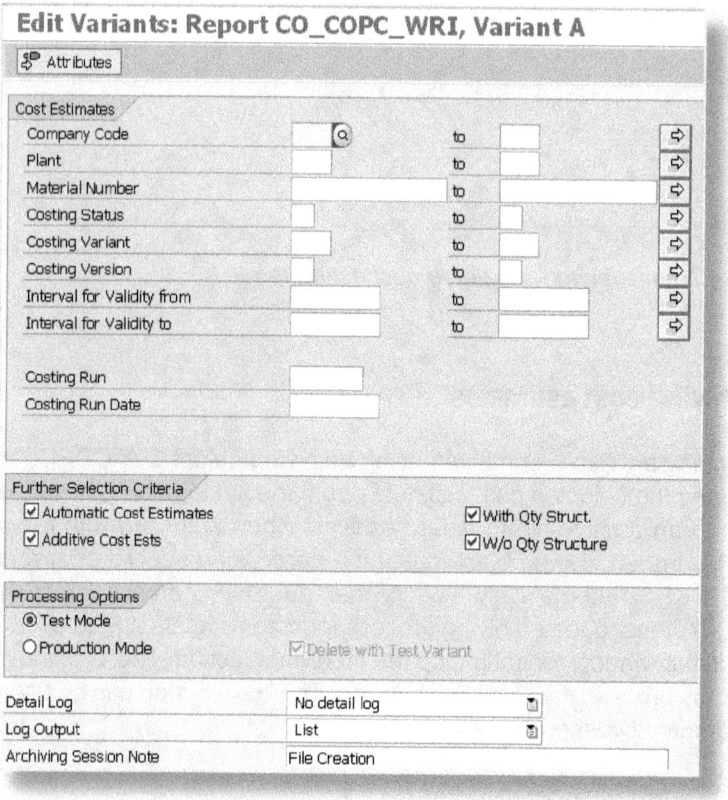

Edit Variants: Report CO_COPC_WRI, Variant A	
Attributes	

Cost Estimates
- Company Code ___ to ___
- Plant ___ to ___
- Material Number ___ to ___
- Costing Status ___ to ___
- Costing Variant ___ to ___
- Costing Version ___ to ___
- Interval for Validity from ___ to ___
- Interval for Validity to ___ to ___

- Costing Run ___
- Costing Run Date ___

Further Selection Criteria
- ☑ Automatic Cost Estimates   ☑ With Qty Struct.
- ☑ Additive Cost Ests   ☑ W/o Qty Structure

Processing Options
- ⦿ Test Mode
- ○ Production Mode   ☑ Delete with Test Variant

Detail Log	No detail log
Log Output	List
Archiving Session Note	File Creation

Figure 11.5: Selection for archiving cost estimates

The second step, DELETE, selects the archive file with the cost estimate intended for deletion, and deletes these from the system. The archive file that was created in step one can then be read, and the archived cost estimates can be displayed using transactions CKR3, SARA, or SARI.

12 Standard costing reports

Being able to produce cost estimates for materials is the most important part of CO-PC-PCP. However, the analysis of these cost estimates, and the ability to compare cost estimates generated in different ways, is also a critical part of managing product costs. The system provides several tools for cost analysis.

12.1 Summary reports

Summary reports provide a list of cost estimate results by material on a line-by-line basis. The analysis step of the costing run creates a summary report. There is basically one summary costing report, although transaction variants have been created to make parameter selection easier based on the purpose of the report. Four SAPGUI transactions have been defined based on these variants. These are:

- S_ALR_87099930—Results of Costing Run,
- S_ALR_87099931—Price vs Cost Estimate,
- S_ALR_87099932—Variances Between Costing Runs, and
- S_P99_41000111—Analyze/Compare Cost Estimates.

These have been converted into two Fiori apps: Costing Run Results and Material Cost vs. Cost Estimate. Figure 12.1 shows a simple interface from the Costing Run Results app that allows for the selection of a costing run, plus a few other items.

Click on the All Selections button at the top of the window to obtain a full list of what is possible for this report (see Figure 12.2). This window is the same for all the different reports.

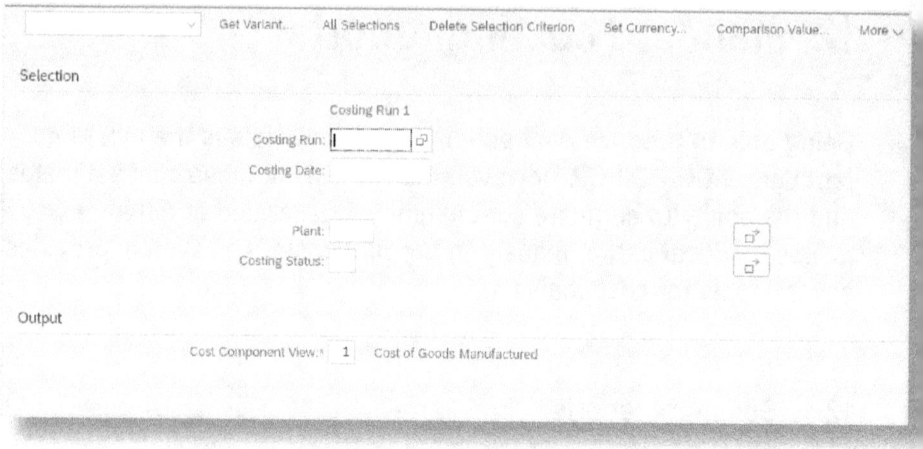

Figure 12.1: Selection window for Costing Run Results app

The report is not restricted to a single costing run or a single costing variant. When two costing runs are selected, there is a side-by-side comparison of the costs per material for each costing run. The EXCEPTIONS section can be set up to define which cost estimates to display based on this comparison. The OUTPUT section enables the selection of the cost component view for the report. The current material price that is displayed on the report can be defined as any one of the price fields in the material master, including the standard, future standard, previous standard, any of the planned prices from COSTING 2, and any of the inventory prices on ACCOUNTING 2. The BASE section determines whether the costing results are displayed using the costing lot size of the cost estimate or the price unit of the material master. If costing lot sizes vary greatly, then price unit can be a much better selection for analyzing and comparing the cost estimates.

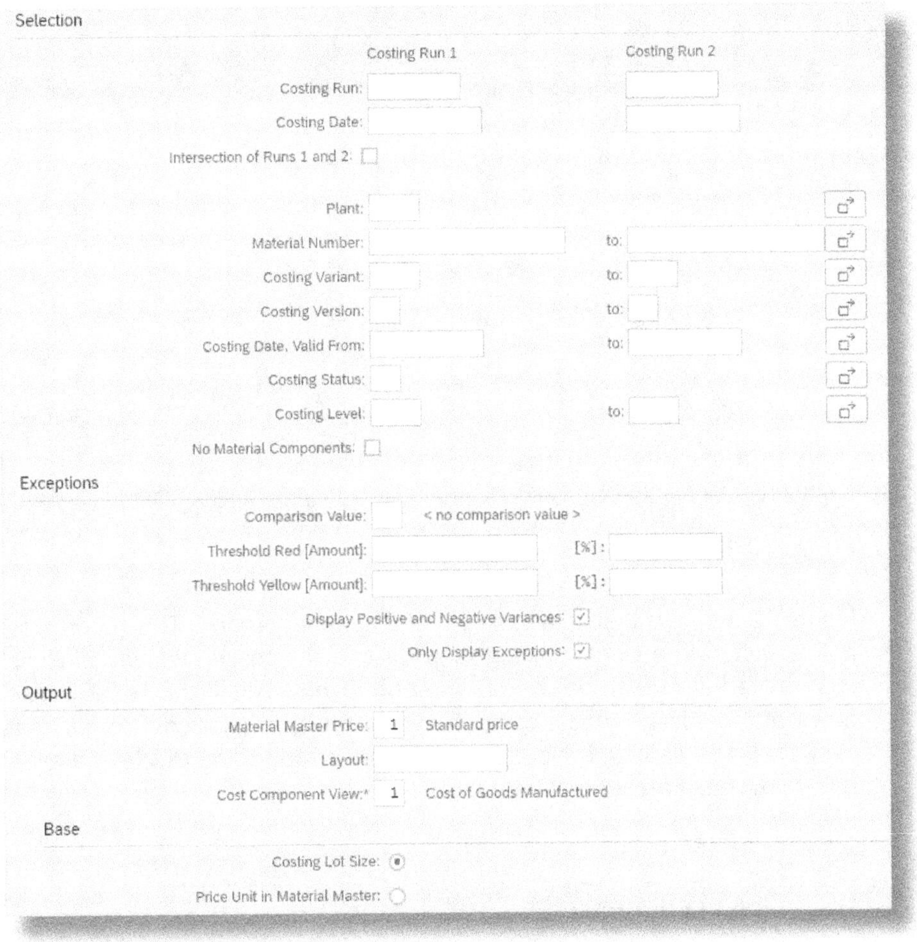

Standard costing reports

Selection

	Costing Run 1	Costing Run 2
Costing Run:		
Costing Date:		
Intersection of Runs 1 and 2: ☐		
Plant:		
Material Number:	to:	
Costing Variant:	to:	
Costing Version:	to:	
Costing Date, Valid From:	to:	
Costing Status:		
Costing Level:	to:	
No Material Components: ☐		

Exceptions

Comparison Value: < no comparison value >
Threshold Red [Amount]: [%]:
Threshold Yellow [Amount]: [%]:
Display Positive and Negative Variances: ☑
Only Display Exceptions: ☑

Output

Material Master Price: 1 Standard price
Layout:
Cost Component View:* 1 Cost of Goods Manufactured

Base

Costing Lot Size: ⦿
Price Unit in Material Master: ○

Figure 12.2: Full list of summary report parameters

Plant	UWU1
	UWU2
	UWU3
Base	Values Based On Costing Lot Size
Cost Component View	01(Cost of Goods Manufactured)

	Cstg Vrnt	Material	Material description	Plant	Sta.	Costing Re	Lot Size	Unit
☐	ZPC1	R109	Red Dye	UWU2	KA	2,500.00	1,000	L
☐	ZPC1	R105	Lubricant	UWU2	KA	750.00	1,000	L
☐	ZPC1	INK MIXING	Ink Mixing	UWU2	KA	9,108.63	100.0	HR
☐	ZPC1	INK MIXING	Ink Mixing	UWU2	KA	9,108.63	100.0	HR
☐	ZPC1	PURPLE INK	Purple Ink	UWU2	KA	1,934.88	1,000	L
☐	ZPC1	R105	Lubricant	UWU3	KA	780.00	1,000	L
☐	ZPC1	R106	Surfactant	UWU3	KA	243.30	1,000	L
☐	ZPC1	R107	Thickener	UWU3	KA	355.00	1,000	L
☐	ZPC1	H221	Ink Base	UWU3	FR	388.18	1,000	L
☐	ZTAX	R105	Lubricant	UWU2	KA	750.00	1,000	L
☐	ZTAX	R106	Surfactant	UWU2	KA	250.00	1,000	L

Figure 12.3: Example of a summary report

Figure 12.3 shows a simple example of a summary report. This report was not restricted to a single costing run or a specific costing variant. Multiple cost-related fields can be used in a report layout. This includes the breakdown of the costs, by cost component, for the particular cost component view that was selected. Double-clicking on a report line displays the detailed cost estimate for that item.

12.2 Object comparison

There are reports that enable comparison of costs of different materials or of different cost estimates for the same material. One example of object comparison uses the Comparison of Itemizations Fiori app or SAP-GUI transaction CK79_99. The report shown in Figure 12.4 compares the standard cost estimate (costing variant ZPC1) to the what-if cost estimate (costing variant ZRMC) for material H101 at plant UWU2. The differences between the two cost estimates are highlighted in the D_{IFF} column.

This report shows the differences for the results of two different costing variants for the same material. This can also be used to compare the costs of two different materials. There are additional reports that compare the cost component split (Cost Component Comparison Fiori app or SAPGUI transaction S_ALR_87013047) or the summarized costs by cost element (Cost Element Comparison Fiori app or SAPGUI transaction S_ALR_87013048).

					Cost Est. 1		Cost Est. 2	
Material					H101 Red Ink		H101 Red Ink	
Pint					UWU2		UWU2	
Costg Variant					ZPC1		ZRMC	
Costg Version					01		01	
Costg Date					04/01/2019		04/01/2019	
Costg Lot Size					1,000 L		1,000 L	
1	2	ItCatText	Res. Text	Material	Total 1	Total 2	Diff	%
		Internal Activity	Mix Ink		454.75	454.75		
		Internal Activity			454.75	454.75		
		Material	Ink Drum		60.00	60.00		
			Lubricant		72.00	86.40	14.40	
			Red Dye		1,214.64	1,260.00	45.36	
			Surfactant		44.00	44.00		
			Thickener		30.80	39.60	8.80	
		Material			1,421.44	1,490.00	68.56	
		Variable Item						
		Variable Item						
					1,876.19	1,944.75	68.56	

Figure 12.4: Material itemization comparison report

12.3 Detail reports

Detail reports are used to display the three main cost windows of the cost estimate. These are:

▶ Costed Multilevel BOM—Material Fiori app (transaction CK86_99),

▶ Cost Components—Material Fiori app (transaction CK80_99), and

▶ Itemization—Material Fiori app (transaction CK84_99).

However, the Display Material Cost Estimate Fiori app (transaction CK13N) is probably the best way to view the information because these views are readily available by displaying the cost estimate. The partner cost component split also has its own app and transaction for viewing—Partner Cost Component Split (transaction CK88_99)— but it is also available from the cost estimate display. A separate report by cost element (SAPGUI transaction KKBC_MAT) can be used to display the cost estimate in a manner similar to that used by the order reports in Cost Object Controlling. This groups the costs by cost element (see Figure 12.5).

Material	H101 Red Ink							
Plant	UWU2 Los Angeles Plant							
Costing Variant	ZRMC Raw Material Changes							
Costing Version	1 Version w/o Customizing							
Costing Date from-to	04/25/2019 - 12/31/9999							
Lot Size	1,000 L l							
Cost Base	1,000 L l							

Cost Element	Cost Element (Text)	Origin		Total Plan		Plan fxd	Currency		Plan Qty	OUM
94113000	Overhead administration			1,250.00		1,250.00	USD			
AdminSales overhead			∎	1,250.00	∎	1,250.00	USD			
51100000	Consumption - Raw Material	UWU2/R105		108.00		0.00	USD		120	L
51100000	Consumption - Raw Material	UWU2/R106		55.00		0.00	USD		220	L
51100000	Consumption - Raw Material	UWU2/R107		49.50		0.00	USD		110	L
51100000	Consumption - Raw Material	UWU2/R109		1,575.00		0.00	USD		630	L
51500000	Consumption - Packaging Material	UWU2/V502		75.00		0.00	USD		5	PC
Direct Material			∎	1,862.50	∎	0.00	USD	∎	1,080	L
									5	PC
94301000	Machine hours 1	200101/MACHHR		262.49		109.38	USD		5.833	HR
Machine time			∎	262.49	∎	109.38	USD	∎	5.833	HR
94311000	Personnel hours	200101/LABRHR		218.01		0.00	USD		9.583	HR
Personnel time			∎	218.01	∎	0.00	USD	∎	9.583	HR
94303000	Setup Production	200101/SETUP		87.94		0.00	USD		1.5	HR
Set-Up time			∎	87.94	∎	0.00	USD	∎	1.5	HR
			∎ ∎	3,680.94	∎ ∎	1,359.38	USD	∎ ∎	1,080	L
									5	PC
									16.916	HR

Figure 12.5: Cost element report KKBC_MAT

12.4 Cost estimate tables for queries

The delivered reports do not always contain all the required information, and the database query functionality provides a way to extend the reporting capabilities. Understanding the tables used and the links between the tables is fundamental to properly design the queries in order to return the desired information. Below is a list of the major tables involved with the cost estimates, as well as the key structures.

12.4.1 KEKO table

The **KEKO** (Product Costing—Header Data) table contains the general information for the cost estimate, such as costing variant used, lot size, and status. It is the link between the material and the itemization and cost component tables. The key structure is:

- ▶ **BZOBJ**—Reference Object. This defines the type of object that uses this cost estimate. 0 is for material cost estimates.

- ▶ **KALNR**—Cost Estimate Number. This is the internal ID of the cost estimate. This connects the cost estimate to the material.

- **KALKA**—Costing Type. This is the costing type assigned to the costing variant for the cost estimate.

- **KADKY**—Costing Date. This is the costing date entered when the cost estimate is created.

- **TVERS**—Costing Version. This is the costing version selected.

- **BWVAR**—Valuation Variant. This is the valuation variant assigned to the costing variant used for the cost estimate.

- **KKZMA**—Additive Costs. This is a flag indicating that this is an additive cost estimate for the material. A value of X indicates an additive cost estimate.

12.4.2 KEPH table

KEPH (Product Costing: Cost Components for Cost of Goods Mfd) is used to store the cost component split for the cost estimate. There are 40 cost fields representing the possible cost components. The definition of which cost field is associated with which cost component is kept in table TCKH3 (cost component configuration table). The key structure is:

- **BZOBJ**—Reference Object. This defines the type of object that uses this cost estimate. 0 is for material cost estimates.

- **KALNR**—Cost Estimate Number. This is the internal ID of the cost estimate. This connects the cost estimate to the material.

- **KALKA**—Costing Type. This is the costing type assigned to the costing variant for the cost estimate.

- **KADKY**—Costing Date. This is the costing date entered when the cost estimate is created.

- **TVERS**—Costing Version. This is the costing version selected.

- **BWVAR**—Valuation Variant. This is the valuation variant assigned to the costing variant used for the cost estimate.

- **KKZMA**—Additive Costs. This is a flag indicating that this is an additive cost estimate for the material. A value of X indicates an additive cost estimate.

- **PATNR**—Partner Number. This is the partner ID assigned to a partner cost component split.

- **KEART**—Type of Cost Component Split. This specifies if it is a main cost component split (H) or an auxiliary cost component split (N).

- **LOSFX**—Link. This is an indicator to determine if this record contains lot-size independent costs. An X indicates that this record stores these types of costs.

- **KKZST**—Lower Level/Level. The cost component split of a manufactured or transferred item can be viewed as a total for the material, or it can be broken down into the costs added at the top-level and the costs generated in all the lower levels of the cost estimate. If this is set to X, it represents the cost component split of the lower level cost estimates.

- **KKZMM**—Costs Were Entered Manually in an Additive Cost Estimate. If set to X, these are the specific costs in the cost estimate associated with an additive cost estimate assigned to the material.

- **DIPA**—Direct Partner. This indicates that the partner is a direct partner and specifies the partner type: company code, plant, business area, or profit center.

12.4.3 CKIS table

The **CKIS** (Items Unit Costing/Itemization Product Costing) table stores the item lines for the cost estimate. The key structure is:

- **BZOBJ**—Reference Object. This defines the type of object that uses this cost estimate. 0 is for material cost estimates.

- **KALNR**—Cost Estimate Number. This is the internal ID of the cost estimate. This connects the cost estimate to the material.

- **KALKA**—Costing Type. This is the costing type assigned to the costing variant for the cost estimate.

- **KADKY**—Costing Date. This is the costing date entered when the cost estimate is created.

- **TVERS**—Costing Version. This is the costing version selected.

- **BWVAR**—Valuation Variant. This is the valuation variant assigned to the costing variant used for the cost estimate.

- **KKZMA**—Additive Costs. This is a flag indicating that this is an additive cost estimate for the material. A value of X indicates an additive cost estimate.

- **POSNR**—Item Number. This is the line item number.

12.4.4 TCKH3 table

The **TCKH3** (Cost Components) table contains the definition of the cost component split. This includes: whether the cost component is set up for variable and fixed costs, the index number of the variable and fixed portion of the cost component, and the various cost component views that the cost component is associated with. The cost component structure is assigned to the costing variant and is stored in **KEKO-ELEHK**. The auxiliary cost component split is stored in **KEKO-ELEHKNS**, if it has been defined. The key structure is:

- **ELEHK**—Cost Component Structure
- **ELEMT**—Cost Component Number

The **EL_HV** (variable) and **EL_HF** (fixed) fields are the indices for the cost components in table **KEPH**.

12.4.5 MBEW table

MBEW is the Material Valuation table. When a material is created for a plant/valuation area, two cost estimate numbers are assigned. These cost estimate numbers are used when referring to the cost estimate with quantity structure (**MBEW-KALN1**) and the cost estimate without quantity structure (**MBEW-KALNR**). This links the material to the proper cost estimate. The cost estimate numbers are constant throughout the life of the material and different cost estimates for the material are differentiated by the other table **KEKO** keys. Different cost estimate numbers are assigned to different valuation types for the same material. Although additive cost estimates are really unit cost estimates, the cost estimate number used is the same as the cost estimate with quantity structure ID (**MBEW-KALN1**). The key structure is:

- **MATNR**—Material Number.
- **BWKEY**—Valuation Area. This is usually the same as plant, but it depends on the valuation area configuration.
- **BWTAR**—Valuation Type.

12.4.6 CKMLMV003 table

CKMLMV003 is the Process model: Receipts/mixing strategies table. Each procurement alternative in mixed costing requires its own cost estimate. To account for this, additional cost estimate numbers need to be assigned to the materials. The top-level cost estimate is reserved for the cost estimate number defined in **MBEW-KALN1**. Table **CKMLMV003** stores the mixing strategies. The key structure is:

- **MGTYP**—Quantity Structure Type. This is the quantity structure type assigned to the costing version of the costing variant.
- **GJAHR**—Fiscal Year. This is the fiscal year the mixing structure becomes effective.
- **PERIO**—Period. This is the fiscal period the mixing structure becomes effective.
- **KALNR_IN**—Procurement Process.
- **KALNR_BAL**—Procurement alternative. This is the cost estimate number for the specific procurement alternative. This is also the link to the specifics of the procurement alternative stored in table CKMLMV001.
- **KALNR_OUT**—Cost Estimate Number. This is the cost estimate number that is assigned to MBEW-KALN1. This is the link between the main cost estimate and the procurement alternatives.

You have finished the book.

Sign up for our newsletter!

Stay up to date!

Sign up for our newsletter for updates on new SAP book releases and exclusive discounts.

http://newsletter.espresso-tutorials.com.

A The Author

Tom King is a graduate of Northwestern University and recently retired from being a senior business analyst with a focus in controlling and product costing. He has over 10 years of experience with the SAP FI-CO modules, mostly as an internal consultant. Prior to that he was involved with the modeling and design of an Activity Based Costing system using a different ERP system for his company's European operations. He has spoken at conferences on several topics relating the CO module and is also the author of "Practical Guide to SAP® CO Templates", published by Espresso Tutorials.

B Index

A

Activity type 113
   fixed allocation 11
   variable allocation 11

Additive cost estimate 137
   cost component structure with texts 153
   costing lot size 139
   costing variant 139
   costing version 139
   costling lot size 142
   dates 140
   lot size independent costs 142
   saving 144
   transfer control 139

Apportionment structure 162
   equivalence numbers 164
   production version 171
   source structure 170

Archive cost estimates 221

B

Bill of material
   operation scrap 25

Bill of materials
   by-product components 157
   component scrap 24
   co-product components 161
   negative operation scrap 37
   net scrap indicator 25, 30, 32
   object dependency 86
   overriding selection 19
   recursion 38
   special procurement key 48
   subcontracting 61
   super BOM 86

   variant linking 89

Business process 113

By-product 157

C

Characteristics 82, 88

Class 82

Component allocation 17
   in cost estimate 18
   scrap calculations 33

Configurable material 81

Control key 71
   configuration 71

Co-product 157, 159
   fixed price 159
   primary 159
   recipe / routing adjustments 161
   secondary 159

Cost component
   definition for inventory cost estimates 202
   delta profit for group costing 212
   update additive costs 153

Cost driver 113

Cost estimate
   assembly scrap 30, 32
   BOMitem recursion 39
   component scrap 23, 24
   co-product (primary) 165, 172
   co-product (secondary) 166, 172
   external processing 75, 77, 79
   in-house manufacturing 55
   manufactured in another plant 53
   mixed-price 123, 134
   operation scrap 26, 27, 32

operation scrap effect on components 35
overhead allocation 109
phantom assembly 57
plant to plant transfer 46
special procurement key 50
specify quantity structure 21
subcontracting 68
template allocation 121
variant materials 93
with additive costs 146, 150
with by-product 158
with costing relevancy factors 206
withdrawal from another plant 49
with reference variant 200

Cost estimate group costing 213

Costing run 173
  analysis step 189
  configured materials 183
  costing by costing level 187
  costing levels 185
  costing results section 177
  costing step 186
  create 179
  deleting 195
  dynamic selections 181
  enable marking 191
  general data section 174
  marking step 191
  no transfer of cost estimates 183
  price update step 193
  processing section 176
  recurrence 180
  reference costing run 182
  release step 193
  selection lists 182
  selection step 180
  structure explosion 184

Costing type
  commercial price update 202
  group valuation 212
  no update 208
  prices other than standard price 204
  tax-based price update 202

Costing variant
  additive cost configuration 149
  mixed price costing 132
  quantity structure type 132
  reference variant 199

Costing version 133, 134

D

Delete cost estimates 217

E

External processing 70
  price from operation 74
  standard purchasing 76
  standard purchasing information 70
  subcontracting purchasing 78
  subcontracting purchasing information 70

G

Group costing 211

I

Inventory cost estimates 201
  costing relevancy factors 204
  determination of lowest value 203
  not using determination of lowest value 204
  raw material pricing 202

Item category
  A 165
  B 143

E 122, 143
F 75, 77, 143
G 109
L 68, 79, 143
M 141, 143
N 143
O 143, 155
P 144
S 142, 144, 147
T 142, 144, 147
V 141, 144, 154
X 122

J

Joint production 157

M

Material master
    assembly scrap 29
    classification 82
    commercial inventory prices 201
    component scrap 23
    co-product settings 159
    overhead group 109
    procurement type 41
    quantity structure override 19
    special procurement key 42, 47
    subcontracting 60
    tax-based prices 201
    variant definition 84
Material variant 83
Mixing ratio 130, 135

O

Object dependency 86
Origin groups 98
Overhead condition 106, 111
Overhead costing sheet
    base 106
Overhead costing sheets 97
    calculation base 98
    configuration 105
    credits 103, 106
    maintaining overhead rates 102
    overhead rate dependencies 99
    overhead rates 99
    percentage overhead rates 101
    quantity-based overhead rates 102
Overhead group 107
Overhead key 107, 109, 121

P

Pricing conditions 63
Procurement alternative 124, 126
Production version
    apportionment structure assignment 171
    overriding selection 19

R

Recipe
    external processing 71, 73
    operation scrap 29
    overriding selection 19
Reference variant 197
    additive costs 199
    revaluation 199
    transfer control 198
Routing
    external processing 71, 72
    material assignment 92
    object dependency 90
    operation scrap 26
    overriding selection 19
    super route 89

S

Scrap 22
   assembly scrap 29
   component scrap 23
   operation scrap 25
Source structures 169
Special procurement key 41
   categories 44
   configuration 43, 47, 50, 52, 53, 56, 60
   in-house manufacturing 53
   manufactured in another plant 51
   phantom assembly 55
   plant to plant transfer 45
   subcontracting 60
   withdrawal from another plant 47
Subcontracting 59
   pricing schema 64
   pricing strategies 63
   purchasing information records 66
   vendor search strategy 65

T

Tables
   CKIS - itemization 230
   CKMLMV003-mixing strategies 232
   KEKO-cost estimate header 228
   KEPH-cost component split 229
   MBEW-material valuation 231
   TCKH3-cost component configuration 231
Template 112
   environments 115
   maintenance 115
   overhead costing sheet 120
   overhead key 120
   rows 117

U

Unit of measure
   recipe operation conversion 12, 14
   routing header 16
   routing operation 16

V

Valuation variant
   costing relevancy factors 205
   external processing 74
   material valuation using tax-based price 202
   overhead costing sheets 108
   subcontracting 62
Valuation view
   group valuation 211
   profit center valuation 211

W

What-if costing 207
   costing version settings 210
   reference variant 211
   transfer control settings 208
   valuation variant settings 209
Work center
   formula 11
   formula rounding 16

C Disclaimer

This publication contains references to the products of SAP SE.

SAP, R/3, SAP NetWeaver, Duet, PartnerEdge, ByDesign, SAP BusinessObjects Explorer, StreamWork, and other SAP products and services mentioned herein as well as their respective logos are trademarks or registered trademarks of SAP SE in Germany and other countries.

Business Objects and the Business Objects logo, BusinessObjects, Crystal Reports, Crystal Decisions, Web Intelligence, Xcelsius, and other Business Objects products and services mentioned herein as well as their respective logos are trademarks or registered trademarks of Business Objects Software Ltd. Business Objects is an SAP company.

Sybase and Adaptive Server, iAnywhere, Sybase 365, SQL Anywhere, and other Sybase products and services mentioned herein as well as their respective logos are trademarks or registered trademarks of Sybase, Inc. Sybase is an SAP company.

SAP SE is neither the author nor the publisher of this publication and is not responsible for its content. SAP Group shall not be liable for errors or omissions with respect to the materials. The only warranties for SAP Group products and services are those that are set forth in the express warranty statements accompanying such products and services, if any. Nothing herein should be construed as constituting an additional warranty.

More Espresso Tutorials Books

Stefan Eifler:

Quick Guide to CO-PA (Profitability Analysis)

- Familiarize yourself with basic organizational entities and master data in CO-PA
- Define the actual value flow
- Set up a planning environment
- Create your own reports

http://5018.espresso-tutorials.com

Paul Ovigele:

Reconciling SAP CO-PA to the General Ledger

- Learn the Difference between Costing-based and Accounting-based CO-PA
- Walk through Various Value Flows into CO-PA
- Match the Cost-of-Sales Account with Corresponding Value Fields in CO-PA

http://5040.espresso-tutorials.com

Ashish Sampat:

First Steps in SAP Controlling (CO)

- ▶ Cost center and product cost planning, actual cost flow
- ▶ Best practices for cost absorption using Product Cost Controlling
- ▶ Month-end closing activities in SAP Controlling
- ▶ Examples and screenshots based on a case study approach

http://5069.espresso-tutorials.com

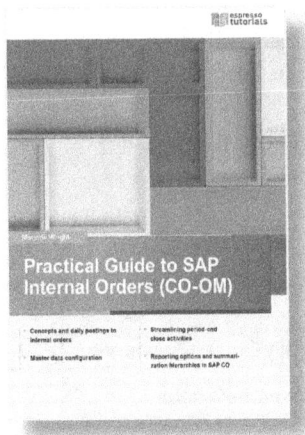

Marjorie Wright:

Practical Guide to SAP Internal Orders (CO-OM)

- ▶ Concepts and daily postings to internal orders
- ▶ Master data configuration
- ▶ Streamlining period-end close activities
- ▶ Reporting options and summarization hierarchies in SAP CO

http://5139.espresso-tutorials.com

Ashish Sampat:

Expert tips to Unleash the Full Potential of SAP Controlling

- ▶ Optimize SAP ERP Controlling configuration, reconciliation, and reporting
- ▶ Transaction processing tips to ensure accurate data capture
- ▶ Instructions for avoiding common month-end close pain points
- ▶ Reporting and reconciliation best practices

http://5140.espresso-tutorials.com

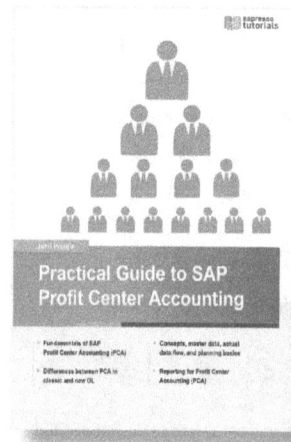

John Pringle:

Practical Guide to SAP Profit Center Accounting

- ▶ Fundamentals of SAP Profit Center Accounting (PCA)
- ▶ Concepts, master data, actual data flow, and planning basics
- ▶ Differences between PCA in classic and new GL
- ▶ Reporting for Profit Center Accounting (PCA)

http://5144.espresso-tutorials.com

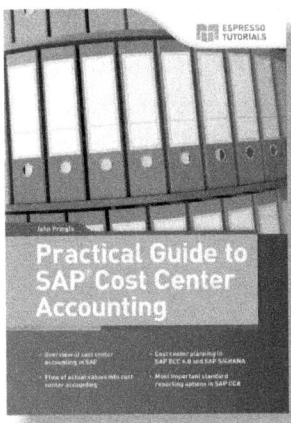

John Pringle:

Practical Guide to SAP Cost Center Accounting

- ▶ Overview of cost center accounting in SAP
- ▶ Flow of actual values into cost center accounting
- ▶ Cost center planning in SAP ECC 6.0 and SAP S/4HANA
- ▶ Most important standard reporting options in SAP CCA

http://5192.espresso-tutorials.com

Stefan Eifler, Christoph Theis:

Value Flows into SAP ERP FI, CO, and CO-PA

- ▶ Value flows based on the sales and production processes
- ▶ Reconciliation between FI and CO-PA
- ▶ Overhead costs and closing tasks
- ▶ Overview of SAP S/4 HANA Finance

http://5199.espresso-tutorials.com

Tom King:

Practical Guide to SAP CO Templates

- Implement and properly use templates
- Scenarios for using templates in SAP Product Costing and Cost Object Controlling
- Template configuration tasks
- Easy cost planning applications

http://5262.espresso-tutorials.com

Tom King:

SAP S/4HANA Product Cost Planning—Configuration and Master Data

- Delve into configuration of costing variants and valuation variants
- Examples of how configuration choices affect costs
- Master data required for generating the cost estimates
- Types of costing supported in SAP Product Cost Planning

http://5376.espresso-tutorials.com

More Value
for your SAP®!

What sets us apart is the ability to put ourselves in the situation of our clients. The result: excellent, tailor-made solutions.

With our combination of specialized IT expertise and ERP know-how, our knowledge of business requirements and more than 15 years of experience, we are ideally positioned to provide lifecycle management for your SAP® system. Due to our international presence, we are able to offer our clients on-site support around the world.

These are our areas of specialization:
- Basis
- ERP Accounting
- ERP Logistics
- Business Intelligence
- NetWeaver
- HANA

Interested?
Visit us **www.consolut.com**
or write an Email: **info@consolut.com**

solutions + value

www.ingramcontent.com/pod-product-compliance
Lightning Source LLC
Chambersburg PA
CBHW052034300426
44117CB00012B/1820